Beyond Born Again

Toward Evangelical Maturity

Robert M. Price

Apocryphal Books

MCMXCIII

About the Author:

Robert M. Price is pastor of the First Baptist Church of Mont-clair, New Jersey, having previously served as Professor of Religion at Mount Olive College. He has attended Gordon-Conwell Theological Seminary and Drew University. He has earned the MTS in New Testament and the PhD in Systematic Theology and is presently a PhD candidate in New Testament.

His articles have appeared in *The Christian Century, The Re-formed Journal, The Journal for the Study of the New Testa-ment, The Journal of Ecumenical Studies, Religious Studies, The Evangelical Quarterly, Christian Scholars Review, The Journal of Psychology and Theology,* and many others. He has also been a contributing editor of *The Wittenburg Door.*

Manufactured by Hypatia Press, 360 W. First, Eugene, OR 97401.

"Wishes and hopes can also mature with men.
They can lose their infantile form . . . and
their youthful enthusiasm without being given
up."
                        --Jürgen Moltmann,
                        The Crucified God

"I know you better now
And I don't fall for all your tricks
And you've lost the one advantage of my
   youth."

                        --Larry Norman, "The Great
                        American Novel"

"When I was a child, I spoke as a child,
I understood as a child, I thought as a child;
But when I became a man, I put away child-
ish things."

                        --The Apostle Paul,
                        I Corinthians 13:11

iii

This book is gratefully
dedicated to

Ed Babinski,

a long-time friend who was
determined to see this
thing published!

CONTENTS

INTRODUCTION: TESTIMONY TIME   1

SECTION I - The Born Again Experience: A Brave New World

Chapter 1: A Mighty Fortress is Our Mentality   11

Chapter 2: The Evangelical Subculture   33

Chapter 3: Devil's Advocates   48

Chapter 4: The Personal Savior   53

SECTION II - The Evangelical Apologists: Are They Reliable?

Chapter 5: Evidence that Demands a Mistrial   63

Chapter 6: Guarding an Empty Tomb   75

Chapter 7: A False Trilemma   89

SECTION III - Can Evangelical Theology Be Born Again?

Chapter 8: Biblical Ventriloquism   99

Chapter 9: Theological Rhetoric   109

Chapter 10: Toward Evangelical Maturity   127

FOOTNOTE REFERENCES   143

APPENDIX - Getting a New Start   159

Beyond Born Again: Towards Evangelical Maturity

1

INTRODUCTION: TESTIMONY TIME

By now, most people have heard of "Born Again Christians." The recent media prominence of these interesting people was, of course, sparked by Jimmy Carter's "testimony" that he had been "born again." Reactions to the new visibility were of at least two types; one can still spot bumper stickers sporting either "I found it" or "I lost it" slogans. Some applaud the new "Evangelical renaissance." Others are uneasy because of the political repression they fear (cf. Malcolm Boyd's prediction of a "demagogic, chauvinistic national religious movement . . . . 'Do you accept Jesus Christ as your personal Lord and Savior?' would be the inquisitorial question asked.")[1] Still others doubt that there has been any revival at all, only increased visibility, or the faddishness of the phrase "born again."

But however one feels about Born Again Christians, one should at least know who they are and what they stand for. In response to this need, we have witnessed a flood of books analyzing Evangelicals and their "old-time religion." Most have been written by Evangelical Christians themselves (e.g., Donald Bloesch, The Evangelical Renaissance; David Wells and John Woodbridge, The Evangelicals; Richard Quebedeaux, The Young Evangelicals and The Worldly Evangelicals; Morris Inch, The Evangelical Challenge), but a few have been written by non- or ex-Evangelicals (e.g., James Barr, Fundamentalism). Of which kind is the book you now hold in your hands? It's hard to say . . . . If you are familiar with Tillich's phrase "on the boundary," perhaps you will understand my reticence to jump into a category. But here, what do such categories mean? For even an "ex-Evangelical" is often merely one more kind of Evangelical with one of several available prefixes. For instance, have you ever seen a "Liberal" religion professor give a hard time to fundamentalist students in his class? Often the most militant of such professors were once fundamentalists themselves and are now trying to settle a score. They have in fact become Liberal fundamentalists!

Let me share briefly with you my background in the Evangelical Christian scene. Every writer is working from a biographical context, and it's only fair that the reader be told what it is. This is especially true on a subject as ticklish as ours. Well, I was converted as an adolescent in a Conservative Baptist Church. Having Jesus Christ as my personal savior gave me "eternal security" from the flames of hell which I otherwise had to fear. During the next few years I absorbed much biblical teaching through the filter of dispensationalist fundamentalism. I learned to pray and read scripture, and to "witness" to my friends (and to feel pretty guilty if I didn't do these things). An acknowledged "spiritual leader" among the youth membership, I found the peer-acceptance that all teenagers so desperately need. Church activities weren't enough, so I joined a student group called "HiBA" (or "High School Born-Againers") in order to see as many as possible of my classmates "come to the Lord." Eventually, several did. Just think, I was a father (spiritually at least) several times by age seventeen! My Campus Crusade for Christ training in evangelism served me in good stead.

Of course, winning others to Christ was only half the picture.

After all, I could only help my converts to mature spiritually as
much as I myself had. I must be a true man of God. Reading devotional works such as Robert Boyd Munger's *My Heart, Christ's
Home*, Miles Stanford's *Principles of Spiritual Growth*, and even
C. S. Lewis's *The Screwtape Letters* considerably advanced my prog-
ress in piety. But never had I found so much spiritual wisdom as
in Bill Gothard's "Institute in Basic Youth Conflicts," a week-long
seminar on God's (and Gothard's) unbeatable principles for a successful Christian life. I took this amassed lore with me when I went
to college.

It did not take me long to become a leader in the campus chapter
of Inter Varsity Christian Fellowship. My knowledge of biblical doctrine and evangelistic technique was welcome here. As I encountered
new influences (though not too many, sheltered as I was), my Christian life grew in new ways. As I erected new barriers, I began to
let down some old ones. On the one hand, there were all of these
"unsaved professors." One should avoid religion courses offered by
such people. Who knows what disturbing things one might hear?
But eventually I was ready for combat on this enemy turf. I had
become interested in "apologetics," the science of defending the
faith. Mentally, I stocked up on the writings of such knights of the
truth as Francis Schaeffer, F. F. Bruce, John Warwick Montgomery,
and Os Guiness. Ready to do battle, I'm sure I irritated my professors no little.

In a battle like this, one must close ranks with the like-minded.
Within the circle of Inter Varsity, I soon encountered new varieties
of Evangelical belief and lifestyle. I learned to tolerate and even
welcome different ideas on eschatology, worldliness, etc. Wider
horizons were a pleasant discovery. Eventually, I had become a
convinced and enthusiastic "neo-Evangelical," going to movies (after
the long cinematic abstinence of my teenage fundamentalist period),
qualifying biblical inerrancy, and teaching the Bible in a Catholic
Charismatic prayer group. My commitment to Jesus Christ gave me
an exciting and satisfying sense of purpose. The Bible was a thing
of constant fascination, and I learned to exult in the love of Jesus,
and of my brothers and sisters.

During my college years, I read voraciously, becoming familiar
with "our" (Evangelical) literature on most subjects. Not satisfied
with encountering the writers only through their works, I took several opportunities to visit other cities where I sought out and con-
versed with various Evangelical leaders. In Wheaton, I met Carl
F. H. Henry, Merrill Tenney, C. Peter Wagner, and Billy Melvin,
President of the National Association of Evangelicals. At a confer-
ence in Ohio, I met my favorite inspirational writer Peter Gillquist.
On a trip to Berkeley I stayed with the Christian World Liberation
Front (now the Berkeley Christian Coalition), talking with Sharon
Gallagher and Jack Sparks (now of the Evangelical Orthodox Church).
In Chicago, I met David F. Wells and Donald Dayton. I talked with
Dave Jackson of Reba Place Fellowship and Jim Wallis of the *Post-
American* (now *Sojourners*). I discussed ministry and theology with
these fascinating people and finally decided to go on to seminary.
I chose Gordon-Conwell Theological Seminary, specializing in New
Testament. This way, I felt I could prepare for a teaching ministry
in my own way by concentrated biblical study. Also, I could con-

tinue my apologetical attack on Liberal, unbelieving biblical criticism and theology. Though I didn't have definite plans for the future (being confident of God's eventual guidance), what eventually happened still surprised me.

One often hears the paradoxical statement that many enthusiastic students lose their faith while in seminary. As the story goes, the wide-eyed seminarian finds his faith in the Bible undermined by the destructive biblical criticism of his Liberal professors. Let me say that there is very little chance of this happening to anyone at my alma mater, where the commitment to Evangelical thought and practice is unswerving. My experience does not therefore fit the stereotype I have just described, but I did undergo quite a change. I found to my unpleasant surprise that by my second year, I was unable to affirm much of that upon which I had spent my life up to that point. I might add that I was dragged to this conclusion kicking and screaming.

As I have said, one of my greatest interests was in apologetics, which in turn greatly contributed to my interest in New Testament studies. The reading of stalwarts like John Warwick Montgomery and Francis Schaeffer convinced me that the stakes indeed were high: if Evangelical Christianity were not true, and based upon historically true events, why then life really held no significance at all! This put me in quite a charged situation. On the one hand, it all *must* be true! Yet, on the other, I must be honest—I could not try to convince an unbeliever with an apologetical argument I would not myself accept. My enthusiasm for the true faith, and the secret fear that the faith might not be true, were sources of fuel that fed each other. My zeal was great, but it was interrupted by periods of doubt that might last for months. The more terrible the doubt, the more zeal was needed to make up for it. As the zeal grew greater, the stakes became higher, and the fear in turn grew deeper. Naturally, I was reluctant to find any weakness in the various arguments in favor of the resurrection of Christ, or the historicity of the gospels, etc. Yet if there were weaknesses, I had to know! Eventually, I believe, I found them in the course of my own research.

At the same time, my suspicions were beginning to mount concerning the viability of the way I had been told to interpret experience. I encountered personal disappointments which I piously assumed God must have sent "for a purpose." Praise the Lord, I figured. Still, I couldn't help but notice that I didn't need "God's will" as an explanatory factor. Human failure and immaturity seemed adequate explanations. Besides, what did it imply about life if every significant experience was significant only as a "test" sent by God? And could you be sure you had discerned God's will, since the last time you thought you had it, everything fizzled anyway? I began to wonder if my picture of life was adequate for the increasingly ambiguous world I lived in. Born-again living seemed to me just a crutch which no longer facilitated healing and growth, but actually protracted immaturity.

During this period, I did not let my doubts and dissatisfactions stop me from sharing the good news of Jesus Christ. But evangelism began to present difficulties of its own. One cold night in Beverly, Massachusetts, I trudged out with a handful of other seminarians to "witness" to local sinners. As I sat conspicuously in a

tavern telling a stranger about the abundant life Christ offered her,
I suddenly found myself at a loss for words. Behind my evangelistic rhetoric, what did it all mean? Just *how* would her life change
if she "accepted Christ"? Well, she would begin to seek guidance
daily in God's Word, and to go to church, and . . . uh . . . well,
basically, to take up new religious habits, I guess. This girl already believed in being kind, loving, and honest. She didn't need
religion for that. What *did* she need it for, I had to ask myself?
Her "problem" seemed to be mainly that she didn't know the requi-
site passwords and shibboleths: "Christ is my personal savior,"
"I'm born again."
        Around the same time, I found myself in a Cambridge cafe having
supper with some friends. We were on our way to a lecture by
Harvey Cox, whose books I'd always found fascinating, though I'd
filled their margins with vociferous criticisms. I suddenly thought,
"Listen, is there really that much difference between 'them' and
'us'?" I had always accepted the qualitative difference between
the "saved" and the "unsaved." Until that moment, it was as if I
and my fellow-seminarians had been sitting in a "no-damnation" section of an otherwise "unsaved" restaurant. Then, in a flash, we
were all just people. My feeling about evangelism has never been
quite the same.
        I had to reevaluate my faith. I had some idea of what other
theological options were like. But since I had always read them
only to refute them, it was going to take some adjustment to be
able to give them a sympathetic hearing. In the summer of 1977, I
took course work at Princeton Theological Seminary, learning much
from Donald Juel and visiting professor Monica Hellwig. The next
fall, I went to Boston University School of Theology and Harvard
Divinity School (members of the Boston area consortium to which I
had access as a Gordon-Conwell student). There I had the privi-
lege of taking courses with Howard Clark Kee, Helmut Koester, and
Harvey Cox. A new world had opened up to me, both theologically
and personally. I felt like a college freshman, thinking through
important questions for the first time. The anxiety of doubt had
passed into the adventure of discovery. It was like being born
again.
        This sharing of my "testimony" brings me now to the theme of
the present book. One might call it an attempt to "put away childish things." Of course, I allude to Paul's eschatological vision in
I Corinthians 13. The imperfect must fade with the advent of the
perfect. Childish things, adequate in their day, must be set aside,
perhaps painfully, when maturity knocks. My experiences and re-
searches lead me to believe that there is a new maturity on the hori-
zon, beckoning to Evangelical Christians. The current, tiring struggles over biblical inerrancy are part of the "birth pangs" of this
"new age." In this book I will sketch several of the difficulties to
be found in traditional Evangelical approaches. I will go on to outline some possible directions for the future already becoming apparent in the thinking of Evangelicals here and there. What I will be
proposing is a really new Evangelicalism, something transcending
Harold J. Ockenga's "Neo-Evangelicalism" (fundamentalism with better manners) and Richard Quebedeaux's "Young Evangelicalism" (po-
litically and behaviorally liberalized Neo-Evangelicals). Let it be

noted that I will *not* be advocating a new candidate for "the one
true faith," but rather a possible option for those who see the problems as I do, and would still like to remain in real continuity with
their Evangelical heritage. (Not that becoming an out-and-out theological Liberal would be a bad thing, mind you. I simply realize
that this is not an option for everyone.)

Now that I've told you who I am, let me take a guess about who
you are, or who I hope you are. Naturally, I hope that Evangelical
students and seminarians caught in dilemmas similar to mine will read
and profit from this book. Its chapters may serve to articulate or
crystalize questions you are asking. This would be no surprise,
since, as Paul says, "No temptation has overtaken you except such
as is common to man" (I Corinthians 10:13). Or in the words of
Ecclesiastes, "There is nothing new under the sun." I do not imagine that I have made many original points here, but I do know that
I had to discover most of them for myself. I had to do this, because
my predecessors in the pilgrimage did not see fit to stick around to
tell anyone else what they found before flying the Evangelical coop.
I hope to save some of you the trouble I went through.

I think next of those convinced apologists who with their inadequate arguments place others in the dilemma I have described. Such
apologists put so much stock in their devices that their reaction to
this book would no doubt be to do apologetics for their apologetics,
to defend their defenses! But I hope to challenge them to do some
honest re-thinking.

What about any non-Evangelicals who might chance to pick up
this book? I remember once reading an in-house fundamentalist
booklet which chided church members for their insufficient zeal and
their worldliness. Halfway through, the writer interrupted himself
to threaten any irreverent unbeliever who might have gotten hold of
this tract. "Don't be too quick to laugh at our foibles, mister, because unless you repent, there's a place in hell waiting for you!"
On the contrary, I welcome non-Evangelicals. I hope to further
dialogue, just as does Morris Inch in his *The Evangelical Challenge.*
Inch sets forth what Evangelicals are *supposed* to believe and do,
inviting a consideration of Evangelicalism at its best. Indeed, one
must understand the best hopes and ideals of a group if one is to
understand the group. But there is also value in seeing the weak
points of a movement. Is there something deeply ingrained which
produces them? To get a well-rounded picture of Evangelicalism,
the observer needs a little dirty linen, I think. Their occasional
claims to the contrary notwithstanding, Born Again Christians are
only human, like everyone else.

Finally, I should think it would be of interest to Evangelicals
themselves to hear in detail just why outsiders do not accept their
claims and apologetic arguments. Their apologists never tire of
complaining that they are ignored by mainstream scholarship. In the
main this is true, but perhaps not for the reasons the apologists
imagine. At any rate, they do deserve a response.

Now, let me explain the set-up of the book. It focuses first on
Evangelical schemas for understanding experience as colored by their
distinctive religious views. Here I attempt to outline what some
would call a "phenomenology of consciousness." I go on to consider
the social and psychological devices with which Evangelicals maintain

the believability of their world of experience. The focus then narrows to consider the nature and function of the Evangelical and Pentecostal belief in demon-possession. This small aspect of Born-Again belief, as we will see, contains larger theological and hermeneutical issues in cameo form. I conclude this section with an observation on the meaning of the claim to have a "personal relationship with Christ."

The second major part of the book deals with a host of apologetics offered by Evangelicals on behalf of several themes. These include the historical reliability of the gospels, the resurrection of Jesus, and the claims of Jesus to be divine. Here my goal is not to challenge the beliefs defended but only their manner of defense.

The third section examines the Evangelical doctrine of scripture, especially the claim that it is the only legitimate and scriptural version of biblical authority. I go on to question other stock criticisms of Liberal theological positions. Then I conclude with some positive proposals for a really new Evangelicalism.

The connection between these sections should be evident, as it is tirelessly made by Evangelical apologists themselves. They maintain that all their edifices are erected to defend their theology which in turn safeguards their pietism. Without Evangelical theology they will have no "answer" to offer modern man in his existential dilemma. We find this sentiment expressed clearly by Clark Pinnock:

> Scripture is not only relevant to the need in theology of a proper epistemological base, and to the need in philosophy of an empirical anchor to resolve the truth question, it is a particularly compelling solution to man's *existential* dilemmas.[2]

It is important to ask just what Evangelicals have in mind when they refer to such a "solution." The answer is not far to seek. Of course, they mean Evangelical pietism, "a personal relationship with Christ." Carl F. H. Henry criticizes dialectical theology because it allegedly

> failed to produce a single evangelist. How irrelevant to the Great Commission can theologians get? . . . . But modern men hungry for spiritual reality will not be flocking there. They will fill up the Los Angeles Coliseum, or Madison Square Garden . . . to hear Billy Graham preach the New Testament evangel . . . .[3]

As one might have suspected, Evangelical theology and apologetics turn out to be cognitive bodyguards for Billy Graham. If these were surrendered it is feared that pietism would become unavailable. I suggest that none of the three areas I am discussing either stands alone or is really intelligible by itself. All three must be taken together.

I would like to make it clear from the outset that I have no desire to "attack personalities." By contrast, I have very much enjoyed meeting people whose views I critique in this book. Such people include Harold Lindsell, J. I. Packer, J. N. D. Anderson, Bill Gothard, Kenneth Hamilton, and especially Clark Pinnock. It is clear to me that, as important as theoretical opinions undoubtedly are, they need not come between people. Along the same lines, I should also point out that in some cases the views criticized in these pages may no longer be held by the writer to whom they are attributed. This is most obviously true of Dr. Pinnock, whose theological quest has in fact led him to change his views on various issues over the past few years. Remember that I am not interested in personalities as such. Rather I want to discuss particular literature which is still commonly used among Evangelicals today, whether or not the writers of it still hold those views. I think this clarification should also protect me from criticisms to the effect that I have not criticized "true Evangelicalism" on this or that point. I am only interested in discussing certain views which are in fact held by many or most Evangelicals. In fact, I suppose that such a would-be critic of mine must agree that the views I critique are indeed deficient. And in view of my last, reconstructive chapter, it becomes clear that in a real sense I agree that the views critiqued here do not (or, better, *should* not) represent true Evangelicalism.

Let me thank my long-suffering mother, Mable Price, who typed various drafts of this book; Ed Babinski for his great encouragement toward seeing it published; Cecil Wysche for his invaluable support toward the same end; Jeff White, who cannot now receive my thanks, for his enthusiastic response to the book; Professor Ted Drange for his helpful suggestions; and Clark Pinnock for his typically open-minded and open-hearted evaluation of it.

Section I
The
Born Again
Experience:
A Brave
New World?

"Hey, wouldn't you like to be born again
Live a new life that's free
Without sin, no ties to philosophy."

--Anne Herring and Matthew Ward,
"Learn a Curtsey"

"You'll be born again into an untroubled world
. . . free of anxiety . . . fear . . . hate."

--"Invasion of the Body Snatchers"

"We want you to experience the total power of
the born-again experience without risk."

--magazine advertisement

Chapter 1

A MIGHTY FORTRESS IS OUR MENTALITY

The most visible thing about "Born Again" Christians is their claims of new and revolutionary religious experience. Yet too often, outsiders are left without much of an idea as to how these claims may be understood or evaluated. I hope to supply an analysis that will be helpful in this respect. The present chapter will attempt to outline the principal schemas by which "Born Again" people interpret and direct their experiences, specifically those of discomfort or adversity.

Some readers may be surprised or even indignant at seeing names associated together which seem at first to represent very disparate viewpoints. E.g., how can I possibly put Calvinist counselor Jay Adams, fundamentalist preacher John R. Rice, and Charismatic exorcist Don Basham in the same classification? I ask only for a little patience. I believe I will be able to show how these and other Born Again Christians actually work from the same basic models of world, self, and the role of religion.

Briefly I will argue that among Born Again Christians (fundamentalists, Evangelicals, and Charismatics), there is a very distinctive model for relating to and coping with the world. I call it "the hard religious line." Here all answers to life's puzzles are strictly religious or spiritual in nature and are directly derivable from personal commitment to Christ and accompanying devotional disciplines. Furthermore, all necessary information for this is in the Bible. The result is a purely religious view of the world and the self which does full justice to neither. This, I will contend, is unhealthy and immature.

Briefly I will outline a derivative model, born in reaction to the one just described, called "the soft religious line." Here, religious commitment is still given fundamental importance in life, but it is also recognized that even the Born Again Christian is subject to problems and solutions that are not especially spiritual in origin or nature. Accordingly, the Bible is not seen to have the answer to everything. One may also look to and trust other sources. The consequent worldview attributes both significant value and independent reality to the world and the self in their own right. In other words, for "softliners" man is not only *homo religiosus*, but more as well. This view is more realistic, healthy, and mature.

Finally, I will consider which of the two models seems more faithful to the common Evangelical understanding of biblical authority. My perhaps controversial conclusion will be that while the weaker, soft religious line is more progressive and healthier psychologically, the hard religious line is actually more faithful to the typical Evangelical understanding of the Bible. Insofar as this view of biblical authority is deemed integral to Evangelicalism, the hard line would have to be seen as more consistently Evangelical.

Let me explain why I will include such a large number of quotations. Basically, the present chapter is an exegetical study of much Born Again Christian literature. While quotations are always helpful in keeping discussions above the level of mere generalization, they will be particularly appropriate here since many of my Born Again readers, biblically-oriented as they are, are accustomed to distrust any important assertion unless it can appeal to several supportive texts.   In other words, no one is going to believe this unless I can document it thoroughly.   Only so can I hope to avoid charges of caricature.   I can only hope the several quotations will not be overly cumbersome stylistically.

Social activist-evangelist Tom Skinner once wrote a book entitled, *If Christ is the Answer, What are the Questions?* Many Evangelical Christians are sure that Christ is indeed the direct answer to all imaginable questions.   The familiar evangelistic slogan, "Jesus is the answer," receives many elaborations, or should I say "paraphrases," for there really is little in the way of elaboration.   Larry Norman, innovative Born Again rock singer and composer, musically runs down a list of national dilemmas and concludes his protest song: "Don't ask me for the answers / I've only got one / That a man leaves his darkness when he follows the Son."[1]   Exorcists Frank and Ida Mae Hammond similarly claim, "Hope for our communities and nation does not lie in social and governmental programs. . . . Our problems are basically spiritual."[2]   But we are more concerned with how the Born Again Christian handles personal problems and difficulties.   Here, too, there is much simplicity.   Bill Bright, the businessman-director of Campus Crusade for Christ, buoyantly promises:

> If we have Christ, we have everything we need, for . . . we are complete in Him.   Do you need love?   Our Lord Jesus Christ is the incarnation of love.   Do you need joy?   He is joy.   Do you need peace?   Christ is peace. . . .[3]

and so on.   Fundamentalist counselor Gilbert Little echoes these sentiments:

> After you believe that the shed blood of Christ was made an offering for your soul, God sends the Holy Spirit to dwell in you. . . . Finally you overcome the evil influence of doubt, fear, anxiety, nervousness, and worry by trusting and meditating on God's Word and by walking each day . . . in the Spirit. . . .[4]

Once again, Jay Adams: ". . . if you have been saved by grace through faith in Jesus Christ, you may be certain that the way out will come just as surely as the problem itself."[5]   Enroth, Ericson, and Peters, in their excellent study of the Jesus People, point out that among these young Born Again Christians, "Whatever the problem, the simple plan of salvation is offered as the whole solution."[6]

It will be no surprise that Born Again Christians who have taken such a tantalizing offer seriously will then expect to be free from problems.   Daniel Stevick, Keith Miller, and Bruce Larson all bemoan their former allegiance to such views, which, they report, proved unworkable.   They, like many fellow believers had been told that new problems would arise only if one is not sufficiently "yielded" or not filled with the Spirit.[7]   This picture is hardly the result of mere distortion by the disgruntled.   It is readily confirmed in the literature.   Bill Bright, in *Experiencing God's Love and Forgiveness*, claims, "When we walk in the fullness and the control of God's Holy Spirit, every day is filled with wonder, meaning, purpose, and fruitfulness."   He provides a diagram illustrating that all of life's inter-

ests automatically fall into or out of place depending upon how recently one has confessed sins and appropriated the filling of the
Holy Spirit.[8] Tim LaHaye asserts that, "The Christ-controlled life
guarantees peace and confidence, thereby avoiding many crises (because it is supernaturally directed). . . ."[9] Sectarian revivalist
John R. Rice agrees: "Every Christian ought to be glad all the
time. But even a child of God . . . cannot be happy if there be
known sin unjudged, unrebuked, unconfessed in his life."[10]
   The reader has undoubtedly noticed that problems in the Christian experience are chalked up to sin, at least according to these
writers. There are other factors, too, all of them religious in nature. Jay Adams is clear in his assessment:

> The Bible knows only two categories of causes for bizarre
> behavior: (1) organic causes, (2) non-organic causes. . . .
> all non-organic problems are represented in the Scripture as
> stemming from the counselee's sin. There is no third, neutral
> category . . . that allows for non-organic difficulties for which
> the counselee may not be held personally responsible.[11]

Gilbert Little seems to agree: "When the Christian succumbs to emotional problems . . ., he has taken his eyes off God."[12]   Other
writers go on to count in the devil. Fundamentalist Bible teacher
R. B. Thieme contends that a Christian who is worried or upset at
anything has thereby already succumbed to Satanic pressure.[13]
Charismatic "Deliverance Ministry" specialists Don Basham, Pat Brooks,
and Frank and Ida Mae Hammond go one remarkable step further.
Problems including self-pity, fear, lust, frigidity, schizophrenia,
spiritual apathy, and a legion of others are often attributable to
demon infestation and must be exorcised![14]
   Positively, exactly how does Christ insure such a thrilling adventure with clear skies all the way? As we have seen, problem-
causing sins are to be confessed, the Holy Spirit is to be appropriated, and demons are to be driven out. Here are a few more reci-
pes. John R. Rice promises that ". . . you may have strength for
every need by constant prayer"[15] but his real enthusiasm is re-
served for "soul-winning" (person to person solicitation of converts):
". . . soul winning is such a worthy goal that it makes all of life
worth living. . . . Everything seems to fall into proper focus."[16]
R. B. Thieme's prescription is a bit different: "What is the stabi-
lizer of Christian experience? Doctrine . . . DOCTRINE . . . DOC-
TRINE . . . AND MORE DOCTRINE!"[17]
   Even more sophisticated writers who assume the hard religious
line still maintain that only Born Again Christians have maximum
opportunity for psychological health and well being. Vernon Grounds,
of Conservative Baptist Theological Seminary, writes:

> I keep asking myself, "Where are all these [factors for
> psychic well-being] to be found?" Conveniently they are to
> be found in the gospel exclusively—or at least with an ade-
> quacy that makes the gospel an unrivaled antidote for neurosis.

Phillip Swihart is sure that "Only Christians have these resources
available to them to dare to be honest in dealing with feelings."[18]
   How are these emotional changes actually effected? It is as easy
as knowing the proper text or principle. Swihart says, "We can

ask God to change our attitudes and feelings, to heal our hurts, to set us free from our obsessions, to melt our anger and hate, to give us feelings of joy, peace and love. . . ." For Merlin Carothers, the Bible is enough to overrule emotion: "Your feelings may tell you that you are lonely, but God's Word says He is with you. Which will you believe? If you aren't sure, you need to repent. . . ."[19] Peter Gillquist offers the example of his wife. She once told him during a particularly trying day, "I should be discouraged, but I told the Lord that I am rejecting discouragement in His name."[20] Bill Bright gives the secret of loving those whom we find less than lovable. Since the Bible tells us to love even our enemies, then, logically, such must be God's will. The Bible also says God will certainly answer prayers that are in accord with his will (I John 5:14-15). Therefore one need only "love by faith," or claim God's love for unlovely persons. It is as simple as that!

To take another kind of example, let's turn to a specific problem and see how "hardliners" deal with it. Tim LaHaye, in *Ten Steps to Victory Over Depression*, recommends almost exclusively religious therapy, including superimposing God onto your self-image, visualizing yourself as God is shaping you, accepting yourself as God's creation, accepting God's forgiveness, thanking God for everything, seeking God's Kingdom, thinking about God's available power, etc.

Jay Adams says that to escape depression one must first know God personally (i.e., be "Born Again"), then decide that you want more to please God than to escape depression, and then you must do whatever God says no matter how you feel.[21] Finally, in dealing with the kindred ailment of anxiety, Vernon Grounds gives almost entirely spiritual advice. The anxious person must repeat Romans 8:38-9 (an assurance of God's providence) at least five times daily, reaffirm Galatians 2:20, pray for faith, surrender anxieties to Christ a la I Peter 5:7, and have Christian fellowship.[22]

Thus far, our evidence has suggested that common to Born Again Christians of very diverse perspectives is a "hard religious line" according to which conversion should eliminate all problems. At any rate, problems are of a purely spiritual nature and may be simply overcome by religious means. As one might expect, the cornerstone for this attitude is the Evangelical esteem for the Bible as the only sufficient norm for faith and practice. I will now turn to representative programmatic statements about the role of the Bible in the "hard religious line."

Once again we begin with Jay Adams as the most forthright spokesman: "The Christian counselor uses the Scripture as the sole guide for both counselor and counselee. He rejects eclecticism. He refuses to mix man's ideas with God's." ". . . the basic principles for the practice of counseling are *all* in the Bible." "The issue resolves itself quite simply into this: if a principle is new to or different from those that are advocated in the Scripture, it is wrong; if it is not, it is unnecessary."[23] Again, Vernon Grounds:

> . . . when it comes to prescribing a panacea for the problems that plague people, you and I as biblicists can speak up with confidence. . . . The gospel, we insist, is not *an* answer, one among many; it is *the* answer.[24]

That Grounds takes his "biblicism" seriously is evident from the fact that almost all his chapter titles introduce their subjects as "The Bible and [e.g.] Anxiety." Bill Gothard, director of the popular "Institute in Basic Youth Conflicts" seminar, claims: "Once the counselor determines the levels of conflict involved . . . he is then able to guide the teenager in applying clear *Scriptural* steps. . . ."[25] Lastly, R. B. Thieme: "All of our assets . . . everything we need for . . . every problem, every trial, every difficulty, every adversity . . . ARE PROVIDED FOR IN GOD'S WORD!"[26]

Lest there remain any doubt as to the hardliners' attitude toward psychology and psychiatry, there follow two representative comments. George Dollar, faculty member at Bob Jones University, protests, "If counseling is so vital as its proponents claim . . . . Does it mean that with the Bible and the Holy Spirit the believer cannot find the answers to his deepest needs without professional counseling?"[27] And in the opinion of Gilbert Little, it is only "Worldly Christians [who] are prone to turn to the psychologies of man, . . . an adjustment to this present world and away from Christ."[28] It is no surprise that, according to Walter Hollenweger, Pentecostal pastors take it as a spiritual defeat when the only alternative left to them is to turn their counselees over to a professional psychiatrist.[29]

The World and the Self in the Hard Religious Line

Sigmund Freud characterized religion as "an attempt to get control over the sensory world in which we are placed by means of the wish world which we have developed inside us."[30]

Whether or not all religion must function this way, I propose that the "hard religious line" offers a clear example of this phenomenon as described by Freud. Let us now proceed to set forth some important aspects of the Born Again "hard line" worldview to see if Freud's characterization fits.

As one should expect, there is a great deal of other-worldliness in this schema. The world is not taken with real seriousness as a reality in its own right. It is sometimes said among Born Again Christians that God does not take them to heaven immediately after conversion simply because he wants them to be here in order to convert others! One may even detect some wistful regret in this explanation.

Peter Gillquist writes: "If we through the Holy Spirit can see our destined [heavenly] citizenship as, eternally speaking, *already* here, life on this planet becomes merely a sideshow that will soon move on." "We see this present life as temporary and fleeting." "The Church of God falls into perspective as being the most important treasure we can know on this earth."[31] Bill Gothard seems to feel that one's vocation is only a means of support, e.g., "I'm a Christian, but I work in the meat-packing plant to get money to pay expenses."[32] Or, to quote another of Larry Norman's songs, "What a mess this world is in! I wonder who began it? Don't ask me, I'm only visiting this planet."[33]

But the Born Again "hardliner," like it or not, is here, at least temporarily. In the meantime, the world is still suffused by the light of eternity. The Born Again worldview assumes the proportions of a "primitive thought-world" as described by anthropologist Mary Douglas:

> The cosmos is turned in, as it were, on man. Its trans-
> forming energy is threaded on to the lives of individuals so
> that nothing happens in the way of storms, sickness, blights
> or droughts except in virtue of these personal links. So the
> universe is man-centered in the sense that it must be inter-
> preted by reference to humans.
>
> In such a universe the elemental forces are seen as linked
> so closely to individual human beings that we can hardly speak
> of an external, physical environment. . . . The physical en-
> vironment is not clearly thought of in separate terms, but
> only with reference to the fortunes of human selves.

Quoting another anthropologist, W. E. H. Stanner, she adds that
primitive man "moves, not in a landscape but in a humanized realm
saturated with significations."[34] This is no less true of our Born
Again "hardliner." He sees the world not so much as an independent reality in its own right, but rather as an elaborate stage or
laboratory. Similarly, events do not happen in and of themselves;
rather they are a series of signals sent directly by God. Their
meaning is that they are devices to educate the believer or shape
his behavior, in a manner reminiscent of behaviorist "operant con-
ditioning." This view of the world even approaches the Eastern
concept of *maya*, i.e., the world as a series of magic tricks, stage
illusions, behind which God must be sought.

No better illustration of this kind of worldview could be found
than those filling the writings of Merlin Carothers, an extremely
popular teacher in the Charismatic movement. Carothers relates how
God himself told him, "My son, what I wanted you to know was that
you never again have to worry whether anyone will overcharge you,
hurt you, or mistreat you unless it is My will." Carothers goes on
to affirm his belief that "if the chair collapses under me it is His
will. If the coffee is too hot or the toast soggy, it is His will."
One day, "God was giving me [a] headache as an opportunity to
increase the power of Christ in my life."[35] He recommends his readers to thank God for letting someone steal one's parking place since
God must have an even better one in store around the corner![36]
Frances Gardener Hunter, another popular Pentecostal speaker, relates how she believed God had delayed her airplane in a snowstorm
so she could have time to read the Bible and to convert a fellow
passenger.[37] Our last example is the testimonial of a "satisfied
customer" of Bill Gothard's Institute in Basic Youth Conflicts. He
says, ". . . just the other day we had a calamity at the office, when
a water pipe broke and my whole carpet was ruined. But I could
come home and joke about it. God just wanted me to get a new carpet."[38] One may be sympathetic to Eli Chesen's opinion of this kind
of thing as "egocentric thinking in its highest form." But, "Despite
the egocentricity, however, such thoughts can give comfort and
reassurance to the person who has faith."[39]

Evangelicals who think in this way do not seem to shrink from
the deterministic implications of these beliefs. Carothers admits
openly that God must be "really responsible for everything that
happens. . . ."[40] Nevertheless, Carothers seems to want to hollow
out spaces for free-will decisions, though he quickly adds that God

will still intervene to work to our advantage any mistake we may make.[41] This scheme is much closer to optimistic "Positive Thinking" or to the idea that ours is "the best of all possible worlds" than Carothers and his many fans would probably care to admit. He even veers amazingly close to Christian Science's gnostic denial of the reality of sickness.   He (with many other Charismatics and Pentecostals) says that the believer must "claim his healing from the Lord" and then believe he has been healed even if Satan continues to counterfeit the symptoms![42] But more about this in Chapter 3.

This cozy universe provides great security.   Carothers assures us that God's appointment schedule is better than ours, so one mustn't worry if he is caused to be unavoidably late.[43] Peter Gillquist quotes Romans 8:28, adding "His promise is that we are not left to chance or happenstance."[44] Tim LaHaye is relieved that the Born Again Christian need never make another decision for himself: "Never ask, 'What do I want to do about this?'" Instead one should let Jesus Christ decide on one's vocation, spouse, and various daily decisions.[45] Similarly, a man who attended the Gothard Seminar concluded that Gothard "erased all areas of gray. I'm convinced that God did not make gray."[46] This desire for total and unambiguous security also surfaced in psychologist John Kildahl's tests on people who "speak in tongues" (glossalalia):

> Our tongue-speakers had a strong need for external guidance from some trusted authority. That is, they had a strong sense of leaning on someone more powerful than themselves, who gave them security and direction in their lives.[47]

This observation raises the question of what sort of self-image is promoted by the "hard religious line." Many Born Again Christians are not in sympathy with any sort of "self-actualization" approach. Jay Adams warns:

> Counselors who focus on improving self-concepts and who try to teach counselees how to love themselves will find themselves spinning their wheels. . . . Not one word in the Scriptures encourages such activities.[48]

Little agrees:

> It is the "I" that gets irritated, filled with hate, rage, and envy. . . . The "I," not the Spirit, makes us sick.
> Too many Christians seem to forget that self must be crucified daily, moment by moment. . . .[49]

The Christian should not trust himself. As already noted, Tim LaHaye urges that all decisions be turned over to Christ, never made on the basis of "what do I want to do?" Gothard shows a similarly dismal view of human judgment when he recommends that in any situation one first decide what he himself would be inclined to do and then take the opposite for God's will![50] Gothard does not stop here, however. He further advises Christians to avoid the possibility of anger and indignation by "yielding all one's rights to God." Henceforth one can only expect poor treatment and be grateful when it is not forthcoming! (This is a kind of rigorist self-criticism and mental discipline akin to ancient Stoicism.) The same sort of self-abnegation is put forth in the book *Have We No Rights?*

which uses a missionary's experiences as an ideal for everyone:
"Every truly consecrated Christian must be willing to give up the
right to the normal comforts of life, to physical health and safety,
to the privacy of business, time, friends, romance, family and home."[51]
While any serious commitment must be prepared for ultimate self-
sacrifice, the thing to note here is that this sort of thing is being
recommended as one's everyday attitude, a constant willingness to be
a door mat.

What then is the value of the self in the hard religious line? As
with the world, the self seems to have little or no real value in its
own right. It is swallowed up in the religious reality. Swihart is
comparatively mild when he says, "We can assume that God gives us
feelings so we will be able to grasp, albeit finitely, something of
who he is in an infinite and thus to us incomprehensible manner."[52]
Is that really the only reason? At any rate, Gothard goes farther
when he holds that God designed our physical appearance before we
were born so that it would function as a (mere) "picture frame" to
accentuate the Christ-like religious character he intends to develop
in us. The purpose is to make the gospel more attractive to outsiders we meet. The self is at best a religious object lesson or
billboard. Accordingly, Gothard's definition of "maturity" is exclusively and entirely religious: "A Christian is mature when he recognizes a personal deficiency or violation of a basic Scriptural principle and has the discernment and the tools to correct the violation."[53]

Coping Mechanisms of the Hard Religious Line

When life and the world are evaluated in a purely religious or
spiritual framework, it follows that all difficulties are to be met in a
religious or spiritual way. I have already touched on this. Now I
propose to deal with these religious coping mechanisms in more detail. The coping mechanisms of the hard religious line are of two
basic types which I shall dub "combat" and "divination." Both are
usually present among all hardliners, though either may temporarily
or permanently predominate.

Combat coping mechanisms see the world primarily as a battleground between the Born Again Christian Soldier and his spiritual
foes, "the world, the flesh, and the devil." First, "the flesh."
John R. Rice puts it succinctly: "Every Christian has a struggle
between these two natures, the old nature and the new nature."
One must "confess before God and judge every sin the moment it
becomes known to you."[54] Merlin Carothers agrees: "Our soul is a
battleground where Jesus Christ has won the decisive victory, but
each of us must [fight] till our attention is focused on God with a
single mind and a united heart." Surrender your immoral thoughts
to God and "When a wrong thought presents itself . . . imagine it
projected on [a] screen. Confess it to God and say, 'I've surrendered that thought. I won't think it. Absolutely not!'"[55] Once
more, Jay Adams: "The Christian life is a daily battle. Daily a
Christian must put to death (crucify) his selfish desires and instead
follow the will of Christ."[56]

"The world" in our trio of opponents might be said to include all
sorts of (negative) circumstances including sickness, poverty, irrita-

tions, and discouraging events. Since "greater is he who is in you than he who is in the world" (I John 4:4), Born Again Christians must "take authority" over such difficulties. Peter Gillquist says: "As we take hold of the authority which has been delivered to us, [we exercise] dominion over the circumstances surrounding us. . . . [e.g.] worry . . . insecurity . . . hesitancy to be free."[57] Kenneth Hagin: "God's plan is for you to rule and reign in your life—to reign over circumstances, poverty, disease, and everything that would hinder you."[58] For Hagin and Carothers, this includes automatic freedom from sickness.[59]

Thirdly, the Born Again Christian must do battle with the devil and his minions. "Demon powers are set in array and given authority by Satan to control the entire world and plague it with pernicious evil."[60] There is a remarkable across-the-boards-agreement here between Evangelical Christians of divergent perspectives. All seem to agree that Satan need not be kept in reserve only for particularly distressing theodicies. On the contrary, according to fundamentalist R. B. Thieme, "The Believer in Jesus Christ is the NUMBER ONE TARGET of the strategy of the Devil. . . . This is the Devil's world. . . ."[61] Philip Swihart agrees that Satan attacks us "in our daily lives" by distorting our feelings and tempting us to be dishonest with them.[62] Hagin, the Hammonds, Basham, and Brooks all warn of the real possibility that demons are behind certain problems in our lives. The Hammonds give a list of over three hundred oft-recurrent demons.[63] Traditional Evangelicals, including Pentecostal denominations like the Assemblies of God, believe that the Christian must "resist the devil," by prayer and other spiritual disciplines, to offset his harassment. But the new "Deliverance Ministry" advocates (e.g., Basham, Brooks, the Hammonds) go further and claim that actual demon-possession occurs in the Born Again Christian. (Traditionalists consider this a possibility only for the "unsaved.") In this case, the evil spirits must be exorcised and then kept out by a faithful program of spiritual disciplines.[64] When one recalls that almost any nagging bad habit or psychological problem is quite possibly (though not always) to be diagnosed as demonic, it is evident that Deliverance Ministry advocates have successfully revived yet another aspect of the primitive and medieval worldview, that of animistic spirit possession. Also, one is reminded of the all-too-human tendency hastily to assume that one has every disease the symptoms of which he hears described. The Deliverance Ministry cannot but find the demons it looks for; it is a self-fulfilling prophecy. (There are other quite interesting aspects of the Pentecostal belief in demon-deliverance which I will consider in a separate chapter.)

The combat coping mechanisms involve such severe and constant self-criticism and introspection, and such vigilance against demonic attack that one wonders just how beneficial these devices can be for coping. Is not the medicine worse than the sickness if one takes these coping mechanisms seriously?

The second major type of hardliner coping device is what I call divination. Here I am concerned with the Born Again view of the world as a "realm saturated with significations." The Gothard-Carothers belief that God causes and/or allows all events and circumstances now comes into its own; the Born Again Christian must thank

God for whatever happens and then try to discern the divine intention—what is God trying to teach him, or how is God trying to mold
and develop him?

It is worth pausing at this point to note an important area of un-
resolved tension. Hardline Evangelical Christians do not seem to
take seriously the apparent contradiction in saying on the one hand
that they must beware the antagonistic, devilish forces literally swarm-
ing about them, and believing on the other that God causes all events
for their good! And most of them do in fact consciously hold both
beliefs. My guess is that they invoke either belief when it seems
appropriate to the particular situation. If there is an unavoidable
difficulty, it is a divine trial or test. If there is temptation, it is
the devil. If it could be either, perhaps the individual's disposition
or mood will decide which to invoke.

The reader may wish to suggest a resolution of this difficulty,
but let me try to beat him to it. "Doesn't the Bible teach that God
sometimes uses Satan for his own purposes, as in the book of Job?"
This may well be so; it is certainly a logically coherent idea. But
the problem is that Evangelical statements about Satanic harassment
such as those examined here seem to carry a rather different tenor.
One definitely gets the feeling that the Born Again Christian feels
himself to be the object of unjust assaults. This becomes apparent
immediately from the characterization of this devilish activity as
temptation to sin, which the Evangelical would never attribute to
God. Though God might *test* (as in Job's case), he is supposed
never to *tempt*. Most Christians would make this distinction, but the
uniquely hardline inconsistency arises from the belief that God causes
all events that come your way. Where in this picture is there room,
logically speaking, for Satanic temptation?

If the combat coping mechanisms saw the world as a battleground,
the divination method sees the world as a proving ground. The
Christian is an apprentice, an initiate, or a soldier in boot camp.
He must successfully reach the end of the obstacle course. "God
puts us in difficult circumstances to strip us of our old nature and
teach us joyful submission to His will." (Carothers)[65] "God is using
the circumstances of this earthly life to equip me . . . for living
forever with Him." (Gillquist)[66] These difficulties range from soggy
toast and ruined carpets (as we have seen) to financial ruin and the
death of one's children.[67] God may be teaching or chastizing. Gothard standardizes the divination formula:

1. Thank God for the irritation. No matter what, there's a
   purpose.
2. Identify possible causes. Did I in any way cause this?
3. Determine ultimate objectives. What qualities does God want
   to develop in me? He has allowed the irritation for my
   ultimate benefit.[68]

Carothers makes a great deal of step No. 1 above in his writings.
One should praise the Lord literally for everything. This can be
observed to result in an alarming, almost childish giddiness in those
who take this seriously. Among other things, he advises individuals
to thank God for an alcoholic father, for being drafted to go to Viet-
nam, and for one's daughter becoming a nude nightclub dancer!
Carothers gives endless examples tending to reinforce the conclusion

that if you are willing to thank God for a horrible situation, then God will be pleased enough at your humility to reward you by changing the situation. At one point, he tries to cover his tracks by denying that this is his intent, but the overwhelming tendency of his work is nonetheless in this direction. He is at least theoretically willing, however, to admit with Gothard that circumstances may not change. Rather God will use them to change you. And what sort of change is involved here? As one might guess by now, the goal is to become more nearly perfect religiously.

Divination has another important role to play. One must also divine the will of God before making important (and sometimes even not-so-important) decisions or choices. Remember how LaHaye advised letting Jesus make all your decisions for you. How do you go about finding out Jesus' opinion on, e.g., which college to enroll in? There are at least two views here. Many, especially Charismatics, simply "feel led" to choose one alternative over another. Moreover, the decision is sure to be the right one if in announcing it, one can add that "I've prayed about it." Prayer is imagined in an almost mechanical way to "clear the lines of static," so that God's signal can get through. And if the situation is serious enough, fasting may be added to the process.

Another group of Evangelicals is more suspicious of the subjectivism implied in all this. They resort to a list of steps for divination (to be found for instance in Paul Little's *Affirming the Will of God*, or Oliver Barclay's *Guidance*). Despite the *de jure* belief in supernatural direction, this approach boils down essentially to common sense. For example, one should assess his or her options (the available "open doors"), seek advice from more mature Christians, make sure one's choice is at least in harmony with biblical principles (though how this would bear on, e.g., which college to attend, I leave the reader to decide), and so forth. The best decision you can come up with must be God's will, since he is in control and would not let you honestly misconstrue the clues. After all, he wants you to find his will, doesn't he?

But the thing to note is that, despite the differences, in both cases the Born Again Christian is told that he *can* and *must* discern the will of God before acting. Witness the constant admonitions to make sure you are "in the center of God's will," or to "find God's perfect will for you." Now here's the problem. What happens if things don't turn out the way you decided God wanted them to? Suppose you are "led" to plan an outdoor evangelistic program, but it rains! Well, it turns out that God's will must have been something other than what you had surmised? The Lord moves in mysterious ways, after all. The Born Again Christian may even chide himself for having presumptuously thought he could second-guess God to begin with. "I've tried to see / your plan for me / but I only acted like I knew / Oh Lord forgive the times / I tried to read your mind" (Keith Green, "Trials Turned to Gold"). His ways are inscrutable to mortals!

All this would be fine except for the fact that the rhetoric of "finding God's will" continues to go on as it did before. The next decision will be approached the same way! The Evangelical will once again assume that God's will is not inscrutable and can be known to us. Again we have a pair of contradictory beliefs, each of which

is invoked at the psychologically appropriate time. When the believer wants to avoid worrying whether he will make the right decision, he uses the divination formula to climb cozily into "the center
of God's will." On the other hand, if things go sour he can assure
himself that it is all for the good since God is working in ways un-
foreseen and *unforeseeable* by a mere mortal like himself!

One would imagine that after a while this contradiction would out-
live its usefulness and cause frustration. Perhaps the most acute
case of this would be the much-publicized disaster at Toccoa Falls
Bible College, where several students were killed when a dam burst.
Now certainly these young people came to study there because they
had arrived at God's will for their lives—he wanted them to serve in
the pastorate or on the mission field. But it was not to be. Instead, it turned out to be God's will to "take them home to be with
himself." How could they have been so wrong? And, let's face it,
in terms of this belief-system either they *were* wrong, or God is
playing some pretty cruel jokes. One would think that this "Lisbon
Earthquake" would severely shake the plausibility of the divination
scheme. But survivors were probably too preoccupied with figuring
out what God meant to teach them through the tragedy, to notice.

One could avoid this trap by deciding to go consistently with one
belief or the other. That is, one could simply decide once and for
all that God's will is inscrutable, and that one can only do his best
to make ethically or biblically appropriate decisions, and *hope* they
conform to God's will. Or one could rely on divination; if and when
things fall apart, one could just conclude "back to the drawing board!"
You must have made a slip-up somewhere in the process and not
assessed God's will correctly. But even here, if one is "wrong"
enough times, one would eventually have to conclude that it cannot
be so easy to find God's will as one was led to believe. In any
event, I believe that the incongruous interplay of beliefs described
above fairly represents the common practice of hard-line Evangelicals.

One of the most disturbing implications of the hardliners' view of
the submissiveness of the self and the divine orderedness of circumstances is that of unquestioning obedience to authority. The most
widely known version of this is Gothard's "Chain of Command." Among
others, this celestial bureaucracy includes God, government, hus-
band/parents, and employers, in that order. God uses his subordinates, our superiors, as hammer and chisel to knock the rough
edges off Christians "so that the true reflection of Christ can be
seen from every angle."[69] Brooks adds that obedience to the chain
of command is also necessary if lasting deliverance from demons is to
be achieved.[70] According to Gothard, wives must acquiesce to
their husbands' decisions, recognizing God's will even in hubby's
mistakes. She should even thank God if her husband beats her!
Carothers adds that if she complains she is sinning, and that she
isn't really submitting to him until she is glad he is exactly the
way he is and enjoys submitting.[71]

What about the government? Carothers, who perhaps significantly is a military chaplain, leaves us in no doubt: "The government
may be wrong, but if we rebel against it, we are disobeying God.
That means communists or fascists or crooked officials. . . . They
are that way because we need to learn submission."[72] Carothers
does not balk at declaring that God not only allowed, but actually

caused Adolf Hitler's rise to power: "What about . . . Hitler? . . .
Are we willing to thank God for raising [him] up? Can we accept
His word that He is doing it for our good? Can we honestly praise
him for it?"[73] Thank God, Carothers grants that Christians may
draw the line at obeying orders such as killing six million Jews or
committing apostasy. One searches in vain for any principle compelling one to draw such a line, however.

It is not surprising that an other-worldly religious outlook would
be indifferent to social change and similar issues, but now we are in
a better position to see just why this is so. The Born Again Christian who advocates the hard religious line is not only apathetic to
larger social questions because he imagines the "real" struggles to
be those of personal, individual piety. In addition to this, the very
worldview by which he rationalizes his privatistic struggles is of
such a nature as to legitimate the social status quo. For instance,
Bill Bright asks, "Do you thank God when you are discriminated
against . . . racially?"[74] The ideal is to avoid letting one's spiritual equilibrium become ruffled by anger, rather than to become
angry enough to change social inequities. It is probably no coinci-
dence that Bright is a supporter of one of the Christian Right's
political organizations called "The Christian Freedom Foundation."
Similarly, Merlin Carothers remarks:

> In recent years we've seen scores of "liberation" move-
> ments pop up. They all teach that we have "rights" as human
> beings and need to stand up for ourselves. But these move-
> ments are all based on the same false concepts of authority
> and submission.[75]

I close these observations with an oft-quoted maxim from Bill Gothard: "Freedom is not the right to do what we want, but the *power*
to do what we ought."

The Psychological Danger of the Hard Religious Line

A very popular chorus among Born Again Christians is Ralph
Carmichael's "He's Everything to Me." Among hardliners, there is a
definite tendency toward totalism, i.e., at least ideally the Born
Again Christian must "lay *all* on the altar," be "*totally* dedicated."
Peter Gillquist, for example, offers an illustration which he thinks
"really communicates godliness." A student once said to him,

> I don't want Jesus Christ to be first in my life any more.
> . . . If He's first in my life . . . then that presupposes there
> must be other things second and third. . . . If that is true,
> then these other things will be vying for first place. I just
> want Him to *be* my life.[76]

John R. Rice extolls "soul-winning" in similar terms: "To be absorbed in the greatest task in the world and have all one's powers,
all one's energy and enthusiasm harnessed in this great work certainly does simplify the matter of living right."[77] This is probably
not the only thing it does. It may be argued that such zeal promotes immaturity and instability since it forces self-integration on
too narrow a basis. The "hard religious line" is a clear example of
what Gordon Allport calls "the immature [religious] sentiment" which

"is not really unifying in its effect upon the personality. Exclud-
ing as it does whole regions of experience, it is sporadic, segmented,
and even when fanatic in intensity, it is but partially integrative of
the personality."[78] It is this too narrow basis of integration that
characterizes what theologian Paul Tillich calls "idolatrous faith."
Such faith must sooner or later collapse since it has elevated to
ultimacy that which is merely one of the self's several finite interests; it cannot long provide real fulfillment. Other unconscious
drives will eventually demand expression.[79]

The hard religious line fosters unquestioning acceptance of pre-
packaged answers. As Eli Chesen points out in *Religion May Be
Hazardous to Your Health*, this kind of acceptance of "arbitrary
answers" and "rigid, confined, and stereotyped religious thinking
patterns can be directly contributory to emotional instability."[80]
The hard-line Born Again Christian will be inhibited in learning for
himself about life, asking ultimate questions, or even working through
and understanding his personal problems, since as we have seen, he
is told to "give them to the Lord" and pray them away. It is imagined that the Holy Spirit will miraculously intervene to solve one's
problems. In fact, to try to solve them oneself would be sin; it
would be acting "in the flesh," i.e., sinful self-sufficiency. Psychologically this kind of "spiritual growth" may result in the re-
tardation of personal growth.

Some examples are in order at this point. Jean Houston, director
of the Foundation for Mind Research in New York City, describes a
teenager who joined the Jesus Movement after a severe family crisis
of some sort.

> She escaped her guilt and horror, but it had the effect
> of a psychological and social lobotomy. Where once she had
> been superbly inquisitive, she now could relate things only
> in terms of her religion—but she now had a focal point for all
> her energy.[81]

The same tendency to put all one's eggs in one tight basket comes
out again in John Kildahl's research on the practice of glossalalia:

> It appeared to us at the conclusion of our study that the
> more integrated the personality the more modest he was in
> both claims and practice of glossalalia. Those who stated
> that they solved virtually every problem with which they wres-
> tled by means of glossalalia were fundamentally immature.[82]

The eventual collapse predicted by Tillich may be observed in the
remarks of Wilfred Bockelman on the Bill Gothard seminar, certainly
one of the most exhaustively and rigidly detailed programs of "hard
line" indoctrination:

> A number of professional counselors . . . told me that
> both they and their colleagues experience an increase in case-
> load whenever Gothard comes to town.
> This includes people of low ego strength. They already
> have a low opinion of themselves. And now they have another
> law laid on them and they can't meet these demands either, so
> they experience yet another failure.[83]

How ironic that this totalism is often advertised with the words of

Jesus: "I came that they might have life and have it more abundantly" (John 10:10). Some Born Again Christians who have become dissatisfied with the hard religious line would want to counter with another quote:

> Why do we try to test God by putting on the necks of the disciples a yoke that neither we nor our fathers have been able to bear? No! We believe that it is through the grace of our Lord Jesus that we are saved (Acts 15:10-11).

It is to this latter group we must now turn.

The Soft Religious Line

Perhaps during the preceding discussion the reader has been hard pressed not to think of William James's classification of "the Sick Soul." But there are the "Healthy Minded" among Born Again Christians. It is not unusual to find in the writings of such people that they are consciously defining their positions over against hardliners whose position they themselves once may have held. In fact, it will take us less time to explain this "soft" religious line since it is almost pure negation of the hard religious line.

First of all, the softliners repudiate the notion that conversion to Christ eliminates problems. O. Quentin Hyder, in *The Christian's Handbook of Psychiatry*, says, "it is absolutely untrue that Christians cannot or should not become mentally ill. We are just as vulnerable as pagans."[84] Consequently religious answers are not always enough. Bruce Larson quite openly says that "worship, prayer, Bible study, and a genuinely pious life" are not enough. Christians also need involvement in the world. Instead of praying for God to remove their fears, Christians should ask for courage to "launch into action despite our fears."[85] He describes his mother's grief at the death of his stepfather. She declined help, claiming that "Jesus Christ was adequate for her needs." Yet what finally brought her out of depression was involvement with others in a tutoring program.[86] Softliners such as Larson and Keith Miller contend that the volitional dismissal of unwanted feelings (a la Gillquist, Bright, et al.) is actually repression. Instead one should seek psychological help if necessary.[87] They stress the need for new methods of helping people and are quite open to the various approaches of modern psychology. For instance, Larson advocates "Relational Theology" which draws methodologically not on religious dogma but on things like personal encounter, leadership dynamics, and communication theory.[88] Keith Miller seeks to interpret the process and benefits of Evangelical conversion to Christ in terms of Maslow's model of "clusters of needs."[89] Thomas Harris's "Transactional Analysis" has also been very popular among Born Again Christians holding to the soft religious line. For instance, Jon Tal Murphree's book *When God Says You're OK*, attempts to make Transactional Analysis's benefits even greater by putting the relationship to God in this framework. Ruth Carter Stapleton's ministry of "Inner Healing" was actually little more than Transactional Analysis with a religious veneer.

The use of secular psychological models and methods by softliners indicates that they do not see the solution of problems as qualitatively different between Born Again Christians and the "unsaved."

Is there any difference, then? Christian psychologist Hyder recalls:
"The actual psychotherapy I had given him was not significantly different from that which he would have gotten from a non-Christian
psychologist."[90] Softliners feel that one's commitment to Christ
facilitates the healing process that everyone has some chance to go
through successfully.   They attribute this to the psychological effects of having strong religious beliefs.   Some soft-line writers attribute psychological potency to the metaphysical truth of their beliefs,[91] but it is hard to see how this is necessary from their own
description of the factors of psychological health.   Miller suggests
that it is the experience of loving God and fellow Christians that
helps the Born Again Christian to meet several clusters of needs
relatively quickly.   Larson feels that commitment to Christ gives a
boost toward being able to become vulnerable and to affirm ourselves
and others.[92] In other words, being Born Again does not give the
convert a new answer to his problems; it merely gives him a shot in
the arm to do a better job at trying the same answers everyone else
has.

Of course, there is also attention to the Bible among soft-line
Born Again counselors.   Witness Hyder once again: "With [Chris-
tian patients] I honestly attempt to integrate sound principles of
psychotherapy with teachings of Scripture."[93] The impression here,
however, is very different from that of hard-line counselors like Jay
Adams who would apparently preach a sermon on repentance to anyone who came to him for any reason.   It is obvious that the role of
the Bible is very different here.   Adams, Thieme, Little, and the
others assumed the Bible and its dogmas to be an adequate medical
kit.   They need to look no further.   This is not so among the softliners.   For example, Gary Collins writes:

> It does not follow . . . that God reveals all truth about
> men or about His universe within the pages of Scripture. Med-
> icine, physics, chemistry, and a host of other academic disci-
> plines have discovered truths about God's world which are
> consistent with, but not *written* in, the pages of the Bible.[94]

Yet these people do consider themselves Born Again Christians with
the adherence to "biblical authority" that is implied, so lip service
at least is given to the Bible's importance.   James Mallory protests:
"Christians have sometimes concluded that the 'real answers' to man's
practical problems are outside the Bible somewhere.   So they soft-
pedal the Bible, and then apply to 'science' or 'psychology' for the
real answers."[95] Yet Mallory himself seems to have done just this.
While he indeed focuses on some basic biblical ideas, he repairs to
secular psychiatry for the "immense amount of truth" to be found
there, including "many complex medical aspects of emotional problems" and "many techniques to help people open up better."   The
contrast between hard-line and soft-line use of the Bible is of more
importance than is usually understood.   I will return to this point
later.

The World and the Self in the Soft Religious Line

Whereas the hard religious line tends to rob the world of any
inherent value or reality, making it "a humanized realm saturated

with significations," the soft religious line reverses this. The Born
Again Christian who adopts the soft line may be compared to the
"layman" of Yves Congar, for whom the things of this world are
"really interesting *in themselves*" because "their truth is not as it
were swallowed up and destroyed by a higher reference."[96]
   As with the hard religious line, the worldview is reflected in the
coping mechanisms. First, one notices in the literature a distinct
shift away from what we called "divination." Instead of urgings to
discern God's will in every event, we find suggestions that *in general* pain and adversity are necessary for personal growth.[97] Secondly, instead of "combat," the task of the Christian is seen as
growth and relationship: "The true man of God . . . can move out
into creative relationships and adventure, implying that he may fail
and will fail. But when he does, he does not justify his failure by
blaming God's guidance."[98] In the soft religious line, life and
the world have their own value and are not solely a theatre for
the performance of a one-man religious drama. Soft-line Evangelicals
still talk about God's guidance, answered prayer, etc., but there
is a noticeable shift away from the world-picture of the hardliners,
where every event is a coded message from God.
   According to the soft religious line, the Born Again Christian has
a real and valuable self. He is not important only as a potential
carbon copy of Jesus Christ, an exemplar or advertisement of the
gospel. Cecil Osborne, in *The Art of Understanding Yourself*, says,
"God is not concerned only with the need for his children to be
decent and moral and honest. . . . He is concerned . . . that our
lives shall be rich and full and creative; that we shall discover our
highest potential. . . ."[99] Miller echoes these sentiments: "If my
faith is in God, then my job is not to build a successful, untainted
religious life; it is to live a joyful and creative human life."[100] By
the criteria suggested earlier (maturity, stability, and an adequate
basis of self-integration), the soft religious line is clearly healthier
than its rival.
   The reader may be thinking, "But surely it's not such an 'either-
or proposition'!" Yes, that's true—most Evangelicals probably com-
bine both approaches, "hard-line" at some points, "soft-line" at
others. The two schemas represent the axes along which most Born
Again Christians would range themselves. I do not seek to make
anyone into a straw man. I only point out, e.g., that *insofar as*
one adheres to the hard religious line, one is *tending* toward un-
healthiness. I hope to have provided a grid upon which the reader
may "plot" his spirituality, so as to see where it would lead if pursued consistently.

Biblical Authority

   Any list of Evangelical beliefs would include the adherence to the
teaching of the Bible taken at face value, the propositional authority
of "the plain sense of the text." All Evangelical Christians are
united on this point regardless of in-house disputes on questions
such as inerrancy. Thus it is a priority for Born Again Christians
to show that their psychological methods and views of self and the
world are at the very least consistent with and suggested by the
teaching of the Bible. All of them try to do this. In this section,

I will ask how well their attempts come off.   ·

First I will describe what may be considered a hermeneutical abuse of the text sometimes called "psychologizing." This is the attempt to use Old and New Testament characters to illustrate authoritatively (and thus somehow to provide evidence for) the modern writer's view of psychology. The literature used in researching this chapter abounds in such psychologizing. For example, Bruce Larson cites Jesus' cure of the Gerasene demoniac as an example of the affirmation of persons. Jesus' naming Simon "Peter" ("The Rock") shows how we should imaginatively envision a person's potential.[101] Swihart sees Elijah in I Kings 19 as an example of a man repressing his feelings. He speculates from Exodus that Moses had been a spoiled child in Egypt. Jesus, by throwing the money-changers out of the temple, was engaging in a non-verbal form of admitting and "owning" his feelings.[102] LaHaye tries to substantiate his use of a four-temperament emotional categorization by pointing out "Bible personalities [who] show temperamental strengths and weakness."[103]

There are at least two major difficulties with such a use of the Bible. First, the portraits of individuals in the Bible are so sketchy and fragmentary that it would be extremely hazardous to try and "psych them out."[104] In lieu of any real evidence, these writers wind up reading in their own preconceived notions. Second, as is almost universally agreed, the "authority of the Bible" refers to the intended teaching of the Bible, i.e., not to the character sketches of cameo-players who appear from time to time in the redemptive drama. In other words, the biblical documents are usually hortatory or polemical in intent and seldom seem to make a point of what "temperament" a character had, or whether or not he repressed his negative feelings! If character sketches are being appealed to merely to demonstrate certain psychological characteristics common to human beings, why is the Bible used as a focus instead of, say, modern novels, newspapers, plays, or diaries? Probably the answer lies in a mystification of the idea of biblical authority. This notion is vaguely invoked to legitimate the writer's psychological analysis since, after all, he is drawing his examples from the Bible! Even if we could be sure that the Bible provided detailed and inerrant records of certain personalities, this would hardly make them better or more compelling evidence than any modern data. This is so by the very nature of what the psychologist is trying to do with the data. Accuracy in data is helpful but doesn't determine what the data will help prove. (On my second point, see Greidanus's excellent discussion in Sola Scriptura, Problems and Principles in Preaching Historical Texts.)

Little aptly sums up the hard-line view when he says,

Many Christians are searching the Scriptures, hoping to find Biblical passages to substantiate their psychological views. Jesus and the apostles did not spend time expounding psychological theories of man; they preached the gospel.[105]

Advocates of the hard religious line seek to enter into the world-view of the Bible at several major points. For instance, the attribution of most or all sickness to demon-influence is quite at home in the apocalyptic worldview of the evangelists, particularly Luke (Luke 4:33-39; 10:9-20; 13:11-16; Acts 10:38). On the other hand, sickness as often, or even usually, inflicted by God as a punishment or for some other reason is clearly present in New Testament texts such as Mark 2:10-11; Luke 13:1-5; John 5:14; 9:1-3; 11:4; II Corinthians 12:7-9; James 5:14-16. Paul sees delays in his travel plans as the work of Satan (I Thessalonians 2:18) and imagines himself to be constantly engaged in battle with demonic forces (Ephesians 6:11-12ff). That God is in deterministic control of all events is a fair inference from texts including Matthew 10:29-30; Romans 8:28; Ephesians 1:11; 5:20; I Thessalonians 5:18. Obedience to the government (even that of Nero!) is inculcated in Romans 13:1ff; I Peter 2:13ff. Submission of a Christian to his superiors even to the point of willingly taking unjust beatings "because he is conscious of God" is commanded in I Peter 2:18-3:6. Rigorous self-denial is urged in Luke 14:26; I Corinthians 9:27. The deprecation of non-religious reality is present in Colossians 3:1-3; Philippians 1:21; 3:7-9. Stoic acceptance of any circumstance is inculcated in Philippians 4:11-12; II Corinthians 12:10; I Corinthians 7:17, 21. Purely religious "solutions" to anxieties are reflected in Philippians 4:6-7; I Peter 5:7. Hardliners, then, seem to be pretty faithful to the "literal, propositional" sense of the text, that sense which is supposed to be normative for Evangelicals.

By contrast, softliners seem to select very basic biblical ideas, and then expound them in terms of a modern, humanistic worldview. For instance, man's creation in the image of God is taken to imply a modern notion of human dignity and rights. Or the Fatherly love of God is sometimes taken to imply that God will not send calamities to judge and chastise his children, even though this certainly was not the inference drawn by the author of, e.g., Acts 5:1-11. The notion of Christians developing into maturity in Christ (Ephesians 4:13) is made the basis for an emphasis on humanistic self-actualization, though Paul's intent seems to be more strictly religious, or even mystical. For the softliners, what is really important in the Bible is not so much its propositional prescriptions for living, but rather its rudimentary message of salvation, which is then applied in the context of a modern worldview.

Indeed many theologians would salute this shift as a very responsible attempt at hermeneutics. (We will see why in Chapter 9.) However, whether it is faithful to the Evangelical ideal of the propositional authority of all biblical texts *in all matters of faith and practice* is quite another matter. I argue that this use of the Bible is not in harmony with the peculiarly Evangelical understanding of biblical authority, whereas the hard-line approach is.

First, I will compare statements of representative soft-line writers with surprisingly similar statements by theological liberals and secular psychiatrists. As already noted, softliners do not feel themselves obliged to stick to the Bible as their primary guide in psychological matters. To repeat a statement of Collins:

> It does not follow . . . that God reveals all truth about men or about His universe within the pages of Scripture. Medicine, physics, chemistry, and a host of other academic disciplines have discovered truths about God's world which are consistent with, but not *written in*, the pages of the Bible.

Bockelman agrees that ". . . the Bible is not a textbook on science or medicine . . . the findings of science are also gifts and revelations of God."[106] Compare these statements with one by Joseph Fletcher of *Situation Ethics* fame:

> . . . the arts and sciences . . . no longer bow down to .
> . . authoritarian principles. Their lifeline is no more handed
> down in advance or dropped from above by "revelation." . . .
> Men have turned to inductive and experimental methods . . .
> appealing to experience. . . . Psychology, for example, got
> its start and growth this way.[107]

Secular psychologist Abraham Maslow comments,

> It used to be that all these questions were answered by
> organized religions in their various ways. Slowly these an-
> swers have come more and more to be based on natural, em-
> pirical facts and less and less on custom, tradition, "revela-
> tions," sacred texts, interpretations by a priestly class.[108]

It should be apparent that all these quotes are moving in the same direction—psychology must have its own life, its own freedom, and not be tied down as the handmaid of the Bible and its dogma.

There is another, more specific point of agreement here, i.e., that the Bible has only limited relevance because of its origin amid an ancient and outmoded way of looking at some questions. Critiquing Bill Gothard on his use of the Bible, Evangelical New Testament scholar Gordon Fee remarks, "You cannot just stamp the first century culture onto the twentieth century and say it is the divine order."[109] On the difficult problem of homosexuality, softliner J. Rinzema feels free to disregard the Bible's absolute prohibition: "The confirmed homosexual was not recognized until roughly 1890. The Bible writers assumed that everyone was [naturally] heterosexual."[110] Liberal Joseph Fletcher makes a similar remark in *Situation Ethics*, "Paul and the Gospel writers were entirely innocent of the problem we are discussing. It never occurred to them."[111] Finally, Eli Chesen speaks from a secular standpoint:

> The Bible was written long before anyone knew anything
> about modern psychology and the psycho-sexual developmental
> process. Even if its writers' intentions were the best, they
> could not have taken these important factors into considera-
> tion.[112]

These statements are so similar that without the appropriate labels it would be difficult to distinguish which one represented which viewpoint. But it would also be hard to guess that any of them was to be associated with people who allegedly take the literal sense of the Bible as their infallible guide to practice! As Evangelical theologian Donald G. Bloesch says, "We must hasten to add that this [biblical authority] includes . . . its interpretation of man, life, and history."[113] But does one get this impression reading soft-line psychological literature? Is not their understanding of man and life derived from elsewhere?

While nearly all Born Again Christian organizations swear by the literal sense of scripture as the infallible rule for faith and practice, it seems that only the hardliners take this seriously in the particular area of "practice" we have been discussing, i.e., psychology and

coping. Soft-line Born Again writers seem to take a position closer
to that of Liberal theologian James Barr who denies that the Bible is

> a resource-book, a work to which one could turn with one's
> problems and receive directions about what was right or what
> should be done. . . . The Bible is not in fact a problem-
> solver. It seems to me normal that the biblical material bears
> upon the whole man, his total faith and life, and that out of that
> total faith and life *he* takes his direction as a free agent.[114]

Can the soft religious line be salvaged as a biblically consistent
option for Evangelical Christians? Charles Kraft of Fuller Seminary,
in his book *Christianity in Culture*,[115] gives us a hint as to how it
can be. Kraft points out how Evangelicals have often found themselves in a quandary over "biblical injunctions" to wear veils, not to
wear jewelry, etc. There has been a sense that such passages are
culturally-bound in their relevance, and that it would be both naive
and legalistic to take them literally. Kraft gives a helpful articula-
tion of the implicit principle of hermeneutics at work here. He says
that the traditional grammatico-historical adherence to the literal
"plain meaning" of the text has deprived Evangelicals of any real
plumbline with which to separate the culture-bound from the trans-
cultural elements of scripture. He suggests a schema whereby God
is seen as "supracultural," revealing supraculturally valid truths in
the context of the various human cultures, including the Hebrew
and Greek cultures of the Bible. God's basic principles will be
clothed in the culturally-conditioned forms of the biblical writers.
For instance, God inculcates the supracultural principle of propriety and modesty via Paul's culturally relative injunction to wear
veils in church. Sometimes the broad principles are simply stated
as such, with a greater degree of abstraction or generality. Where
this is so, the biblical interpreter has little difficulty in finding
direct guidance from the text using the grammatico-historical method.
But when the principle reaches us in a text's culturally-determined
clothing, the interpreter is faced with a puzzle. Kraft proposes
another hermeneutical method, dubbed the "culturo-linguistic," or
"ethnohermeneutical" method. In thus asking what were the cultur-
ally-determining factors in a given passage, the exegete is only pur-
suing the "historical" half of the "grammatico-historical" method.
The point is that the interpreter has a tool at his disposal enabling
him to take seriously the point of the text without taking as literally
binding statements which are dependent on an alien, and thus inap-
propriate, cultural setting. I think this hermeneutical procedure
implicitly underlies the soft-line approach to the Bible as outlined
above. It seems to me plausible that many of the texts which give
rise to the hard-line views of world, self, and coping really represent the cultural-conceptual furniture of an earlier age. One could
consistently abstract what seem to be larger biblical principles from
such cultural baggage, as the softliners seem in fact to have done.
I am not unaware of the problem of "where do you draw the line?"
In other words, how does such an apparently innocent device as
Karft's "culturo-linguistic" method of exegesis differ in principle
from Bultmann's program of "demythologizing," the divorce of the
gospel from its first-century "mythological" supernatural trappings?
I will return to this issue in Chapter 10.

I have sought to explain some important aspects of the experiential world of Evangelical Christians. In so doing I have indicated that it is by no means either as simple or as spiritually free as their evangelistic propaganda would suggest. Obviously this study will be only as valid as my material is truly representative and my interpretation accurate. To these ends I have drawn from popular and influential writers and spokesmen across the Evangelical spectrum and have buttressed my assertions with ample quotations. Perhaps my study will cause some of my readers to reassess the assumptions and principles governing their religious life.

Chapter 2

THE EVANGELICAL SUBCULTURE

In the last chapter, I tried to explain and critique some important aspects of the way Evangelicals interpret and cope with their experiences. Now I want to turn to a slightly different aspect of Evangelical experience. I want to focus on what sociologists call the "social construction of reality."[1] The idea is that every individual operates within a worldview shared by his community. A person is socialized into expecting certain things and not others, holding certain ideas as true, obeying various rules, operating on a set of assumptions and values without much question. If he didn't, there would be no way to organize life. One's world is no less composed of such "doctrines felt as facts" than it is of physical objects like buildings or trees. They are the "rules of the game" without which you just couldn't play.

Any society must have a certain set of ground rules and assumptions for there to be any cultural cohesion or order. Subcultures are groups of people who dissent from the mainstream on some important issues. A subculture may hold minority political, artistic, or religious views. This fact results in something of a "ghetto-mentality," even if the members of the subculture live dispersed throughout the larger society. In the mainstream culture or society, one's foundational beliefs are held without too much difficulty. A person is pretty much able to take them for granted. But a member of a subculture is not so fortunate. The sheer numbers of people who do not share his way of looking at things must act as pressure on him. He must think twice about his viewpoint. His minority status itself must challenge the truth of his viewpoint. The subculturalist must try two strategies to keep his beliefs believable. He must limit contact with all those doubt-casting influences from the outside, and he must be able to explain away on his own terms the input he does encounter from outsiders. Only in this way does his viewpoint maintain any of the apparent self-evidence it needs.

If successful, what the subculturalist will have done is to use social and psychological defense mechanisms to make his views "feel like" reality. Yet he will not want to realize this. The recognition that the "real-seemingness" of his worldview is generated and maintained by such devices would undermine that "real-seemingness." The subculturalist would have to face the fact that his viewpoint is not self-evidently true. In other words, when recognized, the mechanisms for overcoming doubt become themselves a new source of doubt.

It should come as no surprise (though to some it may) that the distinctives of Evangelical Christianity lend themselves to adequate explanation as a subculture as just described. In fact, the subcultural character of Evangelicalism can trace its roots back into the heart of the New Testament. Contemporary New Testament scholarship likes to speak in terms of an "already-not yet" tension within the New Testament. Its writers believed that the New Age of Salvation had already dawned by way of anticipation in their Christian fellowship. The rest of the world still slumbered in the darkness of sin since the full manifestation of the Kingdom had not yet come.

But believers already lived in the Kingdom of God. They partici-
pated in "the powers of the age to come" (Hebrews 6:5), lived by
the rules of the coming Kingdom. They had to shine forth as stars
in the darkness around them (Philippians 2:15). All this theologizing reflects a subcultural situation. New Testament Christians,
certainly a minority in the Roman Empire, explained this fact in this
way: Their small band formed a beachhead of the New Age in the
midst of paganism.

Moving to the Evangelical Christianity of our own day, let us see
how it fits the pattern of a subculture. One might list a great
number of values, tenets, and practices undergirding Evangelicalism.
Some important ones are: the normativity of the Bible's statements,
the emphasis on personal pietism, introspective ethical rigorism, conservative views of biblical criticism, the obligation to share one's
personal faith with others, constant church attendance, avoidance of
smoking, drinking, and perhaps cinema, belief in salvation by faith,
expectation of the second coming of Christ in the near future, and
several others. One may well ask just how a conversion to faith in
Christ implies all or any of these things. Though Evangelicals have
carefully constructed various legitimations of all of them, the real
connection is more accidental than essential. This fact is evidenced
by the existence of other groups professing faith in Christ without
these particular attendant beliefs and attitudes. The new convert to
Evangelicalism finds himself in a supportive community of faith into
whose attitudes and assumptions he is soon socialized. He has believed their message about Christ; aren't they to be trusted when
they tell him to read the Bible, convert his friends, and, perhaps,
vote Republican?

"If anyone is in Christ, there is a whole new world" (II Corinthians 5:17), wrote Paul. And the new convert to Evangelicalism
will probably not think to separate Christ and the Evangelical world.
This new world is constantly reinforced by verbal input such as
sermons, testimonies from fellow believers, hymns, and jargon. The
series of cliche phrases will function like secret passwords. They
include: "Praise the Lord," "fellowship," "That was a blessing,"
"witnessing," and (if one is Pentecostal or Charismatic) especially
glossalalia, or "speaking in tongues." Such jargon isolates the believers from the outsiders, the "unsaved," and, conversely, immediately signals the believer as to the presence of a "brother or sister
in the Lord."

We have here an example of a full-blown subcultural situation.

> Spiritual rebirth, infallible Scripture, signs and wonders,
> explicit doctrine, and awareness of the approaching End, com-
> bine to build around the Evangelical a magic circle invisibly
> cutting him off from those for whom these things have no
> meaning. Here he lives in an alternative world.[2]

It could fairly be said that, despite the universalizing tendency
implied in the Evangelical emphasis on evangelism, this world-picture
could not exist without its severe "us versus them" dichotomy. It
is essential to the whole Evangelical cognitive enterprise that the
faithful be a misunderstood and rejected minority. Or at least it
must seem so to the faithful themselves. For instance, the overwhelming impression given in apologist Francis Schaeffer's widely

read books is that almost everyone outside of the fold has succumbed
to an agnostic secularism. The Christian soldier must sally forth
with the gospel in a "Post-Christian Age." Anyone else, glancing
at recent surveys like the Gallup poll,[3] might think twice about such
a diagnosis of modern society's level of religious interest.

James Barr suggests that this minority self-consciousness is maintained even where Evangelicalism is not a cognitive minority, e.g.,
in the American South. "Part of its preaching dynamic arises from
the continual suggestion that its view is something that has not been
heard before. . . ."[4] He notes that even in areas of Evangelical
religious dominance there is often still no revolutionary social or
spiritual change such as one might expect from the promises of Evangelical propaganda. This embarrassing hiatus is hidden by continual
rhetoric to the effect that Evangelicals are still a fighting minority.
This illusion seems to be becoming more difficult in the face of recent media exposure. It is becoming increasingly evident that the
Evangelical allegiance of even fifty million Americans has somehow
not proved incompatible with the growing crime rate and decadence
decried by Evangelicals' own rhetoric.

Ironically, while Evangelicals tell themselves that they are ignored
and unknown, simultaneously they warn each other to be circumspect
since the skeptical eyes of "the world" are on them all the time!
Frequently one hears admonitions to be "a good witness" since the
Christian life is lived in "a goldfish bowl" before unbelievers. In
fact, some go so far as to attribute to outsiders the strictest fundamentalist mores! One must not have a beer or go to a movie, because what would a non-Christian think if he saw this? Surely he
knows that such things are incompatible with real Christian commitment, and the beer-drinking, movie-going Evangelical will have "dam-
aged his testimony"! Here the mores of one's own worldview are
reinforced by projecting them onto those outside. The Evangelical
somehow imagines the "unsaved" to think in the same categories he
himself does.

Hear No Evil, See No Evil

Ideally, a subcultural worldview may best be maintained if one
can totally regulate the input received by members. This was, of
course, ultimately the point of "Newspeak" in *1984*. Language itself
was to be manipulated so as to eliminate the possible infiltration of
"dangerous" ideas. Few will wish to go so far in real life, but the
basic motive of protection is often the same. Traditionally, Evangelicals have attempted to avoid "worldly" entertainment including theatre, movies, dancing, etc. This is still the approach of stricter
fundamentalist Evangelicals. One still hears tiresome tirades against
movie-going, but a newer crusade is against rock and roll. This
issue will serve well to illustrate our point. Evangelical opponents
of such music are quite clear in their apprehension of the "ideological protection" question. Bob Larson warns:

> Lyrical content which is directly opposed to Biblical stan-
> dards and accepted Christian behavior should definitely be
> avoided.
> Few teenagers listening to the Beatles sing "Nowhere Man"
> or "Eleanor Rigby" would stop to realize the philosophical im-

plications of the lyrics of these songs. Nevertheless, the
philosophical outlook conveyed will influence their thoughts.
. . .

For Larson, the alternatives are clear:

> . . . the time per day spent listening to rock music is . .
> . compounded far beyond the weekly intake of Biblical train-
> ing [and a] moral imbalance results. A mind that has been
> infiltrated by hours of lyrical pornography throughout the
> week cannot be easily remolded with only a few hours allotted
> for Christian instruction on Sunday.[5]

Frank Garlock of Bob Jones University agrees: "The loud beat
and sensual, pleasure-oriented lyrics will drown out the voice of
God and dwarf your spiritual life."[6]

Of late, moderate Evangelicals have allowed "Christian rock" which
of course has Evangelical lyrics. Such music "keeps 'em down on
the farm after they've seen Paree" by making the farm look more like
Paree! The same is now being done with entertainment talk shows
(Oral Roberts, Pat Robertson) and even soap operas!

A newer attitude among Evangelicals is that one may critically
evaluate the arts (i.e., instead of rejecting them outright) on the
ideological basis of Evangelical doctrine. For Instance, Francis Schaeffer comments:

> As far as a Christian is concerned, the world view that is
> shown through a body of art must be seen ultimately in terms
> of the Scriptures. The artist's world view is not to be free
> from the judgment of the Word of God.[7]

Reading through the ideological critiques of art in books like Francis
Shaeffer's *How should We Then Live?* can be a puzzling experience
for a non-Evangelical. One thing becomes clear, however. The
Evangelical's belief-structure is being shielded either by closing the
doors to certain of the arts and amusements, or at least by demanding the proper password.

The same suspicious attitude is discernible in various Evangelical
stances towards higher education. Bill Gothard, influential teacher
of the popular "Institute in Basic Youth Conflicts" seminar, warns
his listeners to stay away from the social sciences and philosophy.
It has been suggested that this attitude reflects Gothard's own experience in Northwestern University's graduate psychology program.
He found he must either endanger his (fundamentalist) faith or drop
out.[8] Indeed, he views his own seminar as, in some respects, an
answer to secular principles of education. But Evangelicals go farther. Many "Christian Liberal Arts Colleges," such as Wheaton,
Gordon, Westmont, Anderson, and Lee Colleges, have been founded.
For those Evangelical students brave enough to venture out into the
world of secular education, there are groups like Inter Varsity Christian Fellowship. Such organizations seek to form an Evangelical student colony, a refuge in the midst of campus secularism. The organization itself acts as an alternative peer group. It also provides
literature arming the Evangelical student with counter-arguments and
answers to questions he may not yet even be aware of. Staff per-
sonnel make available apologetics literature on such topics as behaviorist psychology, biblical criticism, existentialism, and comparative

religion. Of course, all of it is written from the student's own religious viewpoint and tends to read out ideologically objectionable
elements. The student is led to believe that he is fortunate enough
to be heir to the most intellectually cogent position, whether he has
seriously examined other views or not. He doesn't need to examine
them. Others have already done this for him, or at least it seems so.

The same phenomenon occurs outside of the student world in
Evangelicalism as a whole. Whereas their literature once dealt with
predominantly religious themes, there has come to be a flood of pop-
literature on every imaginable subject, complete with a religious,
proof-texting veneer. There are popular self-help books on losing
weight the "biblical" way, Born Again sex manuals, Christian cook-
books, etc. Evangelicals need not resort to "the world" even for
superstition, speculation, and fantasy. One may find ready at hand
books dealing with the "biblical position" on flying saucers and the
Bermuda Triangle, as well as an extensive literature on demonism
and the occult. What next?

Returning to the safeguarding of Evangelical faith in the world of
education, we can detect a principle underlying the same concerns
throughout Evangelicalism. Kenneth Howkins, in a book designed to
prepare Evangelical students for religious studies in secular schools,
writes:

> The Christian [read: "Evangelical"] will need to think in a
> Christian way about everything. . . . It is particularly diffi-
> cult as such a great proportion of the information and opinions
> he receives is from a non-Christian standpoint. He will need
> to think carefully whether the view of history, or politics, or
> society which he is accepting is really in full accord with his
> Christian beliefs.
>
> The student needs an open mind towards those things he
> does not know. . . . But he does not need to empty his mind
> of those matters about which he has a sure knowledge.[9]

Howkins thus assures his readers that they may practice the virtue
of open-mindedness while refusing to budge from a perspective which
must strictly censor all input!

Be Not Equally Yoked

In the last section we discussed the filtering, censoring, and de-
fensive dynamics used by Evangelicals to shield their subcultural
outlook from the thought and culture around them. The same thing
happens on an individual, interpersonal level. Through various
means, the significant contacts with individuals outside of the subculture must be carefully regulated. This begins at conversion,
when one is "born again." Evangelicals often counsel new converts
at least temporarily to withdraw from their old friends so as to avoid
being pulled back into their worldly ways. An alternative strategy
is for the new convert immediately to share his new faith with his
old friends. This will serve, if not to convert them, then (probably
more importantly) to insulate him from them. He will have put a
wall between them and himself by signaling he is henceforth willing
to relate to them only on his new religious terms. They will now
hold him at arm's length. Either way, the new Born Again Christian

is isolated from the personal influence of those outside. Consequently, he is thrust even more snugly into the arms of his new (and
only remaining) peer group.

"Witnessing," or "personal evangelism" functions in the same way
for those who are no longer neophytes. The practice serves to
keep the non-Evangelical at a distance where his influence on the
Evangelical can be kept to a safe minimum. In Evangelical churches
and campus groups, one is constantly told to "witness" to one's
acquaintances. In fact, it is easy to draw the inference that such
"friends" are primarily to be seen as potential converts. It is often
assumed and not infrequently stated that an Evangelical Christian
could not have a really close non-Evangelical friend. The rationale
for this judgment may be that the goals and priorities of such a
pair would ultimately be divergent enough to inhibit the sharing,
discussion, and sympathy there must be between friends. This is
also given as a reason for the unbending Evangelical insistence that
Evangelicals never marry or even date non-Evangelicals, "the unsaved." As legitimate as this concern for compatibility may be,
the overriding concern in such segregation of potential friends and
spouses is that of protecting the faith of the Evangelical. The "unsaved" friend or partner would threaten and challenge one's own
outlook seriously from such close quarters.

Witnessing performs yet another related function. It not only
segregates the Evangelical from non-Evangelicals, thus reducing
their threat to his worldview. It also positively reinforces that
worldview in other ways. First, there is the strategy of "truth by
majority vote." Theoretically, such a notion is repudiated by Evangelicals in order to discount the fact that the majority does not accept their truth. But psychologically, the winning of more and
more converts numerically increases the popular base of the belief-
system. The more his assumptions about reality are unchallenged or
accepted, the easier one may breathe. Psychologist Leon Festinger
says it well: ". . . dissonance can be reduced. If more and more
people can be persuaded that the system of belief is correct, then
clearly it must, after all be correct."[10]

Witnessing reinforces the plausibility structure in a second way.
Roger Ellwood explains that when the Evangelical challenges people
to convert, he is "patterning external reality in other people on the
basis of [his] own secret reality, rather than being molded [himself]
. . . by the outer world."[11] Thus, even if the potential convert
declines the decision thrust upon him, he is at least acting on the
delineation of alternatives proposed by the Evangelical. The Evangelical's reality has been afforded the dignity of recognition. But,
thirdly, even hostile rejection or ridicule will reinforce the Evangelical's belief. It will prove to him that he is indeed one of the
persecuted minority, the "faithful few." Thus every experience is
interpreted in a positive way. Nothing could disconfirm the worldview.

It is not surprising to read in John Lofland's *Doomsday Cult* that
the same dynamics are at work among the Moonies when they prose-
lytize. For instance, since they envision their efforts as part of
the cosmic battle between good and evil, they can always chalk up a
meager number of converts to Satan's opposition. But God might
bless them with new converts. "In general [Moonies] could not lose.

If prospects came along, God was most active. If they did not, Satan was most active. . . . Satan worked hardest against [Moonie evangelists] when they were really striking a blow for God. Therefore if it appeared that Satan was really attacking them—e.g., if few prospects were appearing—that must mean that in some way they were really getting close to a victory for God."[12] Sound familiar? It all seems to work the same way regardless of which religious worldview one is trying to propagate.

Speaking of the Unification Church, it might be instructive to point out another interesting parallel between it and the Evangelical movement. That is the practice of "heavenly deception," i.e., being less than aboveboard with outsiders so as to more effectively influence them for the Truth. When I heard of the shady tactics of the Moonies, my initial indignation was modified by empathy. I remembered only too well all the innocuous-sounding "fronts" operated by Evangelicals in order to witness to sinners, e.g., coffee houses, concerts, philosophical forums, religious surveys. None of these was ever billed for what it was. The idea was to hook the unsuspecting sinner and win an opportunity to tell him the gospel. Similar Machiavellian tactics govern various interpersonal contacts. A campus leader or foreign student may find himself the object of an Evangelical's friendly attention, not realizing he has been singled out for "friendship evangelism" because of his potentially strategic position. A football star, once "saved," may use his influence to convert many others. The foreign student may become a future leader in his pagan home country. What a boon to missionaries he would be if he converted!

Any non-Evangelical reading this book may remember occasions where a conversation with an Evangelical unexpectedly turned to religion. Let me assure such a reader that this was no accident. Most Evangelicals are exhorted to try to turn any conversation with a non-believer "toward spiritual things." As the conversation proceeds and differences of opinion are aired, the "unsaved" person may begin to notice that the Evangelical gives no real consideration to his point of view. Because the stakes are eternal life or death, and everything depends on one's belief-stance regarding Christianity, the Evangelical has no room to recognize that honest minds may differ. No, if a non-Evangelical does not accept the Evangelical's absolute truth, it *must* be because Satan is blinding him, or because the unbeliever is guiltily hiding behind a smokescreen. Evangelicals often assume that an unbeliever is only using his questions as a dodge to avoid repentance from sin.

Bracketing the truth or falsity of Evangelical belief, I think that technically speaking this kind of stance is what we mean when we use the term "narrow-minded." But Evangelicals as respectable moderns would say they frown on narrow-mindedness. They must face the question: is it narrow-mindedness per se that they deplore? Or do they just oppose people narrow-mindedly holding non-Evangelical views?

One may also notice a double standard at work. The Evangelical will try to knock down his friend's objections to Born Again faith, thus asking the potential convert to "listen to reason" and give in. But if a really thorny question comes up, the Evangelical has been coached to admit "Say, that's a good question. I don't have an an-

Robert M. Price

swer, but I'll try to get one. Meanwhile wouldn't you like to convert anyway?" What this shows is that while he appeals to the unbeliever on an allegedly rational basis, he holds his own beliefs by
pure willpower. Otherwise, how could his lack of an answer to a
"good (i.e., genuinely troublesome) question" fail to make him think
twice about the cogency of his beliefs? I will have a good bit more
to say on all this in the second section of this book.

Mirror, Mirror on the Wall,
Who's the Truest of Them All?

Advertising is based on the practice of making the public think
they need what you've got. Evangelicals use a similar ploy to legitimate, or explain on their own terms, the fact that even though "the
world" does not accept Evangelical faith, this faith is still true, and
not, say, a mere eccentric sect. The idea is that outsiders really
want what Evangelicals have. In fact they are just crying out for
it, if they only knew! Evangelicals thus project their valuation of
their religion onto the absence of that faith in the outside world and
the result is an imagined longing for Evangelicalism's "answers."
Evangelicals imagine how they would feel if they were suddenly deprived of their faith and then assume that those without their faith
must actually feel this way. One finds in Evangelical literature a
never-ending refrain to this effect. For instance, Francis Schaeffer
claims:

> Christianity [read: Evangelicalism] has the opportunity . .
> . to speak clearly of the fact that its answer has the very
> thing that modern man has despaired of—the unity of thought.
> It provides a unified answer for the whole of life.

Schaeffer prooftexts art, poetry, theatre, philosophy, movies, tele-
vision, pornography, and music. From his viewpoint secular assumptions must lead logically to despair, and he proceeds to assume,
in effect, that the secularists agree with his conclusions! "The system that surrounds us . . . . is a monolithic one." "These people
are in total desperation."[13]

James Sire, in a book comparing various major worldviews, says
at the beginning(!): "Yes, that is just what those who do not have
faith in the infinite-personal Lord of the Universe must feel—aliena-
tion, loneliness, even despair."[14] Os Guiness in a similar work surveys the options and "false" hopes facing Western culture and comes
up with this dreary result:

> The West today, its self-confidence sagging, its vitality
> ebbing, its order eroded, knows only introspection, lethargy.
> . . . Prone from exhaustion, a prey to its own fears, it is in
> danger of being overwhelmed by the anxiety, apathy, and
> anger of a humanity strangled within it.[15]

Guiness is able to "document" this apocalyptic diagnosis only by
prooftexting pessimistic doomsayers throughout. He picks quotes
from only those secularists dissatisfied with each option he is con-
sidering, giving the impression that all secularists have abandoned
hope. Finally he offers Evangelicalism as the glowing alternative.
He does not think to mention that most of the despairing secularists

he quotes had probably already rejected Guiness's religious viewpoint as an option long ago!   Guiness is not alone in this kind of "documentation" of modern non-Evangelical humanity's despair.

All this is a sophisticated attempt to discount outsiders' views, or to explain them away in terms of one's own viewpoint.   From an Evangelical viewpoint, these secular views *must* end in despair; why then, the Evangelical viewpoint having thus been "demonstrated" to be superior, must be true!   Schaeffer, Sire, Guiness, and others are among the more sophisticated Evangelicals.   Others are cruder in technique.   Some simply need to know that another view is non-Evangelical to attribute it to Satan's invention, a favorite catchall in popular Evangelicalism.   Walter Martin so consigns "cults" such as the Jehovah's Witnesses and the Mormons, amazingly right after deploring the narrow-mindedness which leads the Jehovah's Witnesses to do exactly the same thing![16]   James Bjornstad similarly characterizes Edgar Cayce.[17]   John Weldon and others explain the origins of UFO's as demonic.[18]   Finally, let me draw attention to the recent raft of Evangelical "rebuttals" to Raymond Moody's *Life After Life.*   Evangelicals cannot seem to bear the existence of supernatural-type phenomena outside their theological categories.   Everything must be explained on their terms.   "A place for everything, and everything in its place."

When Evangelicals leave the somewhat abstract discussion of other viewpoints, they go on to deal with other concrete religious groups. A favorite device for negating the views of these groups is to construct one's picture of them entirely from testimony of dissatisfied ex-members.   It should be obvious that such a procedure can only give a distorted picture of a group.   The organization is depicted as being so terrible and oppressive that it is inferred that no one could remain a member under his own free will.   Instead, it is assumed that only brainwashing, deception, and fear can keep people in such groups.

This approach has provided fundamentalists with much of their ammunition against Catholicism.   The most vehement anti-Catholic is the ex-Catholic.   Similarly, current Evangelical literature on groups such as the Unification Church takes testimony of ex-members as normative.   After all, it is reasoned, who is in a better position to tell us about a group than a former member who had to leave when he faced up to the group's failings?   But the testimony of such people is often far from objective.   The convert (or "de-convert") must legitimate his change by negating as evil or ignorance his former life.   The result is that the old group *must have* been bad enough to merit the person's leaving it.   Testimony from dissatisfied ex-members may take the form, then, of biased legitimation.   Such testimony in turn is used by Evangelicals to prove their point.   Evangelicals would rather believe that members of other groups or religions are not experiencing satisfaction, since this confirms the reality of their own experience.   If, however, the Evangelical is confronted with the testimony of a satisfied member of another religion, he is liable to explain such experience as "counterfeit."   And since a counterfeit implies a reality to copy, why then, his own Evangelical faith is confirmed once again!   He wins either way.

The assumption underlying all of this is that one's own view, *simply because* it is one's own view, is seen as qualitatively differ-

ent from the confused miasma of competing alternatives. They are
all alike since they are not *my* view, and that is enough to sink
them.

Rewriting History

Any subcultural worldview comes complete with a past and a future. "It locates all collective events in a cohesive unity that includes past, present, and future" (Berger and Luckmann).[19] Evangelicalism uses history in several interesting ways.
First, the Bible and its stories form a special category of history.
Roger Ellwood describes it perceptively:

> . . . the Bible and its time stand like a lighthouse in the
> midst of history. Bible time is special; it stands in equal re-
> lation to all other points in time. The evangelical is always
> contemporaneous with it, particularly with the time of Christ.
> He wants to collapse into nothing all time between himself and
> the New Testament.[20]

That "Bibletime" so functions is evident from several facts. Evangelicals constantly compare themselves with the primitive church in
The Acts of the Apostles. This picture of the past hovers as an
ever-present ideal. This is a sort of "canonical" picture of the past
such as Robert L. Wilken describes in *The Myth of Christian Origins*.
Another fact confirming Ellwood's observation is the surprising ignorance of church history among many Evangelical laypersons. Sometimes only Martin Luther is sandwiched in between the Apostle Paul
and Billy Graham.
A related use of the past among Evangelicals occurs often in
scholarly Evangelical polemics. Evangelicals claim that they represent direct continuity with historic Christian orthodoxy, particularly
with regard to doctrines such as the inspiration of the Bible. The
object of such polemics is to discredit theological Liberals as revi-
sionists. The same charge has been made against the Evangelicals
themselves, e.g., by James Barr, Ernest Sandeen, and others. At
any rate, history is conceived by Evangelicals as supporting their
own claims of continuity with the "canonical past."
Pentecostal and Charismatic Evangelicals have yet another variation of the "canonical past" schema. This is often called the "Latter Rain" concept. Pentecostalism comes from a revival at the turn
of the century, when people began to have emotional and ecstatic
experiences which they regarded as identical with the "spiritual" or
"charismatic gifts" of the New Testament church. They had to account for several centuries of church history between the early
church and the Pentecostal revival when few such experiences were
in evidence. Someone came up with the "Latter Rain" theory. It
seemed that because of sin, lethargy, or divine providence, the
charismatic gifts were withdrawn from the church after the early
centuries of the Christian era. Spiritual vitality was only gradually
recovered, e.g., the doctrines of justification by faith through Luther, sanctification through Wesley, lay democratization through the
Plymouth Brethren, and finally the spiritual gifts through the Pentecostal revival.[21] This conceptualization is clearly geared to serve
the cognitive needs of sectarian Protestants.

Another ideological use of the past has already been touched on previously. Francis Schaeffer and others try to show a dismal downward slide in the history of culture, away from a pristine Christian purity. Schaeffer clearly longs for the days of the Medieval synthesis, when theology was queen of the sciences and regulated all inquiry and theorizing. In one of his last books, *How Should We Then Live?*, he explained the book as an "attempt to present the flow and development which have led to twentieth-century thinking, and by so doing . . . to show the essential answers."[22] The resulting recital took the form of sketchy overviews of enormous periods of time, prooftexting the histories of art, philosophy, and other disciplines, showing how Western culture fell from grace when it departed from the Bible.

A particularly striking example of the Evangelical shaping of history is the phenomena of paperback apocalypticism. Hal Lindsey's *The Late Great Planet Earth* (as well as a flood of other books with the same contents) sketches out for credulous readers a roadmap for the (short) future, culminating in Armageddon. The picture includes World War III, the decline of American influence, the unification of Western Europe, and the usual eschatological disasters. With such a picture of the future to rely on, the Evangelical who believes this sort of thing (not all do) has little to worry about. He is absolved from any real social responsibilities since the world must worsen till the End. Atomic warfare is nothing to worry about since the Bible seems not to include such a thing in its forecasts. And at any rate, history will culminate in the salvation and reward of the Evangelicals (and no one else). This picture places the Evangelical securely in a history that revolves about himself, and ultimately holds no fears for him. And when one searches the newspaper daily for the latest imagined fulfillments of Bible prophecy, as some do, one has a simple interpretive *gestalt* for all events. For example, he need not worry about Palestinian rights; all he needs to know is that the Bible supposedly promised Palestine to the Jews in the End Times. And so what if peace efforts fail? The sooner Armageddon explodes the better for the Evangelical who will be "raptured" out of the apocalyptic chaos, as in a cosmic Dunkirk.

To turn from eschatology to protology, we cannot ignore Scientific Creationism, a subject much too vast to pursue here in the required detail. My own reading has persuaded me that the whole thing is one vast exercise in explaining away clear but unwelcome evidence. Based on a highly dubious exegesis of Genesis chapter 1, Creationists reject the theory of evolution, or as they like to dub it "macro-evolution," implying they accept enough evolution ("micro-evolution") to retain a shred of scientific respectability. They cannot stomach the notion that all present life forms evolved from unicellular ancestors through millions of years. They wish to preserve the notion of a direct hands-on creation of all major species prototypes by God at crucial junctures. He is imagined to have created an original "dog-kind," from which various breeds including the Chihuahua and the Pit Bull subsequently evolved, willy-nilly. And the whole process took a meagre six days. Archbishop Ussher's famous, or infamous, chronology is preserved intact, really an astonishment in the modern age. The resulting age of the earth is a scant six thousand years. Here, perhaps, we find the weakest and

most embarrassing apologetics of all.   I and others have dealt with
them in detail elsewhere.[23]

Here let me just observe the relevance of Creationism for the
Evangelical apprehension of history.   I think it is no accident that
when one embraces both Creationism and Lindsey-style apocalyptic,
one has drawn history close about oneself like a snug blanket.   Neither the past nor the future is very long.   Humanity thus seems to
be center-stage for the whole duration of the play.   Only the most
radical fundamentalist sectarians still believe the earth is the center
of the planets and the sun, but this curtailing of history on both
ends serves the same end.   The implications of Copernicus's revolution may be safely ignored: man is the center of things after all.

I sometimes think that many Evangelicals would rather live in a
prescientific age, though those engaged in organizations like the
American Scientific Affiliation have striven manfully to make the best
of it where they are.   But the more an Evangelical pursues science
for its own sake, and not to refute it or exploit it for apologetic
ends, the less easily one is able to hold onto the kind of schema I
have described here.   One's copy of Henry Morris's The Genesis
Flood winds up in the attic or the garbage can.   It is replaced by
Bernard Ramm's The Christian View of Science and Scripture.   One
leaves behind the hard religious line and embraces the soft religious
line, if I may borrow my own terminology.   One begins to toy with
accommodations like "theistic evolution," and "progressive creationism," etc.   The world gets older, and one's fundamentalist colleagues
begin to look askance and to doubt one's commitment to inerrancy.

You can see what is really afoot in this foreshortening of the past
and the future if you look at the worldview of cultures who still do
live in a prescientific age.   Anthropologist Jan Vansina says,

> We can use one kingdom as an illustration for the telescoping
> of the past into a very shallow time depth because one could
> not express greater depths of time.   The Tio of Congo recog-
> nize only two generations backwards from an adult Ego. . . .
> Beyond that one goes straight to origins, to mythical founders.
> Anything earlier than the structural time depth . . . is ig-
> nored . . . or telescoped to remain within the frame.   Time
> and space become congruent with society.[24]

I am suggesting that Evangelicals are editing history to fit their own
Procrustean time-frame.   They are cruising along in a cozy history
without much previous mileage on it and with little road ahead to
threaten the vehicle with either accident or obsolescence.

A Glimpse Outside

In the previous chapter, I explored the mechanisms of Evangelical
consciousness that enable a believer to cope with experience.   In
the present chapter I have explored some of these subtle mechanisms
whereby that subcultural system of consciousness as a whole is maintained.   These mechanisms are necessarily subtle, since as we have
observed, the very recognition of them would undermine their effectiveness.   The subcultural way of seeing things must seem self-
evident to the believer.   Only so can all the outside alternatives
seem ipso facto in error.

Anyone who knows an Evangelical Christian knows that Evangelicals assume their religion to be qualitatively different and superior to others, uniquely true and effectual. To be more specific, there are a number of features of Evangelicalism which are seen by believers as marks of its unique truth. A few of the most important components of the Evangelical stance would include: (1) the idea of biblical authority and possibly inerrancy; (2) historic Protestant dogma; (3) the conversion experience; (4) the promise of power for victorious living; (5) a personal relationship with Christ; and (6) radical discipleship and social activism. (Granted, the last one is not common to all Evangelicals.) Together, do not these six features compose a viable, even vibrant religious expression? Anyone can see why Evangelicals are secure in, and proud of, their religion. But Evangelicalism is in fact only one of several viable religious options in which the very same religious components appear. Sometimes they appear in completely different doctrinal contexts, or are combined in very different ways.

For example, it is well known that (1) biblical authority and inerrancy are affirmed by several "heretical" sects including Jehovah's Witnesses. It is amusing to note, incidentally, that Watchtower publications even approvingly cite the work of Evangelical F. F. Bruce on the reliability of the gospels. Similarly, (2) historic Protestant theology is the common property of many non-Evangelical, confessional Protestants.

Moving on to the experiential features outlined above, (3) the conversion experience (to which, of course, the term Born Again refers) is common to nearly all modern "cults," such as the Unification Church, and many mass therapies including est. (On this point see the fascinating book by Conway and Siegelman, *Snapping: America's Epidemic of Sudden Personality Change.*) These conversions are no less "life-changing" than those experienced under Evangelical auspices.

Evangelical devotional literature is filled with promises of and techniques for attaining (4) "power for victorious living." It may be rather surprising to observe how prominent the very same theme is in the mass of pop-Liberal "inspirational literature" by Norman Vincent Peale, Henry C. Link, and others, which peaked in popularity in the 50s. These writers recommended different psychological-religious techniques than the Evangelical devotionalists do. For instance, Bill Gothard teaches "scriptural meditation"; Bill Bright advocates "spiritual breathing"; Inter Varsity writers inculcate the habit of a "daily quiet time." Liberal writers prescribe techniques like "positive thinking," "scientific prayer," etc. The theological context and the jargon are different, but the promised blessings are pretty much the same: "power for living," divine guidance in decision making, emotional security, sometimes even material prosperity. And judging by the immense popularity of these works, it must be assumed that quite a number of people did indeed find "power for victorious living" in this very non-Evangelical alternative. An interesting and important analysis of the appeal and the theological character of this "inspirational literature" may be found in Schneider and Dornbusch, *Popular Religion: Inspirational Books in America,* 1958.

A similarly striking non-Evangelical parallel to Evangelical rhetoric

occurs in the Catholic Charismatic Renewal. There we find (5) the
experience of a "personal relationship with Christ." For instance,
Catholic Charismatic leader Ralph Martin speaks of the need for
people "personally commit[ting] their lives to Jesus, accepting him
as . . . Savior and Lord."[25] Many Evangelicals understandably rejoice at hearing such words from Catholics, but it is imperative not
to overlook the difference in theological context here. Unlike Evangelicals, Charismatic Catholics often do *not* equate conversion/salva-
tion with a personal relationship with Christ. Rather, all Catholics
are understood to be "saved" by virtue of their (infant) baptism.
The personal relationship with Christ is sort of "icing on the cake."
Though Evangelicals somehow often overlook this, from the standpoint of Evangelical theology, this difference really cannot be over-
stressed. Besides this, many if not most Charismatic Catholics continue to embrace traditional Catholic theology, ecclesiology, Mari-
ology, etc.

Finally, what about (6) radical discipleship, made popular among
younger Evangelicals in recent years through the circulation of publications like *The Other Side*, *Radix*, and *Sojourners*? Just how little this part of the picture depends on an Evangelical context is
clear from a glance at almost any issue of *Sojourners*. Karl Barth,
Daniel Berrigan, Thomas Merton, and Walter Wink appear side by
side with Clark Pinnock and Mark Hatfield. In fact, one receives
the impression that while this magazine is the pride and joy of many
"progressive" Evangelicals, its main sources of inspiration are hardly
Evangelical at all!

The upshot of this survey is that these features, though they
appear with integrity in Evangelicalism, are not *necessarily* interdependent in any one religious system much less the Evangelical one.
This in turn suggests, at least to outsiders, that Evangelicalism is
not "the truth," but rather only one of several viable and vital religious options in America, many of which really offer the same spiritual, cognitive, and experiential benefits in different packagings and
combinations. Though this realization comes as no news to outsiders,
most Evangelical Christians do not see it this way at all. Instead,
they tend to see themselves as the "real Christians" while others are
only "nominal Christians." Otherwise, how can one explain the constant use of the adjective "Christian" with obvious reference to Evangelicals only? Or the oft-posed question of strategy in personal
evangelism, "How do I get through to my Catholic friend who says
he already believes Christ is God's Son, etc.?" Yet this situation
might change if Evangelicals recognized the things I have pointed
out in this chapter. The exclusive truth of their viewpoint would
no longer be so self-evident.

On the level of academic theology, significant changes may be in
the offing. It is becoming apparent that many Evangelical thinkers
are themselves beginning to shed this essentially sectarian outlook.
This can be observed by tracing the change in Evangelical attitudes
toward "dialogue." Early fundamentalists stigmatized Liberalism as a
completely different (non-Christian) religion, Catholicism as the
Whore of Babylon, and confessional Protestantism as "dead formal-
ism." There was no dialogue, only polemics. Later "Neo-Evangelicals" like Carl F. H. Henry, Harold J. Ockenga, E. J. Carnell, and
Bernard Ramm came to advocate "dialogue," but intended this pri-

marily as apologetics for essentially fundamentalist doctrine. Recently, however, "Young Evangelicals" have advocated and have actually engaged in genuine give-and-take dialogue with other religious
traditions. For instance, Lewis Smedes and Richard Mouw were
signers of the ecumenical "Hartford Appeal for Theological Affirmation" (cf. Mouw's essay "New Alignments: Hartford and the Future
of Evangelicalism" in Berger and Neuhaus, *Against the World, For
the World*). Marvin Wilson led Evangelicals into the dialogue recorded in *Evangelicals and Jews in Conversation*. Robert Webber
(*Common Roots*), Donald Bloesch, and some of their fellow contribu-
tors to "The Chicago Call" and *The Orthodox Evangelicals* have explicitly called for the end of Evangelicalism's ghetto mentality. According to them, Evangelicals must now humbly take their place in a
spectrum of *legitimate* Christian traditions wide enough to include
Liberal Hans Küng and theosophical mystic Meister Eckhart. One
last example would be the Evangelical sponsorship and participation
in the 1978 "Conference of the Laity" which welcomed Roman Catholics and Ecumenical Liberals as legitimate "brothers and sisters in
the Lord."

But perhaps even more astonishing is the admission by Clark Pinnock, David F. Wright, and other Evangelical theological scholars
that Liberals are genuine Christians after all! Wright says, "Unnecessary offense has clearly been given by statements like 'He is
not a Christian,' when what is meant is 'He is not an evangelical
(Christian)' . . . God alone knows who are his."[26] Liberals who
demythologize and desupernaturalize Christianity can still be admitted theoretically to have adequate ("saving") faith! In this case
the seriousness of Evangelicals' denials of the legitimacy of Liberal
theology has obviously been radically undermined. Whether or not
one demythologizes the Bible is reduced to the same kind of inter-
necine difference as how many dispensations one should divide the
Bible into.

And this potentially constitutes a major shift, even a revolution
in Evangelical self-consciousness. To realize the implications of
this, imagine how it would translate into the practice and perception
of Evangelical laity and students. If Pinnock, Webber, et al. are to
be taken seriously, it is no longer so clear that the Born Again
Christian office worker should witness to his cigar-smoking Catholic
co-worker, or that the IVCF member should pray for the conversion
of his Liberal Presbyterian roommate or campus minister. Maybe
they are really Christians already, after all. The "us-versus-them,"
saved/unsaved dichotomy that has been crucial to the shape of Evangelical religious life would be seriously blurred, whether rightly or
wrongly. My suggestion is that this would be no small change in
the shape and style of Evangelical religion. I will return to this
matter in the final section of the book.

Chapter 3

DEVIL'S ADVOCATES

In Chapter 1, I had occasion to mention the common Evangelical belief in the reality of Satan and his demons. I showed how this belief fit into the set of "combat" coping mechanisms that are part of the "hard religious line." Referring to the uniquely Pentecostal "Deliverance Ministry," I compared it to primitive belief in spirit possession, a comparison which incidentally would probably not be repudiated by those involved. Writers of this persuasion are quite happy to point to instances of spirit-possession among preliterate tribes as valid examples of the demon activity in which they believe.

I would now like to turn to some special difficulties created for Evangelicals by their inclusion of demons in their worldview. First let me indicate a point where belief in demons becomes theologically controversial. In his famous essay "New Testament and Mythology," theologian Rudolf Bultmann contended that "modern man" no longer believes in the New Testament's picture of evil spirits and their destructive intervention in human life. Evangelicals indignantly challenge this, pointing out that they too are moderns, yet they share the New Testament's belief in demons. As a matter of fact, I suspect that most Evangelicals do *not* share the New Testament's view of demons. Their belief about demons has been significantly adjusted. But more about that momentarily.

Evangelicals, when challenged on the reality of demons, invariably reply that Jesus the Son of God believed that demons existed. Being omnicient (or very nearly so) Jesus would have known that "there ain't no such things as ghosts" if indeed there ain't. And ever-eager to satisfy human curiosity, Jesus would certainly have let us in on the secret. Otherwise he would have been dishonest. "Either deceived or deceiving" runs the usual description of the two unacceptable alternatives. No, had Jesus known better, he would have told us so. Of course this kind of logic must also blame Jesus for millions of deaths since he didn't let humanity in on all the advanced medical knowledge which must have been at his disposal! At any rate, it has become apparent that demons in and of themselves are not the real issue. The Christological question seems uppermost. Evangelicals are stuck with demons because Jesus believed in them. Or are they? Would Jesus have been "wrong" or "deceived" if he believed in non-existent evil spirits?

Things may become a bit clearer if we shift our categories. Should Jesus' ministry of demon exorcism be seen as part of Jesus' teaching ministry, or of his healing ministry? That is, was Jesus putting forth and defending a doctrine about evil spirits? Or was he concerned about delivering the afflicted from their ailments? The latter, it would be safe to say, is closer to the truth. Seen from this perspective, Jesus' assumptions about the activity of demons can be regarded simply as part of the first-century model of illness. Modern psychologists might substitute models of "abreaction" or "psychosomatic medicine." To say Jesus was "wrong" because he worked with first-century middle-eastern categories is not only culturally chauvinistic but theologically naive. Should the Son of God not have thought in the framework into which the Incarnation brought him?

One might as well charge Jesus with error because he spoke Aramaic instead of English! So it is not self-evident that an Incarnational Christology would require Evangelicals to believe in demons.

The preceding discussion could be repeated with regard to the Bible, since often Evangelicals claim its authority for their view of the demonic. We would have to repeat that for the Bible to describe things in prescientific cultural categories alien to us would not be tantamount to error in the Bible. Then what is the basis for belief in demons? Apparently, Evangelicals do not want to surrender any detail of the New Testament's first-century world picture. If they did, where would one draw the line? Perhaps eventually one would find himself with Bultmann deeming the whole New Testament world-view (Incarnation, resurrection, miracles, and all) as mythological. Give Bultmann an inch and he'll take a mile![1]

Without entering here into the very important debate on "demyth-ologizing" (i.e., restating Christian faith for the modern age in non-supernatural categories—see Chapter 9), I would like to take up my earlier suggestion that at least on this point Bultmann has accurately described most modern men. Moderns, including most Evangelicals, do not in fact share the New Testament's particular belief in demons. In the synoptic gospels it is obvious that demon possession was thought to be one of the most common causes of disease. It seems like Jesus is thronged by demoniacs on every street corner! When an Evangelical, say a middle class suburban Baptist, gets arthritis or pneumonia, does it even occur to him or her to call in an exor-cist? No, demons are believed by such people to inhabit mainly far-flung strongholds of paganism, or to prey upon those involved in the occult. Demons are just not encountered in everyday life as was the case in Jesus' milieu. When was the last time you offered your sympathies to your neighbor whose son was demon-possessed? Evan-gelical psychologist Basil Jackson admits,

> In all honesty, I have to say that I certainly do believe in demon possession . . . because the Bible teaches it. How-ever I remain unconvinced that I have ever seen or, at least recognized, demonization in a patient with whom I was work-ing.[2]

It is no surprise that there are at least a couple of rationaliza-tions forthcoming for this embarrassing hiatus. For instance, some suggest that there was a special flurry of demonic activity in first-century Palestine because of the presence of the Son of God, as if to offset his influence. Demons are less apparent today since Jesus is not physically here. Yet the gospels contain no hint of such a special state of affairs. In fact, the reverse seems to be assumed; Jesus made such an impact because he was able to interrupt the long-endured oppression of demons, at least for a few. Another attempted explanation is that the historic Christian influence on the West has curbed the activity of demons. While theoretically possible, both arguments are pretty implausible. They sound like special plead-ing; Evangelicals insist that the New Testament's worldview (includ-ing demons) must be preserved as normative for all eras, yet these arguments try to show how this one particular aspect of that world picture does not apply today. Let's face it—you just can't cast out your demon and have it too.

For all I have just said, there is one small group of Evangelical
Christians who do take the reality of the demonic quite seriously.
They are people like exorcists Frank and Ida Mae Hammond who pro-
mote the "Deliverance Ministry" already referred to. These people
are the exception which proves the rule, as can be seen from the
enormous hostility and suspicion they arouse from other Evangelicals.
Even mainstream Pentecostals (yes, there is such a thing!) are very
uncomfortable with the Deliverance Ministry practiced by some within
their ranks. Most Evangelicals deny that Born Again Christians may
be demon-possessed, but Deliverance advocates teach that no one is
immune, not even a regenerate believer in whom the Spirit dwells.
It should be noted that the exorcists do have a respectable basis
for their view in Evangelical theology which has always recognized
a gap between "positional vs. experiential truth" (see Chapter 4),
as well as in the New Testament distinction between "indicative and
imperative." In both cases the point is that there is slack to be
taken up between the experience of a believer and what he is ideally
supposed to be "in Christ" (in this case, free from demons). His
Christian birthright will not be actualized in experience until he
"appropriates" it by faith. "Deliverance" would be the "appropriation" in this case.

I have not actually challenged the Evangelical belief that demons
exist. I only question the consistency of their assertion since on
this point, Evangelicals seem to have one foot in either worldview.
I am not going to prove or disprove the reality of demons (or even
try to figure out how one might go about doing this). Certainly
the mere fact that demons are generally not considered to be among
the "furniture" of the modern Western worldview proves nothing.
Peter Berger offers an insightful comment here:

> We may say that contemporary consciousness is such and
> such; we are left with the question of whether we will assent
> to it. We may agree, say, that contemporary consciousness is
> incapable of conceiving of either angels or demons. We are
> still left with the question of whether, possibly, both angels
> and demons go on existing despite this incapacity of our con-
> temporaries to conceive of them.[3]

But just because they can't be ruled out of court, this doesn't mean
they can be proven either. Evangelical psychologist John White
admits: "I can conceive of no demonic state which cannot be 'explained' by a non-demonic hypothesis. I can likewise conceive of
no experiment to give conclusive support to demonic rather than
para-psychological hypotheses."[4]

So instead of proving or disproving, I think it will be more interesting to ask about the social and psychological function of believing in these demons. When it would seem so much easier to
adopt the modern disbelief in malign spirits, what possible benefit
can accrue from holding on to the demonic? This question is especially acute with regard to the Deliverance Ministry, where Christians are led to suspect that they themselves need deliverance. Why
would anyone feel inclined to maintain such an apparently repugnant
belief and practice? I will suggest some continuities with the Pentecostal tradition within Evangelicalism which explain the appeal of
the Deliverance Ministry.

The Deliverance Ministry is the latest in a series of spiritual elitist movements in Protestantism. Shortly before the Civil War, many churches had to deal with friction resulting when some members claimed a new experience of "holiness," or "entire sanctification." Others were in effect second-rate Christians. The Holiness movement was soon followed by the Pentecostal revival at the turn of the century. This time, the new illuminati claimed a "Baptism of the Holy Spirit" which set them apart from their brethren. The badge of elitism was the practice of glossalalia. This division has recently been repeated in mainline Protestant congregations with the spread of the neo-Pentecostal, or Charismatic, movement. Militant Charismatic prayer cells regard other parishoners as not yet having arrived at the group's own spiritual plane. Now, as if not satisfied with such an elite status, some Charismatics have found a new shibboleth which makes them the elite among the elite. This shibboleth is the ministry of deliverance from demons. Deliverance advocates feel that they are privy to the devil's best-kept secret. Most Christians are being victimized by Satan but are prevented by their doctrinal views from recognizing it! The faithful few have found out the secret and try to warn their fellow Charismatics. But few will listen; thus Deliverance advocates become a persecuted, elitist minority. This is very satisfying for some people who seem to thrive on this sort of messianic self-conception.

There is also what we might call a "guilt factor," that plays a major role here. As mentioned above, the Deliverance Ministry is only the latest development in the American Holiness-Pentecostal tradition. This tradition has been one of perfectionism. It has been believed that once one has experienced "entire sanctification" or "the Baptism of the Holy Spirit," or both, one is responsible for, and capable of, maintaining a largely sin-free life and attitude. To eradicate sinful actions and attitudes, one need only remain faithful in devotional practices and "claim the victory" by appropriating God's power over spiritual and moral problems (see Chapter 4). The Deliverance Ministry admits that even after the Spirit-filled believer has done all this, some problems and sins seem to remain. The attribution of particularly stubborn problems to demons allows one to avoid personal culpability. To err is not human, it is demonic. If the believer has been sanctified, what other culprit is left? If on the other hand he has "backslidden" from his sanctified state, the believer may readily enough admit his guilt and repent. But if he has tried his best without results to deal with a "besetting sin," the appeal to demons can get him off the moral hook.

The same dichotomy occurs in the specific case of sickness. Here, too, Pentecostals have been perfectionists. That is, they have often claimed that it is never God's will for the believer to be ill, but that the believer can "claim his healing" which, like salvation itself, was automatically provided for at Calvary. The healing is readily available if only one's faith is strong enough. As one might well imagine, this last catch has saved face for the Pentecostal claims only at the cost of great guilt for those "seekers" who came away without being healed. They had thought their faith was sufficient, but it must not have been after all! Since they weren't healed, what other possibility is there? Once again, Deliverance advocates (and here many other Charismatics as well) step forward with an alternative to guilt. They cheerfully announce that the seeker really *was* healed! The only reason this is not apparent is that Satan is counterfeiting the symptoms, in order to make the believer doubt! This is a rationalization widely used in Charismatic circles. In short, the devil has again been used as an alternative to human failure, so that one may resort to exorcism instead of feeling guilty. Which was it— a lack of faith, or Satanically-counterfeited symptoms? Probably only conscience will tell.

Seen this way, the Deliverance Ministry has been able to supply a shrewd theological device for escaping the frustration that inevitably accompanies perfectionism. Yet how long can the device work? What is the believer to conclude if the demonic sin or problem, or the Satanically "counterfeited" symptoms do not leave when "rebuked in Jesus' name"? At this point, I imagine, the whole system may backfire. Mustn't the would-be exorcist (or self-exorcist) conclude that his faith in the power of the name, or blood, of Jesus wasn't strong enough? Or maybe even that such a lack of faith is itself demonically-produced? Believe it or not, something very much like this reasoning has already appeared in Deliverance literature, where Don Basham warns any skeptical reader that stubborn refusal to believe in the Deliverance Ministry is quite possibly caused by demons! But as far as I know, no Deliverance minister has yet attributed the failure of exorcism to demonic crippling of faith. This would indeed be a vicious circle. One is reminded of the gospel text (Matthew 12:43-45) wherein the expulsion of one demon only results in its return with seven others worse than itself.

Chapter 4

THE PERSONAL SAVIOR

"I have a personal relationship with Jesus Christ." If you are an Evangelical Christian you can remember saying these words probably more times than you can count. If on the other hand you are not "Born Again," you may have heard this phrase from an Evangelical inviting you to establish such a relationship with Christ. You may have had to ask just what the Evangelical Christian meant—how is it possible to have a "personal relationship" with an individual of the past? Even if Jesus actually rose from the dead and is alive today, how can one "relate" to him as to another flesh-and-blood person?

I first heard this question broached in a fascinating work by Richard Coleman (*Issues of Theological Warfare: Evangelicals and Liberals*). Even as a convinced Evangelical of several years' standing, I could not help but admit this was a good question. Yet I have seldom either heard or read a discussion of it. In this chapter I want to explore what Evangelicals seem to mean, and to think they mean, when they claim to have a "personal relationship with Jesus Christ." Hopefully such an analysis can serve to clarify the use of Evangelical religious language on a major subject.

When asked what his "personal relationship" terminology refers to, an Evangelical will often press for an almost literal application. If Jesus is alive today, why should one not be able to know him personally? Much Evangelical rhetoric suggests literal interaction between individuals. A beloved hymn describes how "he walks with me, and he talks with me, and he tells me I am his own," etc. A common evangelistic slogan defines Christianity as "not a religion; it's a relationship." A couple of problems immediately become apparent, at least to an outsider.

Everyday relationships between individuals depend upon conversational interaction available by sense impression. Conversations may be carried on at long distances and with time intervals (say, by letter or telephone), but there must be such interaction. Is Jesus available in this way? Obviously not. When a Born Again Christian claims that "I speak to him in prayer; he speaks to me through the words of the Bible," this is really metaphorical and does not satisfy the requirement.

A second difficulty is the individualized, concrete picture of Jesus implied in such a claim to have a personal relationship with him. If the risen Jesus is still another *individual analogous to ourselves* (and this is dubious on the basis of New Testament texts such as I Corinthians 15:45), we find ourselves asking absurd questions like, has Jesus gotten older and wiser in the two thousand years since the Incarnation? Or, how does he listen to all those prayers at the same time?

Richard Coleman at least sees the first problem here.

A personal relationship with Jesus is different insofar as we will never have the opportunity to know him in his earthly existence. The relationship must therefore be formed on what we can learn about Jesus secondhand rather than by a firsthand experience; but this is no different from forming a personal relationship with someone by correspondence.[1]

Though Coleman does sense the difficulty, his solution is wholly inadequate. As we have suggested, correspondence is in fact first-
hand experience of another in that he is communicating specifically
and intentionally with *you*. Coleman's suggestion would also imply
the possibility of "personal relationships" with Julius Caesar by
reading the *Gallic Wars*, or with Abraham Lincoln by reading Sand-
burg's biography of him. My point is not that Coleman has not said
anything significant. It is merely to point out that he has failed to
justify the use of "personal relationship" language for the kind of
religious experience he means to describe, i.e., an "encounter" with
the Jesus of the gospels.

Let me dwell a moment upon the real religious value in Coleman's
argument. His idea is very similar to that of nineteenth century
theologian Wilhelm Herrmann, one of Karl Barth's mentors. Herrmann
contended that Christians experience the power and love of God only
in the New Testament's portrayal of the "inner life" of Jesus. As
we are transfixed by the pictures of the personality there revealed,
we are flooded by the grace of God. According to Herrmann, "the
communion of the Christian with God" is mediated by our loving
apprehension of the portrait of Jesus in the gospels. However,
Herrmann vigorously denies that this devotion is tantamount to a
"personal relation with . . . Christ"[2] which pietists claimed to have.
This latter, he says, is an illusion. The apprehension of a portrait
of someone's "inner life" is not a relationship with that person himself. Coleman's argument really amounts to Herrmann's view that
the New Testament picture of Jesus is essential to Christian devotion. This would certainly be a valid point worth making, but since
there is no interpersonal give-and-take, "personal relationship" language is not appropriate, as Coleman tries to argue.

What else might an Evangelical refer to as a "personal relationship
with Christ"? A second option might be that he knows Christ as a
spiritual being with whom he is in psychic communication. Several
UFO cultists and New Age channelers have claimed that Jesus literally communicates with them via internally "heard" voices. But Born
Again Christians do not seem to want to make Jesus into a disem-
bodied "spirit guide" or "space brother." An analogous phenomenon
that is accepted among them concerns occasional visions of Jesus.
These are granted to certain individuals, usually Pentecostals. In
these appearances, Jesus actually speaks to the individual, giving a
particular direction or word of comfort. Again, we may gladly recognize the spiritual value of such occurrences, but this kind of
thing is not likely to be what Evangelicals refer to with their "personal relationship" language. They themselves recognize such experiences to be rather extraordinary, different from that "relationship"
enjoyed daily by all believers.

Perhaps the Evangelical means that he experiences the reassuring
presence of a divine providence in his life. This is obviously true;
there is no question but that Evangelicals experience this. But
again we have to ask if "personal relationship" terminology is appropriate for this. One may pray to such a divine presence, and one
may even interpret general feelings of comfort and reassurance as a
response to one's prayers. But is this really the kind of give-and-
take interaction between individuals implied in a "personal relationship"? Along the same lines, it must be asked why such a spiritual

presence is to be characterized as "Jesus Christ"? Do not all religious people of whatever persuasion claim to experience such a divine
presence guiding and comforting them? Obviously in principle there
cannot be much continuity between the historical figure we know
as "Jesus Christ" on the one hand, and such a rather amorphous
benevolent "presence" on the other. One may reply, "Yes, but it is
through faith in Jesus Christ that I experience this 'benevolent
presence.'" Once again we have an altogether valid, and valuable,
point here. But it could more accurately be communicated with a
phrase like "I know God through Jesus Christ." This phrase, unlike the phrase "I have a personal relationship with Christ," has a
solid exegetical foundation in the New Testament. And like the latter, the former is already a venerable part of Evangelical vocabu-
lary.

A final inadequate meaning of the Evangelical claim we are discussing amounts to what I call the "figment of faith." I do not
think I am in error when I suggest that many Born Again Christians,
in effect, mentally imagine a picture of Jesus listening to them.
They pray to this imagined figure and even think themselves to receive some kind of answer or guidance from it. This phenomenon is
perhaps most analogous to that of a child's "imaginary playmate"
with whom he pretends to frolic when there are no flesh-and-blood
playmates about.[3] I suggest this based upon my own observation
during twelve years in the Evangelical movement, but I also find
other writers referring to it. Herrmann comments:

> It is of course not difficult for an imaginitive person so to
> conjure up the Person of Christ before himself that the picture
> shall take a kind of sensuous distinctness. . . . Someone
> thinks he sees Jesus Himself, and consequently begins to com-
> mune with Him. But what such a person communes with in
> this fashion is not Christ Himself but a picture that the man's
> own imagination has put together.[4]

C. S. Lewis describes a similar state of affairs in *The Screwtape
Letters*. "Screwtape" describes a Christian at prayer:

> If you examine the object to which he is attending, you
> will find that it is a composite object containing many . . .
> ingredients. There will be [e.g.] images derived from pic-
> tures of [Christ] as He appeared during . . . the Incarnation.
> . . . I have known cases where what the [person] called his
> "God" was actually *located* . . . inside his own head. . . .
> [Such a Christian will be] praying to *it*—to the thing that he
> has made, not to the Person who has made him.[5]

I do not want to deny the religious value of even such a devotional "figment of faith" if one is able to avoid making an idol of it
as Herrmann and Lewis warn against. A la Paul Tillich, such an
imaginary figure might truly function as a transparent "symbol"
through which the worshipper encounters the Holy itself. But once
such a figment is recognized for what it is, a better alternative
might be sought.

Do I have any such alternatives to offer? Let me suggest two.
The first is suggested by the insightful analysis of theologian Don
Cupitt.[6] The reader has probably heard the familiar distinction

made by Evangelicals between "knowing" and (merely) "knowing about." The idea is that the impersonal, abstract, and secondhand knowledge *about* someone is vastly inferior to personal knowledge *of* that individual. This is no doubt true in the realm of knowable individuals like ourselves. But we have just seen how difficult it is to place a "relationship" with Christ in this realm. Cupitt suggests that a slightly different distinction be drawn. There is a *personal* kind of "knowing about" that is superior to an *impersonal* kind of "knowing about." For instance, one may know about love theoretically, say from movies or psychology books, but it is quite a different thing to know about love from being in love yourself. Note however that even in the latter case one is not "acquainted" with "love" as if it were a "Thou" in its own right. One "knows love" in that he knows *about* it from experience.

In the same way one could meaningfully claim that he "knows Jesus Christ" without claiming personal acquaintance with him. One could "know" him in that one truly discerns and grows in the presence of his Spirit as encountered in his Word or his Body, the Church. The difference is obvious between this, and a *trivial* "knowing about" Christ in that one merely knows, e.g., that he lived two thousand years ago.

Though Cupitt's redefinition salvages the term "knowing Christ," it does not deal directly with our phrase "having a personal relationship with Christ." Here our second alternative can help. I want to call attention to what I believe was the original connotation of this phrase. Keep in mind the revivalistic context of its origin. Revivalists felt that the churches were full of "nominal Christians" to whom commitment to Christ was a rather abstract proposition. It was a mere religious inheritance from one's culture. "Faith" in Christ was impersonal and cold. In this context, revivalists pressed home questions like "You may intellectually believe Christ is the Savior, but do you take him as *your personal* Savior?" Was one's relationship to Christ merely one of social convention, or was it a *personal* relationship? In short, the issue was not whether you related to Christ as to an individual person, but whether you took your commitment to Christ as a matter of *personal* (i.e., existential) concern. The "personal" is focused on *my* side of the relationship, not Christ's.

I am not ignoring the fact that this element is still very much present in Evangelical rhetoric. In fact, I am happy to be able to recognize this. I merely suggest that greater clarity would result if "personal relationship" language could be restricted to meaning "personal commitment." The phrase itself need not be discarded, as long as in using it Evangelicals are careful to avoid the conceptually confusing dead ends reviewed earlier. The cause of evangelism could not but be helped.

Before concluding this chapter I would like to examine a little more closely what is supposed to be going on in a pietist or devotional "relationship with Christ." Just *how* is a relationship with Christ a life-changing thing? I am going to take a brief dip into the area of Evangelical spirituality, specifically, the "deeper life." Incidentally, in view of my earlier observations, I think it will be interesting to note just how little the following devotional dynamics seem to depend on one's being able to relate to Jesus Christ as an individual person. Though, e.g., Miles J. Stanford calls it an "intimate fellowship"[7] I suggest that the devotional process about to be described is pretty much a solo performance even as described in its own terms.

According to many devotional writers and speakers (e.g., Andrew Murray, *Abide in Christ*), the secret of the "victorious Christian life" is "abiding in Christ" (cf. John, chapter 15). The idea is that no one can live the Christian life except Christ himself. But since Christ is supposed to dwell in Christians, the believer can "let go, and let God." i.e., let him produce spirituality *through* the believer. As Watchman Nee says, God "has given only one gift to meet all our needs: his Son Christ Jesus. As I look to him to live out his life in me, he will be humble and patient and loving and everything else I need—in my stead."[8]   Stanford says it in a slightly different way, giving us an important clue about the *how* of it: "It is now a matter of walking by faith and receiving, appropriating, from the everlasting source within."[9] "Appropriating" says it all. The idea is that in his crucifixion and resurrection, Jesus Christ has won a "once-for-all" victory over sin. By personally "appropriating" that redemption, a person becomes a regenerate, justified child of God. As such he has access to "the unsearchable riches of Christ," a sort of ethical and spiritual treasure-trove, imagined in almost pictorial terms as being stored in "the heavenlies." This last is an archetypal realm where in Platonic fashion the ideal spiritual realities, including Christ himself, dwell. This picture accurately reflects the double-tiered apocalyptic worldview of the New Testament, as described by New Testament scholar Johannes Weiss:

> . . . there existed a twofold world, and thus also a twofold occurrence of events. The world of history is only the lower floor of the world's structure. The world of angels and spirits is erected above that. . . . Moreover, what happens on earth has its exact parallel in heaven. All history is only the consequence, effect, or parallel copy of heavenly events. . . . But while those realities have transpired in the realm between heaven and earth, they must now be fought out on earth.[10]

Thus, upstairs "in the heavenlies" God already sees Christians as perfect; on the earthly, lower plane, believers must "catch up" by appropriating these "riches of Christ," a divine potentiality for spiritual growth. This is the distinction between "positional" and "experiential truth" mentioned briefly in Chapter 3. It is this heavenly "positional truth" which is "appropriated" as you become experientially what you already are "in Christ." Here, too, I suggest that this picture is pretty accurate to the Pauline strand of New Testament thought. Bultmann agrees that according to Paul, "The way the believer becomes what he already is consists . . . in the constant appropriation of grace by faith."[11]

In his "quiet time" of devotional Bible reading, meditation, and prayer, the Evangelical thinks deeply about all this. He may concentrate steadily on a particular virtue, say patience, and reflect on how "in Christ" it is his for the asking. He may "strive for the victory" or "rest in the victory," depending on the preferred idiom. And after a while, presumably, his life begins to manifest more patience. Psychologically speaking, how should we understand the process?

We find a surprising parallel to this kind of "devotional victory"
in a shamanistic litany analyzed by anthropologist Claude Levi-Strauss
in his essay "The Effectiveness of Symbols."[12] The incantation is
used to facilitate troublesome births. Without ever touching or medi-
cating the afflicted woman, the shaman summons all sorts of potent
spirit-entities to battle the woman's illness (also personified as a
spirit). The woman hears what is in effect a blow-by-blow account
of the mythological contest. At the end of the ritual, the shaman
announces that the afflicting spirit has been vanquished. The woman,
relieved at last, gives birth! How did it work? Levi-Strauss suggests that while the woman's worldview and culture allow her no
understanding of the actual medical-psychosomatic causes of her illness, the mythical beings of the incantation give her, as it were, a
handle on her condition. Once she is given a personalized, objec-
tified schema to interpret the otherwise mystifying condition, she is
psychologically able to deal with it effectively.

I think that functionally speaking, pretty much the same process
is at work in the struggles of the Evangelical pietist. From experience he knows only defeat in his attempts to be more virtuous (in
our example, to be patient). How can he hope to control his unpre-
dictable emotions? "For that which I do, I understand not" (Romans
7:15). The belief in Christ as a champion over sins, presiding over
a supramundane "treasury of merit" provides an interpretive schema
with which finally to "get the victory." The pietist envisions Christ
on the cross defeating the sin, e.g., of impatience. By "appropriating" this victory for himself, the pietist at last has a handle on
his condition. "He's shared with me / His victory / He won in days
of old" (Keith Green). The cosmic drama enacted thus in his imagination functions pretty much the same way as the shaman's litany of
spirit-warfare. Eventually, patience evidences itself.

All this begins to answer the question of how Evangelicals can
say things like "I experience the power of Christ's cross." Short of
experiencing the stigmata, what can this mean? Wouldn't the Evangelical pietist in our example only be able to say that he has experienced patience? But his devotional meditation on the riches of Christ
has led him so closely to associate "patience" with "the cross," that
experiencing the first seems to him tantamount to having experienced
the second. While he yearned repeatedly for patience he was vividly
picturing the crucified Christ and his "spiritual riches." As the
first "sank in," so did the second. Watchman Nee illustrates this
process when he discusses "the facts of the Cross." He says that
"faith can 'substantiate' them and make them real in our experience."[13] In the same way, of course, experience is taken to be
proof of various religious belief-systems in the context of which it
occurs.

I suppose that the above analysis does not really reflect on the
ultimate truth of the positional truth-appropriation schema, except
that the analysis indicates that it is all explainable without recourse
to divine intervention. That is, I think that most Evangelicals believe that "sanctification" results from the supernatural infusion of
the Holy Spirit, whereas I have suggested that the process is quite
explainable in natural terms. But perhaps it would not be a bad
thing merely to posit that God uses "secondary causes" in the sanctification process. We find a similar situation in Bill Gothard's teach-

ing about scriptural meditation. Citing Joshua 1:8 ("This book of
the law shall not depart out of thy mouth, but thou shalt meditate
therein day and night . . . for . . . then thou shalt have good
success."), Gothard promotes meditation on the Bible practically as
a good luck charm. God wants people to meditate on his word and
rewards them if they do. This seems to be the only connection between the action and the result. But later in the seminar Gothard
seems to feel uneasy with this and supplies quite a different link,
an intrinsic one, between the two: the reason meditation brings
success is that biblical principles contain down-to-earth common
sense about how to succeed in life, and the more one familiarizes
himself with these principles the more astute and successful he will
become. Suddenly there is no need for special divine intervention
in human fortunes. Yet Gothard and his fans seem satisfied with
this. And perhaps they should be! I only use this example to
illustrate how "spiritual growth in Christ" need not presuppose a
framework of supernatural power as pietist rhetoric often suggests.

Now that I have reached the end of this section on Born Again
Christian experience, let me suggest how it might prepare the reader
for what is to follow. Back in the introductory section, "Testimony
Time," I proposed that Evangelical apologetics and theology (the
subjects of the next two sections) seemed to function as bodyguards
for pietism. If my analyses have been at all cogent, the reader may
not be sure that the much-vaunted Evangelical pietism can really
bear the weight of the claims made for it. Can *this* really be the
only answer for modern man's existential dilemmas? Is it so com-
pellingly superior to other ways of understanding and coping with
life? I think these questions might make the reader willing to take
a second look at the apologetics and theology predicated on this
piety.

Now, I am quite aware that the truth question is not so easily
answered. Even if the experiential results were not satisfying,
Evangelical doctrine might still be true. (In fact something like this
is surely envisioned in exhortations to bear one's cross for Christ.)
However, I suspect that in fact many Evangelicals do not separate
the truth question from the pragmatic one. Though theoretically
they might hold their doctrinal views on their own merits, my guess
is that they were first pietists, and only became interested in apologetics and theology as means of propagating and defending that
pietism. The egg came before the chicken. And if the preceding
chapters have made such a reader a bit less unwilling or afraid to
rethink his religious experience, may I invite him to feel free to
rethink his apologetics and theology as well.

Section II
The
Evangelical
Apologists:
Are They
Reliable?

"My message and my preaching were not with wise
and persuasive words, but with a demonstration of
the Spirit's power, so that your faith might not
rest on man's wisdom, but on God's power."

                                    --The Apostle Paul,
                                    I Corinthians 2:4-5

"The believer, like the lover, has no conclusive
proofs to give him complete security. But the
believer too, like the lover, can be completely certain of the Other by committing himself entirely to
the Other. And this certainty is stronger than
all the security established by proofs."

                                    --Hans Küng,
                                    On Being a Christian

"In this respect fundamentalism has demonic traits.
It destroys the humble honesty of the search for
truth, it splits the conscience of its thoughtful
adherents, and it makes them fanatical because
they are forced to suppress elements of truth of
which they are dimly aware."

                                    --Paul Tillich,
                                    Systematic Theology

Chapter 5

EVIDENCE THAT DEMANDS A MISTRIAL

In the first section of this book, I outlined the structures of perception through which Evangelical Christians experience the world. I went on to describe several psychological and social strategies employed to make the whole works seem self-evidently real. These included various kinds of legitimations of their own views as well as attempts to explain away the views of others. This brings me to the present section on apologetics, the attempt to legitimate faith on intellectual grounds. With a large host of arguments, Evangelicals try to reassure the faithful against the attacks of unbelievers, and to convert unbelievers themselves. Suppose an Evangelical is inviting a friend or classmate to undertake a "personal relationship with Christ" (see Chapter 4), but the potential convert is putting up a fight. How can he be sure there is any Christ to have a relationship with? Can he be expected to accept all this talk about the resurrection and the deity of Christ? Let's have some proof! The Evangelical is only too ready to comply. Apologetics was once the restricted province of scholars and clerics, but with the popularity of works like Paul Little's *Know Why You Believe* and Josh McDowell's *Evidence That Demands a Verdict*, many rank-and-file believers are now "ready to give the reason . . . concerning the hope that is within you" (I Peter 3:15). While no one could deny that it is good to have a reasoned faith, I see some disturbing features in all this.

First, I wonder how appropriate it is to try to "argue someone into the kingdom." Many apologists hotly deny any such charge, but I don't believe them. The tenor of almost all apologetics literature makes it plain that this is their intent. Just look at the title of McDowell's catalog of apologetics: *Evidence That Demands a Verdict*. Similarly, Clark Pinnock writes concerning the resurrection that, "Its evidence is sufficiently impressive to demand an answer from every non-Christian."[1] Fans of the Evangelical apologists delight in reciting the stories of former skeptics like John Warwick Montgomery, C. S. Lewis, Lew Wallace, and Frank Morison, who were "dragged kicking and screaming into the Kingdom of God" by the sheer weight of the evidence. It is apparent that such people would just love to drag in others the same way! But how biblical is all this? If one is interested in following the lead of the Apostle Paul at this point, and generally Evangelicals are supposed to be interested in this, one must question these tactics. Doesn't such evangelistic polemicizing amount to resorting to "wise and persuasive words" instead of the "demonstration of the Spirit's power"? Won't a faith established on such apologetical arguments "rest on man's wisdom" instead of "on God's power"? (I Corinthians 2:4-5). And what happens if one day these arguments no longer seem to be so compelling? Good-bye faith!

Second, I suspect that most apologists do not really know whether their arguments are inherently convincing or not, since they themselves came to faith on different grounds entirely. To hear them tell it, some were persuaded by the arguments of, for instance, Montgomery and Morison. But in my experience, apologetic arguments are used for propaganda or legitimation purposes by people

whose faith comes from a Christian upbringing or a conversion based
on existential factors.   I doubt that they themselves believe in,
e.g., the resurrection of their Savior because of supposedly cogent
arguments.   I think this implies some subtle but real dishonesty.
More importantly, it would help us understand how it is that such
bright people can be caught using such a raft of absolutely terrible
arguments, as I hope to show.

   Third, a qualm about the method of argument used by apologists.
I often have the feeling that apologists, whether scholarly or popular, are willing to use any argument no matter how dubious as long
as it stands a chance of convincing an unbeliever.   Whatever the
evidence might suggest in and of itself, the apologist's faith makes
him subconsciously assume that the truest interpretation of the facts
must be the one which best fits his convictions.   However, he proceeds to offer this interpretation as the one which makes the best
inductive sense of the facts themselves.   This ground-shifting no
doubt goes unnoticed by the apologists themselves, who have sincerely good intentions.

   In this and the next two chapters, I will be challenging the principal apologetics used by Evangelicals to defend three key beliefs:
the historicity of the gospels, the resurrection of Christ, and the
deity of Christ.   I have no desire or intention to attack these beliefs.   I will critique certain lines of reasoning and evidence used
(I think illegitimately) to defend these (quite legitimate) beliefs.   My
point is that these things are not the only things Christians are
supposed to believe in.   Truth is another one of those things.   And
I am afraid that Evangelical apologists are often in danger of sacri-
ficing belief in the truth to defend belief in other matters.

   Evangelicals repudiate the notion that the gospels contain legendary or fictitious material about Jesus Christ.   They want to be able
to believe he did and said everything attributed to him there.   Since
most modern New Testament scholarship concludes that the gospels
are at least to some degree legendary, Evangelicals must work extra
hard to defend their beliefs. They must fight on two fronts: against
skeptics who do not believe *period*, and against Liberal New Testament scholars who do believe, but not quite what Evangelicals believe.   In recent years, Evangelicals have published reams of apologetical material defending the historical reliability of the gospels'
story of Jesus.   An attentive reading of the many articulate works
of Josh McDowell, John Warwick Montgomery, F. F. Bruce, J. N. D.
Anderson, Michael Green and others reveals certain stock arguments.
These include the importance of the short time span between Jesus
and the writing of the gospels, and the centrality of eyewitnesses in
the formation of the gospel tradition.   Such factors, it is held, make
it extremely unlikely if not impossible that the gospels contain fabri-
cated or legendary material.   These arguments start from generalized
premises as to what is or is not probable in the development of historical records.   Such abstract criteria are then applied to the gospel narratives in a blanket fashion.

   There is a serious blind spot in this approach.   Almost completely
deductive, it pays insufficient attention either to specific data in the
documents under consideration, or to other documentary data which
might cast doubt on the generalized criteria.   Will these criteria
work on other materials analogous to the gospels?

I begin with a representative statement by Josh McDowell:

> One of the major criticisms against the form critics' idea of
> the oral tradition is that the period of oral tradition (as de-
> fined by the critics) is not long enough to have allowed the
> alterations in the tradition that the radical critics have al-
> leged.[2]

Similarly, John Warwick Montgomery confidently asserts: "With the
small time interval between Jesus' life and the Gospel records, the
Church did not create a 'Christ of faith.' . . ."[3] This "small time
interval" would be about thirty or forty years! Some conservatives
protest that this is not really a long period at all. McNeile in his
New Testament introduction, a favorite of Montgomery's, states that
"It is not unusual for men even of slight intellectual ability to recall
and relate clearly important events occurring thirty-five years previously."[4] But surely this is not the real point. Form critics suggest not so much that eyewitnesses forgot the details of what they
saw. Their idea is that other people spun out legendary material
during the same period, or that as Strauss suggested, people who
witnessed only a little of Jesus' activity formed legendary "remem-
brances" to fill in the gaps in their knowledge.

But weren't the gospel events too well known for any "creative
community" to plausibly get away with alteration? F. F. Bruce, al-
luding to remarks by C. H. Dodd, draws the analogy of how easily
World War II was remembered twenty to thirty years afterward. If
someone suggested some seriously distorted version of the events of
those days, no one would be fooled. Buell and Hyder invoke the
example of Richard Nixon's resignation:

> Suppose that, thirty years after Nixon's presidency ended,
> a nonfiction bestseller portrayed a thoroughly consistent pic-
> ture of Nixon having left office before his second term ex-
> pired for reasons of personal health while at the height of
> popularity. . . . Although most of us did not know Nixon
> personally, we would certainly know enough to contribute to
> the rebuttal.[5]

Apart from the will-to-believe already present among their Evangelical readers, how can the apologists hope to get away with analogies
like these? In both cases we are dealing with events of immediate
national and world impact that were continually impressed on the
senses of whole populations through massive disturbances in lifestyle and by the mass media. Thus World War II and Watergate
were known and remembered in detail by most of the world. The
public ministry of Jesus is hardly a comparable case! Had Jesus,
like Billy Graham, had the benefit of William Randolph Hearst's jour-
nalistic machine, perhaps we would have a parallel here. But as it
is, we are dealing with an itinerant preacher in first-century Palestine. To quote a line from "Jesus Christ Superstar": "If you'd
come today, you'd have reached a whole nation / Israel in 4 B. C.
had no mass communication." Besides, many of the important words
and deeds of Jesus in the gospels are depicted as occurring in the
presence of rather small or private groups, e.g., the disciples.
(Also see the numerous admonitions to secrecy in Mark 5:43; 8:26,
30; 9:9; etc.) Apologists seem to think they can secure their argu-

ment with the mere citation (I am not exaggerating) of Acts 26:26:
"This thing was not done in a corner." Does no one notice that
Paul is here referring not to Jesus' career or resurrection, but to
his own conversion and the attendant uproar which brought him
before Agrippa? Does context matter so little?

In any case, if McDowell, Montgomery, Buell and Hyder, et al.
are right, biographical records of similar religious figures written
within a comparable time span should also be free of legendary embellishment. What do we find? Gershom Scholem's study of the
seventeenth century messianic pretender Sabbatai Sevi provides a
productive parallel here. Sevi was able to arouse apocalyptic fervor
among Jews all over the Mediterranean during the 1660s. The movement suffered a serious setback when the messiah apostasized to
Islam! But still it did not die away. The history of Sabbatai Sevi
is more readily accessible to the modern historian than are the gospel events. Sabbatai Sevi lived much closer to our own era and
much documentary evidence of various kinds survives him. Here,
too, according to the apologists, legends should have waited at least
a couple of generations till they reared their heads. But Gershom
Scholem speaks of "the sudden and almost explosive surge of miracle stories" concerning Sabbatai Sevi within weeks or even days of
his public appearances! Listen to his description:

> The . . . realm of imaginative legend . . . soon dominated
> the mental climate in Palestine [during Sevi's residence there].
> The sway of imagination was strongly in evidence in the let-
> ters sent to Egypt and elsewhere and which, by the autumn
> of 1665 [the same year] had assumed the character of regular
> messianic propaganda in which fiction far outweighed the facts:
> [e.g.] the prophet was "encompassed with a Fiery Cloud" and
> "the voice of an angel was heard from the cloud."[6]

Letters from December of the same year related that Sabbatai
"commanded a Fire to be made in a publick place, in the presence of
many beholders . . . and entered into the fire twice or thrice, without any hurt to his garments or to a hair on his head." Other letters tell of his raising the dead. He is said to have left his prison
through locked and barred doors which opened by themselves after
his chains miraculously broke. He kills a group of highwaymen
merely with the word of his mouth. Interestingly, the miracle stories often conformed to the patterns of contemporary saints' legends.[7] The spread of such tales recalls the statements by the synoptic evangelists that many of their miracle stories came from popular reportage (cf. Luke 1:65-66; 2:18, 38, 47; 4:14, 37; 5:15, 26;
6:17-18; 7:17, 22; 8:34-39, 47; 9:6-7, 9; 9:43; 12:1; 13:17; 18:43;
19:7, 37, 48).

A similar phenomenon occurred with Jehudah the Hasid (died
1217). In his own lifetime, legends made him a great purveyor of
religious magic, though actually Jehudah was a staunch opponent of
such things![8] More recently, African prophet and martyr Simon
Kimbangu became another "living legend" despite his own wishes.
One group of his followers, the "Ngunzists," spread his fame as the
"God of the blacks," even while Kimbangu himself disavowed the
role. Legends of Kimbangu's childhood, miracles and prophetic visions began within his own generation.[9] Faith-healer William Marrion

Branham was held in exaggerated esteem by legions of his followers, many of whom believed him to be Jesus Christ returned or even a new incarnation of God. He, however, did not teach such notions. In fact, once on a visit to such a group of devotees in Latin America he explicitly denied any such wild claims made for him, but his followers reasoned that he was just testing their faith! Many believed in Branham's virgin birth despite his published recollections of his alcoholic mother.[10] A final example is more recent still. Researcher Ed Sanders encountered a number of legends about Charlie Manson during the writing of his book *The Family*. On one particular bus trip in Death Valley, "several miracles were alleged to have been performed by Charles Manson." One story relates that "Charlie levitated the bus over a creek crag."[11]

So it seems that an interval of thirty or forty years could indeed accommodate the intrusion of legendary materials into the gospel tradition. (Whether or not this actually occurred is a different question.) But Evangelical apologists do not restrict their arguments to matters of dating and time intervals. They also appeal with great relish to the role of eyewitnesses in the gospel tradition. Montgomery, McDowell and some other apologists employ what they call the "external evidence" test, in dependence on military historian C. Sanders. Montgomery writes that "as to the authors and primary historical value of the Gospel accounts, confirmation comes from independent written sources."[12] He goes on to quote Papias and Irenaeus to the effect that the gospels of Matthew and John were written by the disciples of those names, and that Mark was written in direct dependence on the apostle Peter. It would obviously be strategic for the apologetic task if these texts could be established as the direct testimony of eyewitnesses. This would be even better than being able to say, as F. F. Bruce does, that the oral tradition underlying the gospels stems from eyewitnesses. (We will consider Bruce's approach momentarily.) But this effort by Montgomery and company is dubious. This is something of which we will see several more examples: the adducing of something as unambiguous evidence that is itself a matter of serious debate.

For instance, Montgomery gives no hint of the relevance of source-criticism (of which he seems to be aware)[13] for this whole question. By contrast, the fact that the first gospel makes use of the second almost in its entirety makes F. F. Bruce restrict Matthean authorship to the Q source of sayings, rather than extending it to the whole Greek Gospel of Matthew. Montgomery also ignores the possibility of tendentiousness in ascription. Papias, Irenaeus and others may have attributed the gospels to apostolic individuals for reasons of theological pedigree. Evangelical New Testament scholar Ralph P. Martin doubts for this reason that the Gospel of Mark is dependent on Peter as Papias claimed. But Montgomery's readers will suspect nothing of all this.

Edwin M. Yamauchi makes the same error. He assures his readers that

> There is some dispute over the identity of the authors [of the gospels], but it is generally held that Matthew, a converted tax-collector, and John, a fisherman, were two of Jesus' apostles. Mark was an eyewitness as Jesus and the apostles met

in his home, and later he learned more about Jesus from Peter,
whom according to Irenaeus, he served as interpreter.[14]

Veteran apologist Wilbur Smith echoes this opinion: "Most scholars
believe that the first Gospel, by Matthew, was written by a disciple
of Jesus, who was an eyewitness of what he wrote."[15] Is all this
"generally held" by "most scholars"? Hardly, yet if Yamauchi's and
Smith's readers are not familiar with the relevant literature, they
will not know any better. In another article Yamauchi discounts the
claim of Philostratus, the third century biographer of the miracle-
worker Apollonius of Tyana, to have used the memoirs of Apollonius's
eyewitness disciple Damis. The issues here are very similar to those
involved in the patristic ascriptions of the gospels to eyewitnesses.
Yet here Yamauchi is quite satisfied that the claim for eyewitness
sources is false: "Most scholars reject the account of the notebooks
of Damis, Apollonius's contemporary, as a fabrication."[16] Actually,
as before, (though I happen to agree with him in this instance)
scholarly opinion is not so unequivocal as Yamauchi would like us to
think. Why does he overgeneralize scholarly opinion in favor of
eyewitness sources for Jesus, but against them for a rival miracle-
worker? Here we have an example of what Evangelicals constantly
decry among Liberals, i.e., the claim that "most scholarship" supports one's own preferences.

Yamauchi comments on the fourth gospel that "Although it has
been customary to date John's Gospel approximately A.D. 90, some
scholars have recently favored a date in the 70s or 80s."[17] Yamauchi is referring to what John A. T. Robinson has called "a new look
on the fourth gospel." Thanks to the work of C. H. Dodd (*Historical Tradition in the Fourth Gospel*) and others, several scholars
have rethought the dating of this gospel, or at least of the traditions underlying it. Evangelical apologists rejoice in this. It seems
to them to support their contention that this gospel was written by
(or stems from) an eyewitness, as the book itself claims (19:35;
21:24).

Evangelicals have uniformly opposed the view held since D. F.
Strauss, though anticipated as early as Clement of Alexandria (in
his remarks on the "spiritual gospel"), that John represents the
theological musings of a later theologian, put into the mouth of Jesus.
They figure that if the gospel stems from an eyewitness, then the
discourses recorded there must represent an accurate transcript of
Jesus' words. But this does not follow at all. The assumption is
challenged by Plato's later Socratic dialogues. Plato was an "eyewitness disciple" of Socrates whom he portrays in debate. Yet scholars agree that in the later dialogues, Plato merely uses the figure of
Socrates as a literary mouthpiece for his own ideas. By analogy,
even if the fourth gospel's claim to eyewitness authorship is vindicated, the issue is not settled whether the Johannine discourses
really represent Jesus or John. Considerations such as the differences of theology and idiom between John and the synoptics, the
heavy stylization of the Johannine discourses, etc., could not be
swept under the rug by any confirmation of eyewitness authorship.
We would still have to ask whether and to what extent the fourth
gospel represents the meditations of the evangelist himself.

A kindred appeal to eyewitnesses technically does not depend on

the direct eyewitness-authorship of the finished gospels. Here apologists are content to argue that the gospels represent the end product of a process of oral tradition. Some, like F. F. Bruce, actually
seem to accept this idea; others, like Montgomery, seem only to be
accepting this premise for the sake of argument. But in either case
the objective is to show that the formation of any such oral or com-
munal tradition was firmly under the control of eyewitnesses all the
way, and thus did not admit of legendary embellishment. For example, F. F. Bruce writes:

> . . . it can have been by no means so easy as some writers
> seem to think to invent words and deeds of Jesus in those
> early years, when so many of his disciples were about, who
> could remember what had and had not happened.[18]

The idea is that the apostles and other eyewitnesses would have seen
to it that the rank-and-file believers did not let their fancy run
wild in creating stories about Jesus. It seems to me that this argument rests on a rather anachronistic picture of the apostles' activity.
They are imagined to be sort of a squad of ethnographer-detectives,
ranging over Palestine, sniffing out legends and clamping the lid on
any they discover. If the apostles declined to leave their preaching
to wait on tables, I doubt if they had time for this sort of thing
either!   Again the story of Sabbatai Sevi offers an illuminating parallel to the situation envisioned here. In this case we know that the
chief apostle of the movement, Nathan of Gaza (a contemporary of
Sevi), *did* repeatedly warn the faithful that the messiah would have
to merit their belief *without* doing miracles.[19] But, as we have
seen, miracle stories gushed forth without abatement! So in a very
analogous case, the efforts of the chief apostle could do nothing to
curb the legend-mongering enthusiasm of the faithful. I have already
mentioned the deification of Simon Kimbangu in his own lifetime and
despite his own wishes.   The additional relevance of this fact in
this context is obvious.
    It is wise to keep in mind the caution of Bollandist scholar Hip-
polyte Delehaye. In discussing the sources and historicity of saints'
legends, he remarks:

> The intellectual capacity of the multitude reveals itself on
> all sides as exceedingly limited, and it would be a mistake to
> assume that it usually submits itself to the influence of supe-
> rior minds.   On the contrary, the latter necessarily suffer
> loss from contact with the former, and it would be quite illogi-
> cal to attribute a special value to a popular tradition because
> it had its origin amid surroundings in which persons of solid
> merit [in our case, the apostles] were to be met with.[20]

Bruce and Montgomery go on to add a negative version of the
eyewitness argument: what about non-Christian eyewitnesses who
could have called the Christians' bluff?   "Had there been any tendency to depart from the facts in any material respect, the possible
presence of hostile witnesses in the audience would have served as
a further corrective."[21]   Would it?   Evidence indicates this to be
pretty doubtful.   Bruce is not reckoning with the contagious fervor
of apocalyptic movements; one hears what one wants to hear.   In
the case of Sabbatai Sevi, we know that "hostile witnesses" tried to

keep things under control but to no avail. The rabbis of Constantinople announced that during Sevi's stay there ". . . we have not
beheld a single miracle or sign . . . only the noise of rumors and
testimonies at second hand."[22] No one seemed to listen.

In our own day we can find several parallel cases, none of which
seem to accord with the apologists' claims about what "would" or
"would not have happened." Readers may recall the brief flurry of
interest, during the great "cult" hysteria of the 70s and early 80s,
over the young divinity Guru Maharaj Ji. He was a rotund little
Buddha of a man, a boy really, who had a notorious preference for
Baskin-Robbins ice cream. As it happened, he also had a preference
for his secretary and married her, much against the Old-World wishes
of his mother. She promptly booted the young godling off the throne
of the universe and replaced him with his charisma-less older brother. What, one might ask, was the reaction of the Premies, as the
disciples were called, to this train of events? On a visit to Berkeley a year or so later I saw them still handing out literature featur-
ing the boy-god's grinning visage. I asked how this was still possible and was told that the Premies simply refused to believe the
whole debacle had happened! All was the same as far as they were
concerned.

Or take the Rastafarians of Jamaica. They venerated Ethiopian
emperor Haile Selassie as God incarnate, despite his own puzzled
reaction to this news once when he visited the island. What became
of their faith when the deposed emperor died? On a "Sixty Minutes"
broadcast an intelligent-looking Jamaican journalist with allegiance to
the religion matter-of-factly said he believed Haile Selassie was still
alive, his supposed death a "premature report" (Mark Twain) engen-
dered by the unbelieving Western media!

Or who can forget the remarkable case of religious talk-show host
and con-man Jim Bakker? Even after his conviction on the basis of
a veritable mountain of evidence, the faith of a stubborn group of
his followers remained unshaken. They formed the "Bring Back the
Bakkers Club"!

In all such cases what we have is "cognitive dissonance reduction." More about that later on, but for now suffice it to say that
when one has so much at stake in a belief being true ("Lo, we have
left everything to follow you . . ." Mark 10:28), one simply cannot,
psychologically speaking, afford to admit one was mistaken. Any
fact may be denied or rationalized to avoid such an admission.[23]
Finally one is impervious to the evidential barrages of "hostile witnesses."

The eyewitness argument is dubious in yet another respect. Evidence shows that the proximity of eyewitnesses to the events does not
even guarantee the factuality of their own enthusiastic reports.
Turning again to the Sabbatian movement, we note Scholem's description:

> The transition from history to legend took place with extra-
> ordinary rapidity in what are practically eyewitness accounts.
> Already the earliest documents confuse dates and chronologies,
> and abound in legendary accounts of miracles.[24]

One may trace the growth of the legends in some cases by comparing
different versions of what is known to be the same event.[25]

William Peter Blatty's novel (and the subsequent movie) *The Exorcist* was loudly trumpeted as having been based on an actual case of exorcism. Henry Ansgar Kelly, himself a Roman Catholic priest, set out to determine just how closely *The Exorcist* had been based on fact. He interviewed the priest who had conducted the rite, who freely confessed that all the supernatural effects had been added by rumormongers and scriptwriters. More important for our purposes is that the exorcist, himself obviously no Bultmannian skeptic, given his profession(!), admitted that "he recognized a strong myth-making tendency even in himself. If he did not record the events of each session of exorcism as soon as possible after it occurred, he declared, he found the details changing in his mind, becoming more 'impressive.'"[26]

We find eyewitness attestation of numerous wonders in the battles of the Sudanese Mahdi in the last two decades of the nineteenth century. Here, we are told, fire licked out from the wounds of enemy soldiers to finish them off. The corpses of the unbelievers miraculously piled up into a huge mound within an hour of the battle, untouched by human hands.[27] Are we to believe these stories on the strength of eyewitness testimony? One more example of suspicious eyewitness reporting comes from the Roman satirist Lucian. After watching the self-immolation of the charlatan-prophet Peregrinus, Lucian dupes a couple of yokels, telling them he has seen a vulture ascend from the pyre, crying that Peregrinus had been exalted to heaven. The next day he is startled to overhear an old man solemnly testifying that he himself had witnessed this (invented) marvel![28]

Here I think it is crucial to bring in psychological studies of eyewitnesses and what they can and cannot accurately remember. Ironically the problem is implicit in an analogy apologists often use to rationalize away differences between parallel gospel accounts of the same events, such as the number of angels at the empty tomb, or how many demoniacs were healed by Jesus at Gerasa. Apologists maintain that the situation is like that of several reports of a car accident or a train wreck. Reports of eyewitnesses will naturally vary as each recalls only the aspect he saw or what impressed him most. If we could view a videotape of the event, we might be able to harmonize all the details. Implicit in this very argument is the awareness that eyewitness testimony varies. How much does it vary?

Studies have shown that eyewitness testimony is often remarkably unreliable, most especially when it is testimony of a surprising and remarkable event. The witness will have to reach for some familiar analogy or category (perhaps from myth or science fiction) in order to be able to comprehend the oddity at all. Psychologists have staged unusual events and then immediately interviewed the observers with wildly disparate—and one might add distinctly unharmonizable—results.

And it may take only half an hour for recollections to begin to blur and metamorphose! After a series of experiments, Hall, McFeaters, and Loftus report that,

> Whatever the source, additional information is acquired and is often readily integrated with original memory for the event. Thus, both pre- or post-event information has in fact altered the content of what is recalled or recognized. Once created,

the new memory can be as real and as vivid to the person as
a memory acquired as the result of "genuine" perception.[29]

For "pre-event information" here we might read "prior messianic expectations." For "post-event information" we might read "the early
Christian kerygma." In other words, memory altered in the light
of the suggestions of faith.

Far from supporting the apologists' position, the dynamics of eyewitness testimony would seem to point rather strongly in the direction of the critical view of gospel-embellishment: the witnesses of
Jesus saw a most remarkable man endowed with unusual gifts and
proceeded to interpret him in categories drawn from Old Testament
miracle tales and from Jewish apocalyptic and Hellenistic mythology.
Once the gospel of a miracle-working savior began to be preached,
it is no surprise if the eager memories of "eyewitnesses" would begin to reflect dogmatic amplifications.

Let us turn now to the related question of the tradition of the
sayings of Jesus. Wouldn't special care have been taken to preserve
Jesus' authentic sayings and to exclude bogus ones? Form critics
suggest that sayings were created by the early Christians by the
prophetic inspiration of the Spirit, and then were ascribed to Jesus.
The idea is that it mattered little to them whether the saying came
from the earthly or the exalted Lord. Conservatives reject this
suggestion. F. F. Bruce is typical here:

> Indeed, the evidence is that the early Christians were care-
> ful to distinguish between sayings of Jesus and their own
> inferences or judgments. Paul, for example, when discussing
> the vexed questions of marriage and divorce in I Corinthians
> vii, is careful to make this distinction between his own advice
> on the subject and the Lord's decisive ruling: "I, not the
> Lord," and again, "Not I, but the Lord."[30]

But surely one text (and the same *one* is invariably quoted when
apologists argue this point) is not enough to indicate what the general practice was. Elsewhere Bruce himself recognizes the very
ambiguity stressed by the form critics. Citing I Thessalonians 4:14-
18, Bruce says "We cannot be sure whether Paul is quoting a *ver-
bum Christi* which had come down to him in the tradition . . . or
one which was communicated by the risen Lord through a prophet."[31]
Who knows if prophetic sayings were in fact later credited to the
earthly Jesus; my only point is that the evidence is not so clear as
to rule out this possibility.

Montgomery, Charles Anderson, and I. Howard Marshall have
pointed with appreciation to the work of Swedish New Testament
scholars Riesenfeld and Gerhardsson. They argue that Jesus and
his disciples must have used the strict methods of repetition and
transmission used in rabbinic tradition. The rabbis' teaching, as
Marshall summarizes the argument,

> was transmitted with great fidelity, each pupil learning ac-
> curately by heart what he heard from his teacher, and then
> passing it on. There was, on this view, little scope for the
> wild developments and addition to the tradition which had
> been envisaged by some scholars [i.e., form critics]. Riesen-
> feld argued that if the tradition was treated in this sacrosanct

manner, the explanation must be that it could be traced back to Jesus himself. . . .[32]

Let us grant for the sake of argument that Jesus and his circle of pupils did operate this way (though many scholars doubt that these rabbinic practices can be traced with certainty back to Jesus' day). This argument still does not go as far as the apologists would have their readers believe. The work of Riesenfeld and Gerhardsson would effectively refute those radical theories which hold that community-tradition was so creative and freewheeling that "the disciples must have been translated to heaven immediately after the resurrection."[33] According to such critical theories, the primary transmission of Jesus-material was a popular and essentially creative one, fabricating countless new sayings and letting the authentic teaching disappear. This extreme view is probably something of a caricature. But it is properly refuted by Riesenfeld and Gerhardsson. These scholars make it plausible that there was a careful, custodial transmission of Jesus-material by people authorized to do this. The problem is that Evangelical apologists use Riesenfeld and Gerhardsson as an excuse to jump from one extreme to the other. They assume that we can now be sure that there was *only* such custodial transmission, with no creative folk-tradition alongside it. But the work of Riesenfeld and Gerhardsson certainly does not allow us to assume this. Nor does it allow us to assume that the gospels contain only the carefully-preserved, authentic traditions stemming from Jesus' circle of disciples and not also some of the other (creative popular) tradition. Basically, the problem is this: whatever the practice of the "college of apostles," it does not necessarily have unmediated connection with the finished gospels, which seem to contain material popularly transmitted outside this original circle of disciples.

What is the goal of the Evangelical argument at this point? Scholars like Robinson, Jeremias, Gerhardsson, and Riesenfeld suggest that the gospel-tradition contains more authentic Jesus-tradition than critics have been accustomed to think. But Evangelical apologists have a less modest goal in mind. They want essentially to approximate by means of historical-type arguments an estimate of gospel-accuracy held by them on the basis of a belief in verbal inspiration. They would ultimately like to see the critic of the gospels embrace verbal inspiration, but it will be almost as good if with historical reasoning the outsider can be convinced that, yes, Jesus did do and say all the things attributed to him. (See the section "If Miracles Are Possible, Are Legends Impossible?" in Chapter 9.)

Riesenfeld and Gerhardsson applied rabbinic methods of tradition-transmission to the early Christian situation. But this is not the only possible analogy in the history of middle-eastern religion. Early Muslims were concerned to hand down the *hadith*, or oral traditions of the Prophet Muhammad. How did they accomplish this? R. D. Smith has this to say:

> . . . regarding the character of the transmitters of the traditions, especially during that vulnerable century when they were transmitted only by word of mouth and memory, two ancient Moslem authorities agree that "a holy man is nowhere more inclined to lie than in the matter of traditions." There are many venerated Moslems who actually are known to have

succumbed to this temptation, some of them explicitly admitting
that they did so. It is important to note, moreover, that in
spite of the fact that these men were known as forgers, they
were nevertheless revered as holy men because their lies were
considered to be completely unobjectionable. It was a quasi-
universal conviction that it was licit in the interest of encour-
aging virtue and submission to the law, to concoct and put into
circulation sayings of the Prophet.[34]

Jan Vansina, in his *Oral Tradition as History*, comments:

> Historical truth is also a notion that is culture specific. . .
> . When G. Gossen reports that the Chamuleros (Maya Chiapas)
> believe that any coherent account about an event which has
> been retold several times is true the historian does not feel
> satisfied. . . . In many cultures truth is what is being faith-
> fully repeated as content and has been certified as true by
> the ancestors. But sometimes truth does not include the no-
> tion that x and y really happened. . . . One cannot just as-
> sume that truth means faithful transmission of the content of
> a message. The historian must be on his guard; he cannot
> assume anything on this score, but must elucidate it for the
> culture he studies.[35]

Thus, by ancient middle-eastern standards, it is not at all certain that faithful "ministers of the word" would never dare let a
"phoney" saying slip in. This might be the very thing they *should*
do! It is only a modern Western distaste for this kind of thing
that makes George E. Ladd gratuitously assume that the Spirit's
guidance would have kept the gospel tradition "pure" of new sayings. He arbitrarily dogmatizes that the Spirit could not inspire the
attribution of new sayings to Jesus.[36] We certainly do not know
that ministers of the Jesus-tradition necessarily did follow the same
practices as the transmitters of *hadith*. But the existence of such
a possible parallel in this milieu means that the creation of new sayings cannot be deemed *a priori* contrary to a concern for "faithfulness" in transmission.

Well then, are the gospels in fact filled with legends, completely
fictitious? I have not once addressed this question. I do believe
that the major conservative apologetics for the historicity of the
gospels are in error at virtually every point. But this conclusion in
itself says nothing about gospel historicity. Whether this or that
item in the gospels is authentic must be settled case by case, and
on the basis of appropriate historiographical criteria. The quest for
history in the gospels has been going on now for generations in
mainstream New Testament scholarship. One should try one's best
to avoid the excesses and abuses into which such research has sometimes fallen. But it is inadmissible to try and short-circuit the
whole process as conservative apologists do with bogus arguments
like the ones examined here. These arguments would be fine (though
not very compelling) if one were to replace their "must haves" with
"might haves." That is, it is quite *possible* that the disciples suc-
ceeded in shielding the gospel tradition from legendary accretions.
I have merely sought to challenge the apologists' claim that this
must have been the case. Critical study of the gospels is needed
if we hope to find out what actually *did* happen.

Chapter 6

GUARDING AN EMPTY TOMB

In Chapter 5, I dealt with the most common arguments for the reliability of the gospels. Now I want to discuss a special case, the arguments advanced for the resurrection of Jesus Christ. At the outset of his widely circulated booklet, *The Evidence for the Resurrection*, J. N. D. Anderson gives attention to the view that the resurrection narratives are legends. Anderson rules that "this is . . . impossible. . . . [because] the records were too early for legendary growth."[1] We have already seen the fatal difficulties that beset this contention. There is no point in repeating it all here, except to remind ourselves that the time interval between Jesus and the gospels is certainly sufficient to allow for the growth of legends. But since the historicity argument is absolutely crucial to Evangelical apologetics for the resurrection, we will devote a little space to the particulars of the resurrection narratives.

What suggests to non-Evangelical scholars that the resurrection narratives contain legendary elements? First there is a variety of apparent contradictions in the stories which in any ancient narrative would have to arouse the historian's suspicion. Perhaps the most detailed investigations of these are still to be found in Reimarus's *Fragments* and Strauss's *The Life of Jesus Critically Examined*. They include the well-known discrepancies of which and how many women visited the tomb, and at what hour. Was it Mary Magdalene alone, or was she with others? Did she/they see the angel(s?) before or after she(they) called Peter and the others? Where was Jesus buried, in a tomb that conveniently happened to be nearby, or in Joseph's tomb? Did the risen Jesus tell his disciples to go to Galilee, or to stay in Jerusalem? The most embarrassing divergence between the narratives revolves around the spectacular scene in Matthew. In this version, the women are treated to the sight of a luminous angel flying down, causing an earthquake, and heaving the stone away from the empty tomb, and all this in full view of posted guards! The problem is that the other evangelists somehow seem to have forgotten to mention the guards and the whole sequence of events! Certainly if all this had really taken place, the women could not help but have included it in every telling of their story, and no gospel writer could have failed to use these facts had he known them. In a gospel otherwise known for midrashic expansion (e.g., the addition of Peter walking on the water), it would not seem improbable that we have an unhistorical addition here.

The reader has probably seen some attempts to harmonize some of the discrepancies between the gospel accounts. The precarious and contrived nature of the result should make anyone hesitant to base much on it. But let us suppose these texts could all be harmonized. The value of the accounts as evidence for the resurrection would still be greatly lessened. The very admission of the need to harmonize is an admission that the burden of proof is on the narratives, not on those who doubt them. What harmonizing shows is that *despite appearances*, the texts still *might* be true. This is a different thing than saying that the texts *as they stand* probably *are* true, that the burden of proof is on the person who would over-

turn this supposedly unambiguous evidence for the resurrection.
Conservative apologists often ignore all the discrepancies, or after
they have harmonized them, they continue to pretend the texts constitute unambiguously positive evidence.

Worse yet, the gospel resurrection stories seem to be in conflict
with an earlier version. Evangelical apologists are happy to be able
to point to a resurrection text from about 56 A.D., i.e., I Corinthians chapter 15, where the resurrection of Jesus is used to refute
Corinthian errorists who denied the future resurrection of believers. Paul was able to appeal to his preaching of Jesus' resurrection
which his readers had accepted years before. The list of appearances there can be pushed back with reasonable probability to within
a few years of the crucifixion. (Paul's material does not *describe*
any appearances, however, and this will be important to keep in
mind.) Though Paul's own writing does not go back so far, it is
still several years earlier than the gospels' resurrection narratives.
Any divergences between the two sets of material (i.e., between
I Corinthians 15 and the gospels) may prove to be significant.

Apologists usually focus on the list of appearances quoted by Paul
from tradition in verses 6-7. But one must not stop there. The
way he goes on to use this material in the rest of his argument
helps us reconstruct his understanding of the resurrection. In describing the future resurrection of believers, Paul raises the question, "How are the dead raised? With what kind of body will they
come?" (verse 35). The answer is that it will be a "spiritual body,"
not a natural or corruptible body such as we have now (verse 44).
Paul says he knows this because believers will recapitulate the resurrection of Jesus himself (verses 48-49). He had a "spiritual body"
of the kind Paul describes. Though Paul is not so presumptuous as
to try and plumb this mystery completely, there is one thing he can
say in description of this "spiritual body"—it does not have flesh:
"I tell you, brothers, that flesh and blood cannot inherit the Kingdom of God, nor does the perishable inherit the imperishable" (verse
50). It follows that Jesus' body was not flesh either. In fact, Paul
can say that Jesus by his resurrection "became a . . . spirit" (verse
45). We may have a similar idea expressed in I Peter 3:18, "In the
body he was put to death; in the spirit he was raised to life."

To put it plainly, this conception of the risen Jesus is in direct
contradiction to that presupposed in the later accounts of the gospels. The conception is exactly the opposite. Whereas Paul had
said that the risen Jesus was "a spirit," *not* "flesh," Luke reports
Jesus saying, "It is I myself! Touch me and see! No *spirit* has
flesh and bones as you see that I *have*" (Luke 24:39). To underline
the point even more, the three evangelists who record appearances
of Jesus describe the tactile reality of his flesh, even of his wounds
(Luke 24:39-40; Matthew 28:9; John 20:27). They make Jesus "flesh,"
not a "spirit"!

I am quite aware of the harmonization offered here. As a matter
of fact this harmonization is taken so much for granted that Evangelicals do not realize that it *is* a harmonization. It so controls
their reading of the texts that they never seem even to see the
problem. Not noticing the "spirit" vs. "flesh" problem, they just
assume that the "spiritual body" in I Corinthians 15 refers to Jesus'
"ability to walk through walls" and his inability to be recognized at

first glance as allegedly reported in the gospels. But this harmonization rests on too superficial a reading of the gospel accounts. The sudden appearances and disappearances of the risen Jesus have little necessarily to do with any changed quality of his body. Rather, what seems to be in view is spatial teleportation.

The same thing happens elsewhere in Hellenistic religious biography, such as in Philostratus's *Life of Apollonius of Tyana*, where the philosopher Apollonius suddenly vanishes from the courtroom of the Emperor Domitian only to reappear elsewhere among his friends. His companions are startled, but Apollonius laughingly reassures them that despite his mode of travel, he is a flesh and blood mortal like themselves. Luke himself, who makes the most of Jesus' teleportation, gives another example of it in Acts. There Philip (who certainly has no risen "spiritual body") is supernaturally caught up after he baptizes the Ethiopian, reappearing near Azotus (8:39-40).

As for the failure to recognize the risen Jesus, Luke attributes this not to any quality of the risen Jesus, but to an interference with the faculties of the witnesses. Luke 24:16 says, "They were *kept* from recognizing him," in practically the same terms as Luke uses elsewhere, in one of the passion predictions: "It was hidden from them, so that they did not grasp it" (9:45). Evangelicals who use this argument are probably subconsciously influenced most by the spurious passage Mark 16:12: "Afterward Jesus appeared in a different form to two of them while they were walking in the country." Even if this text were originally part of Mark, the context indicates that for some reason Jesus' appearance on this one occasion was different from that of the other resurrection encounters where he was recognizable.

In short, none of these data from the gospel accounts serves to harmonize them with Paul's earlier and quite different concept of the risen Jesus. The implication should be evident, as in fact it has been to several generations of New Testament scholars. Serious doubt must be cast on the historical reliability of these narratives; they are not only chronologically later than the I Corinthians 15 tradition but they seem to be based on a later and contradictory understanding of the resurrection.

If the gospel resurrection narratives turned out not to be factual accounts based on eyewitness reporting, what is their origin? Evangelical apologists suppose that the only alternative is that they formed part of some kind of hoax as suggested long ago by the hostile skeptic Reimarus. This is evident from statements like the following:

> "Legends" put in circulation and recorded by the original eyewitnesses are [tantamount to] deliberate inventions. (Anderson)[2]

> . . . what would have motivated the disciples, in the face of their overwhelming discouragement, to create imaginary—yet closely detailed—resurrection accounts such as [Luke 24:36-43]? (Montgomery)[3]

There are two controlling yet unfounded assumptions at work here. The first is that if the resurrection accounts are not factual reports, then this must mean the resurrection itself never happened. The second is that if these accounts are not factual reports, they

still were written by the immediate disciples of Jesus, and therefore
must be lies.   The apologists are only able to make these assumptions on the basis of their mistaken conclusion that the gospels are
too early to admit of the intrusion of popular legends.   Therefore
they must realize that popular legends would not involve anyone in
a charge of intentional fraud.   Yet if the unbeliever can be induced
to see the alternatives as "history or hoax," the apologist's task is
easier.   It is a little difficult for any intelligent person to imagine
that Christianity is based on a huge fraud.

In the last chapter I argued for the theoretical possibility of a
popular legendary element in the gospels.   Now I will look at some
positive data which make it not unreasonable to see the resurrection
narratives as legends.   I will not be attempting to prove that these
accounts are legends, only that to view them as legendary is not
historically outrageous as the apologists hold.

Charles Talbert, in *What is a Gospel?*, has demonstrated that in
Jesus' era philosophers, kings, and other benefactors were often
glorified in terms of ancient legend.   Heroes of antiquity such as
Romulus and Hercules were rewarded for their labors by "*apotheosis*"
—i.e., they were taken up into heaven and divinized.   Their ascent
into heaven was supposedly seen by gaping eyewitnesses (as in the
case of Romulus) or was at least evidenced by the absence of any
bodily remains.   The hero might even reappear to his mourning
friends to encourage or direct them.   Not only were such legends
circulating about mythical figures of the past, but the same stories
would be applied in popular imagination to more recent or contemporary figures such as Apollonius of Tyana, the Emperor Augustus,
and the prophet Peregrinus.   In fact, so many contemporary figures
were divinized that the whole practice came to be satirized, e.g., in
Seneca's *The Pumpkinification of Claudius*.   Thus Michael Green is
simply mistaken when he reassures his readers that "nobody had
ever attributed divinity and a virgin birth, resurrection and ascen-
sion to a historical person whom lots of people knew."[4]   The application of this kind of glorification legend to Jesus (as to other historical figures like Augustus and Apollonius) is to be distinguished
from the older, wholly speculative theory that Jesus' resurrection
was derived from vegetation cults centering around mythical dying-
and-rising deities like Adonis, Sandan, or Attis.

In the light of these tendencies it is not difficult to understand
the gospels' resurrection narratives as based on legends that had
grown up to glorify Jesus.   To recognize the possibility of this, one
need not assume that there was no resurrection.   Indeed it was precisely because of experiences of some kind (such as those intriguing-
ly listed but not described by Paul in I Corinthians 15) that anyone
cared to glorify Jesus.   But the growth of legends describing appearances of Jesus in physical terms would help explain the development between Paul's "spiritual body" version of the resurrection and
the physicalized conception in the gospels.

Such historical data go a long way toward stultifying apologetical
standbys like the old "empty tomb argument."   One hardly need exercise himself over whether "either the Jewish or Roman authorities
or Joseph of Arimathea removed the body"[5] (Anderson), if the whole
story may be understood as an apotheosis legend.   The inability of
anyone to find a single one of his bones had convinced his compan-

ions that Hercules had indeed been taken to Mt. Olympus. Men assumed that Aristeaus had gone into heaven because he was no more to be seen. Aeneas was known to have joined the gods when after a battle his body was nowhere to be found. Romulus ascended from another battlefield as evidenced by the fact that no one could find so much as a fragment of his body or his clothes. One might include here the Old Testament stories of Enoch and Elijah (both of whom were objects of considerable speculation in Jesus' milieu). Both were taken up to be with God, the result of which was that no trace of either could be found (Genesis 5:24; II Kings 2:16-18; cf. Deuteronomy 34:5-6).

In more recent (i.e., non-mythical) times, the philosopher Empedocles disappeared after an evening meal with his friends and could not be found, and together with a voice from heaven, this proved he must have ascended. Another philosopher, Apollonius of Tyana, a contemporary of Jesus, was said by later legend to have heeded the summons of heavenly voices to "go upwards from earth"; his friends searched the temple from which he had disappeared but could find no remains. Is it surprising that Christians would eventually circulate a story wherein mourning friends came to Jesus' tomb only to find no trace of his body and to be told by an angel that he has been "raised"?

Stories of the physical reappearance of Jesus to comfort or command his followers would also fit into this pattern. Ovid records this appearance of Romulus, after he had ascended from the battlefield.

Proculus Julius was coming from the Alba Longa; the moon was shining, he was not using a torch. Suddenly the hedges on the left shook and moved. He shrank back and his hair stood on end. Beautiful and more than human and clothed in a sacred robe, Romulus was seen, standing in the middle of the road. He said, "Stop the (Romans) from their mourning; do not let them violate my divinity with their tears; order the pious crowd to bring incense and worship the new [god] Quirinius." . . . He gave the order and he vanished into the upper world from before Julius' eyes.[6]

In another text strikingly reminiscent of the gospel accounts, Philostratus tells the story of a doubting pupil of the departed Apollonius of Tyana:

This young boy would never agree to the immortality of the soul, "I, my friends, am completing the tenth month of praying to Apollonius to reveal to me the nature of the soul. But he is completely dead so as never to respond to my begging, nor will I believe he is not dead." Such were the things he said then, but on the fifth day after that they were busy with these things and he suddenly fell into a deep sleep right where he had been talking. . . . he, as if insane, suddenly leaped to his feet . . . and cried out, "I believe you!" When those present asked him what was wrong, he said "Do you not see Apollonius the sage, how he stands here among us, listening to the argument and singing wonderful verses concerning the soul? . . . He came to discuss with me alone concerning the things which I would not believe."[7]

The research done by Talbert and others makes the set of alternatives proposed by the apologists (i.e., "hoax or history") a false
one. It is considerations like this which make works like Anderson's
The Evidence for the Resurrection hopelessly out of date. In this
book, and a large number of others like it, the apologists manage to
effect a resurrection of their own—they bring back the deists and
rationalists of the eighteenth century as their opponents in debate.
The apologists assume that their opponents, the imagined advocates
of the "wrong tomb" and "swoon" theories, etc., agree that the gospel resurrection accounts are substantially accurate even down to
the details. Otherwise, for instance, Edwin Yamauchi could hardly
dismiss the possibility that grave robbers removed Jesus' body,
merely by an appeal to the Johannine notation that Jesus' shroud
was left behind. Yamauchi assumes that his opponents will accept
the Johannine narrative at face value as he himself does. Unfortunately, such easy targets have long since vanished. Rationalists
and deists like Paulus and Venturini used to argue this way since,
oddly, they held to the near-inerrancy of the texts' reportage of
events, yet claimed that apparent miracles were to be explained
naturalistically! That Anderson has such people in mind is obvious
from a quote like this: "The only rationalistic interpretations of any
merit admit the sincerity of the records, but try to explain them
without recourse to the miraculous."[8] New Testament scholarship
has long since left both Anderson and Venturini behind, since it
has shown at least that the facticity of the resurrection narratives
cannot be simply taken for granted. Granted they are not lies,
they may yet be legendary.

Montgomery, Stott, Lewis, and others point to the "vivid detail"
in the narratives as proof of eyewitness authorship. A favorite text
adduced in this regard is John 20:3-8, "[an] eyewitness account in
a vivid, yet restrained, passage [which] . . . records the visit of
Peter and John to the tomb"[9] (Anderson). "The account [John]
gives of this incident . . . bears unmistakable marks of first-hand
experience"[10] (Stott). I invite the reader to open his New Testament to this text and compare it to a passage from Chariton's *Chair-
eas and Kalliroe*, a fiction novel written probably in the first century B.C. It concerns a girl, mistakenly entombed alive, who has
been removed by grave robbers.

> Chaireas was guarding and toward dawn he approached the
> tomb. . . . When he came close, however, he found the stones
> moved away and the entrance open. He looked in and was
> shocked, seized by a great perplexity at what had happened.
> Rumor made an immediate report to the Syracusans about the
> miracle. All then ran to the tomb; no one dared to enter
> until Hermocrates ordered it. One was sent in and he re-
> ported everything accurately. It seemed incredible—the dead
> girl was not there. . . . [When Chaireas] searched the tomb
> he was able to find nothing. Many came in after him, disbe-
> lieving. Amazement seized everyone, and some said as they
> stood there: "The shroud has been stripped off, this is the
> work of grave robbers; but where is the body?"[11]

I am not suggesting that John or the other evangelists used this
novel as a source. I mean only to show that vivid descriptions of

empty tombs and abandoned graveclothes prove nothing about "eye-witness authorship" since we find them also in an admitted work of fiction.

Does anyone think the story of the two disciples meeting the un-recognized Christ on the road to Emmaus (Luke 24:13-35) reads too much like vivid eyewitness testimony to be considered legend? Then let him consider the parallel provided by a votive tablet posted in the healing shrine of the god Asclepius in Epidauros, Egypt, in the fourth century B.C.:

> Sosastra, of Pherae, had a false pregnancy. In fear and trembling she came in a litter and slept here. But she had no clear dream [the usual medium for revealing the inspired pre-scription from the god] and started for home again. Then, near Curni she dreamt that a man, comely in appearance, fell in with her and her companions; when he learned about their bad luck he bade them set down the litter on which they were carrying Sosastra; then he cut open her belly, removed an enormous quantity of worms—two full basins; then he stitched up her belly and made the woman well; then Asclepius re-vealed his presence and bade her send thank-offerings for the cure to Epidaurus.[12]

The apologists assure us that the resurrection appearances could not have been hallucinations. They seem indignant that anyone should think to trouble them with such absurd notions. First, they claim that the disciples were hardly the kind of "highly strung and imaginative types" to have hallucinations. Anderson claims that too many of Jesus' disciples were too "hardheaded" and "prosaic" for this.[13] But just how "hardheaded" would we call someone who left his family and livelihood to join a wandering Galilean healer? How "prosaic" is a man who exclaims, "Lord, even the demons are sub-ject to us in your name," or "Lord, do you want us to call down fire from heaven on them?" Such a person is obviously moving in a realm far removed from the "prosaic"!

Another contention of the apologists is that:

> Hallucinations are highly *individualistic* because their source is the subconscious mind of the recipient. No two persons will experience exactly the same phenomena. But the crowd of five hundred [mentioned in I Corinthians 15] claimed to have experienced the same "hallucination," at the same time and place. And other groups, both large and small, experienced the same "hallucination." (Anderson)[14]

Unfortunately the facts again fail to bear out such generalized assertions. I am not sure where Anderson, McDowell, Green and others get their information on the supposed "laws of hallucinations," but in fact collective hallucinations are a well-known phenomenon discussed, for instance, in G. N. M Tyrrell's *Apparitions* and D. H. Rawcliffe's *The Psychology of the Occult*. But to take one particu-larly relevant example of mass visions, let us return momentarily to Gershom Scholem's remarks on the messianic revival of Sabbatai Sevi:

> The people of Smyrna saw miracles and heard prophecies, providing the best possible illustration of Renan's remark about the infectious character of visions. It is enough for one mem-

ber of a group sharing the same beliefs to claim to have seen
or heard a supernatural manifestation, and the others too will
see and hear it. Hardly had the report arrived from Aleppo
that Elijah had appeared in the Old Synagogue there, and
Elijah walked the streets of Smyrna. Dozens, even hundreds,
had seen him. . . . A letter written in Constantinople notes
apparitions of Elijah "whom many have seen."[15]

Visions of Sabbatai Sevi himself after his death were "very common
in many circles of the believers."[16] These instances of mass visions
are all the more striking since they occur in circumstances closely
analogous to those of the resurrection appearances themselves.

The key thing to recognize is that in a group hallucination not
all the participants necessarily see the very same thing! We can
easily imagine a mass-psychological chain-reaction in which every
one present seems to see an absent person according to the particular image of that person contained in his or her memory. Paul does
not tell us "He was seen by over five hundred brethren at one time,
and they all compared notes, and after an exhaustive series of in-
terviews it was determined that all without exception saw Jesus wear-
ing a red cloak over a white tunic, holding out nail-scarred hands."
All we can be sure of is that they all saw their mental image of
Jesus, doing or saying something.

In fact one ancient Christian document envisions precisely this
possibility on an analogous occasion. In the apocryphal Acts of
Peter we read of a scene in which Peter leads a group of charis-
matically endowed women in a collective visionary experience.

Then Peter said to them, "Tell us what you saw." And
they said, "We saw an old man, who had such a presence as
we cannot describe to you"; but others said, "We saw a growing lad"; and others said, "We saw a boy who gently touched
our eyes, and so our eyes were opened," . . . So Peter praised
the Lord, saying, . . . "God is greater than our thoughts, as
we have learned from the aged widows, how they have seen
the Lord in a variety of forms." (chapter 21)[17]

Or compare a series of visions of the Virgin Mary which began in
Dordogne, France, in 1889. Here is the description of George Bar-
ton Cutten in his classic treatment *The Psychological Phenomena of
Christianity*:

A neurotic child of eleven years, named Mary Magoutier,
was the first to see the vision. She saw a figure like the
statues in the churches in a hole in a wall situated in a lonely
place. The vision next appeared to children of her own age,
and then to a large number of peasants, both men and women.
The suggestion was general, and each one filled in and par-
ticularized for himself. For this reason, while the visions were
similar, the details differed. To some the Virgin appeared
dressed in white, to others in black; sometimes she was veiled
and sometimes not; sometimes the figure was large and at other
times small; sometimes the body was luminous, or lights were
attached to the shoulders or breasts; at times the surround-
ings also changed. . . . On August 11 more than fifteen hundred persons visited the wall, and many of these saw the
Virgin. . . ."[18]

But were the disciples in the proper psychological state to experience hallucinations? Clark Pinnock does not think so:

> It is striking that all of the factors favorable to the hallucination hypothesis are absent from the New Testament. The resurrection caught everyone off guard. The disciples were surprised and disbelieving for joy (Mark 16:8; Matthew 28:17; Luke 24:36-43; John 20:19). They needed convincing themselves. Jesus did not come into an atmosphere of wishful thinking.[19]

Or to put it slightly differently, C. S. Lewis maintains that:

> . . . any theory of hallucinations breaks down on the fact (and if it is invention it is the oddest invention that ever entered the mind of man) that on three separate occasions this hallucination was not immediately recognized as Jesus (Luke xxiv. 13-31; John xx. 15, xxi. 4).[20]

Pinnock and Lewis mean that while hallucinatory visions are supposed to occur only to those primed for them by sentimental or enthusiastic longing, the disciples are pictured as being so disillusioned as to be skeptical that it was really the risen Christ they were seeing! If the resurrection appearances were really the result of wishful thinking, how could the disciples have been doubtful, as the narratives depict?

Once again, these arguments are vitiated by their assumption that the resurrection accounts must be historically accurate. But what if these narratives are legends? In this case (and contra the apologists, it is well within the realm of possibility), the picture changes considerably. In the context of religious legend, the reported skepticism of the disciples is *not* "the oddest invention that ever entered the mind of man." (Lewis)

Such an "invention" would not be odd in the least. We find several other examples of it in miracle stories that no one would deny are legendary. At the ancient healing shrine of Epidauros, there survive numerous testimonial inscriptions, either actually left there by "satisfied customers" or composed by the priests for advertisement purposes. One tells of a man whose fingers were crippled. He came to the healing temple, but "he disbelieved in the healings and he sneered at the inscriptions." Yet in his mercy, the healing god Asclepios restored his hand, despite the man's unbelief. Similarly, the one-eyed Ambrosia of Athens came to the shrine with doubts in her mind: "as she walked around the temple of healings, she mocked some things as incredible and impossible, that the lame and blind could be healed at only seeing a dream." Yet Asclepios takes pity and heals her anyway. Another suppliant who actually has an empty eye-socket goes to the shrine for help. This time it is the bystanders who mock—surely this is too great a task even for Asclepios. Nonetheless the man is given a completely new eye!

In Philostratus's *Life of Apollonius of Tyana*, the hero pinpoints the cause of a plague·in Ephesus as a demon. We are told that Apollonius points out an old blind beggar and directs the crowd to stone him to death! Understandably, the crowd is skeptical! But Apollonius knows best. He prevails, and the old man is revealed as a "devil in disguise"; beneath the heap of stones is found no human corpse, but rather that of a huge dog!

Another example occurs in a legend about Rabbi Hanina ben Dosa, who lived in the first century A.D. Some friends are on their way to his house to ask him to pray for the recovery of a sick boy. But as they arrive, the rabbi meets them with the announcement that the fever has left the boy! They are surprised and a bit skeptical, since they haven't even made their request! They retort, "What? Are you a prophet?" But Hanina is right—it turns out that the fever left the boy "at that moment."[21]

In all these stories, the skepticism of the characters functions as a literary device to magnify the miracle worked by the hero. He was able to "pull it off" despite the doubts of everyone! By his mighty works the hero (Asclepios, Apollonius, or Hanina ben Dosa) silences the skeptics. If the gospels' resurrection accounts are legendary in character, a possibility that the apologists have not satisfactorily eliminated, then "the disbelief of the disciples" would be a perfectly natural element in the story. Their disbelief functions to highlight the glory of the resurrection, since it is able to overcome their skepticism. Now maybe the disciples are shown as doubting and then being convinced because this is the way it happened. But this is not the only way to account for the skepticism motif. It would also make sense seen as part of a legendary story. In this case we cannot take the resurrection accounts as unambiguous proof that the resurrection visions of the disciples were not preceded by a favorable psychological state, whatever that might be.

Another commonly rehearsed apologetic argument is that only the resurrection of Jesus can explain the "transformation of the disciples." Anderson poses the question:

> What about the apostles themselves? What changed the little company of sad and defeated cowards into a band of irresistible missionaries who turned the world upside down because no opposition could deter them?[22]

This is what Frank Morison, in his imaginative book *Who Moved the Stone?*, calls "the miracle of the conversion of the disciples."[23] The point is that the disciples were so badly disillusioned after Jesus' execution that nothing short of a resurrection could have snapped them out of it. This judgment is surely premature, psychologically speaking. Before asking the question of what psychological dynamics would be at work in a situation like that of the disappointed disciples, let me recount a few analogous cases of messianic disillusionment.

I have already had occasion to mention the shocking apostasy of messiah Sabbatai Sevi. I think it would have to be admitted that the apostasy of the messiah would be a pill quite as bitter as the crucifixion of the messiah. What happened to the Sabbatian movement when Sabbatai Sevi donned the Muslim turban in order to save his life? For one thing, there was a flood of theological rationalizations forthcoming from the faithful. Suddenly, it seemed that Nathan of Gaza and others had made "passion predictions" long before, though these claims were doubtful. Old Testament passages were interpreted in such a way as to have predicted the apostasy. Also, a plethora of redemption-theories made the rounds. Sabbatai had become a Muslim in order to redeem the Turks and other Gentiles.

Or, he had committed apostasy so as to plumb the lowest depths of evil and transform it into good. Or, he had actually been translated to heaven, while a phantom look-alike went through the motions of apostasy! Perhaps some of this sounds familiar! At any rate, it is important to note that no supernatural event was necessary to stop the movement from collapsing over this event, which one would imagine to have been fatally disillusioning. But the Sabbatian movement endured for several generations! Gershom Scholem suggests that the messianic fervor in which believers had spent so many months was so powerfully real in their minds that no external events could shake it.

There are several other instances of disappointed apocalyptic movements nearer to our own day. The Millerite movement staked everything on the return of Christ occurring in 1843. Two different target dates fell through, but this was not the end of Adventist faith. With a theological adjustment or two, the movement became what is today known as the Seventh-Day Adventist Church, a worldwide missionary movement. A convenient vision led Adventists to believe that the coming of Christ in judgment had indeed occurred on the date predicted, only the "investigative judgment" took place in heaven, not on earth as previously assumed. The Jehovah's Witness sect has used a similar maneuver to save face several times. The most famous of these was in 1914 when Christ should have come to rule the earth in person. The date passed, but no Christ. Well, it seemed that on that date Christ had indeed taken up his reign *invisibly*, from heaven!

Psychologically, what is going on here? How can the obvious disconfirmation of religious belief matter so little to believers? Festinger, Riecken, and Schachter have devoted a famous study (*When Prophecy Fails*) to this very question. Their theory rests on the notion of "cognitive dissonance" reduction. This is the psychological mechanism whereby a person reduces the tension caused by the clash of a belief with contrary facts, either by jettisoning the belief or by reinterpreting or ignoring the facts. When a group has staked everything on a religious belief, and "burned their bridges behind them," only to find the belief disconfirmed by events, they may find disillusionment too painful to endure. They soon come up with some explanatory rationalization, the plausibility of which will be reinforced by the mutual encouragement of fellow-believers in the group. In order to increase further the plausibility of their threatened belief they may engage in a massive new effort at proselytizing. The more people who can be convinced, the truer it will seem. (Remember the "truth by majority vote" strategy of "witnessing" described in Chapter 2.) In the final analysis, then, a radical disconfirmation of belief may be just what a religious movement needs to get off the ground!

The disciples had certainly committed themselves irrevocably to follow Jesus: "Lo, we have left everything to follow you" (Matthew 19:27). Their expectations were great; Jesus was the Messiah who would soon bring eschatological liberation to Israel: "We had hoped that he was the one who was going to redeem Israel" (Luke 24:21). It was therefore unthinkable for Jesus to die: "God forbid, Master! This must never happen to you!" (Matthew 16:22). Yet Jesus *did* die! And what happened? As the Roman historian Tacitus put it,

Christian faith "thus checked for the moment, again broke out."
Luke records the amazing surge of proselytizing emanating from
Jerusalem.   Of course, the message had changed somewhat—now
Jesus wasn't immediately going to "restore the Kingdom to Israel"
(Acts 1:6).   Instead, he had established a *spiritual* kingdom, reign-
ing now from heaven instead of earth as had first been expected.
But, as Anderson said, this message did soon "turn the world up-
side down."   Does the historian need a miraculous resurrection to
explain all this?   Or would the psychological dynamics of cognitive
dissonance reduction serve just as well?

None of this proves that the resurrection didn't happen, but it
implies that the line of reasoning pursued in the "transformation of
the disciples" argument is not compelling.   They *could* have been
"transformed" as other disillusioned disciples have been, by a more
modest means than a resurrection.

A relatively new apologetic argument for the resurrection is offered by George E. Ladd.   His book, *I Believe in the Resurrection
of Jesus*, contains a fascinating survey of Old Testament and inter-
testamental Jewish opinions on the resurrection of the dead:

> Some believed in the resurrection of a gross physical body;
> others in a transformed body.   However, wherever resurrec-
> tion appears, *it is always eschatological*.   It is resurrection at
> the end of the age.   We have found nothing in either the Old
> Testament or contemporary Judaism to help us explain the
> rise of the belief in the resurrection of Jesus.[24]

The implication is that the belief in Jesus' resurrection was so dis-
similar to common ideas that it could have only arisen from the fact
of the resurrection itself.

Amazingly, the most relevant piece of evidence lies unnoticed
directly beneath Ladd's scholarly nose!   Why range far and wide
into Jewish pseudepigraphical literature, when texts such as this
one lie ready at hand?   "Jesus' name had become well-known.   Some
were saying, 'John the Baptist has been raised from the dead, and
that is why miraculous powers are at work in him'" (Mark 6:14b).
Thus we know from the gospels themselves that people *did* believe
in the resurrection of individuals before the general resurrection of
the end time.   Not only so, but the Marcan passage indicates that
the public appearances of Jesus were interpreted by many as resurrection appearances of John, a prophet martyred by a tyrant!   John
had been vindicated by God as could be seen by the exercise of
miraculous power.   We find the same idea expressed regarding Jesus
in Romans 1:4—Jesus has been declared Son of God "with power
[Greek *dunamis*, the same word for "miracle" in Mark 6:14] by the
resurrection"   The New Testament itself tells us that some had already suspected that John was the Messiah (Luke 3:15).   What do
we have here?   Certain extraordinary events lead people to believe
that a cruelly martyred holy man, suspected to be the Messiah, has
been raised from the dead, displaying miraculous power.   And all
this only months before Jesus' crucifixion.   The disciples' belief in
Jesus' resurrection was not absolutely unprecedented in their milieu.

Much is made of the "empty tomb" argument.   I said that the
possibility of accounting for the empty tomb stories as legendary
"apotheosis narratives" considerably lessens the force of arguments

about whether the women could have visited the wrong tomb, or "who moved the stone." The apologists cannot prove that we know enough of the circumstances of Jesus' burial and of Easter morning to lend weight to such speculations. For all we know, the disciples may not have known where Jesus was buried. One tradition preserved in Acts hints that it was the enemies of Jesus who buried his body (13:29). Or, as Strauss argued, perhaps the disciples took off immediately for Galilee, far from the grave of Jesus, where their visions could build their resurrection-faith with no danger of disconfirmation from an occupied tomb. It is hard to imagine that the disciples could have believed in Jesus' resurrection in any form, much less persuaded others, if the occupied tomb of Jesus had stood there refuting them by its very presence! But we just can't be sure we know enough about the setting of the rise of resurrection faith to be sure that this was the situation. Maybe the disciples didn't know what happened to the body; their faith in the resurrection would have made it superfluous for them to try to find out!

Suppose the Sanhedrin knew the whereabouts of Jesus' corpse. Why didn't they make short work of the apostles' preaching by producing the body? Michael Green feels sure they would have: "They could easily have rectified the situation by triumphantly producing it when the Christians started spreading the story of the resurrection."[25] One strategic detail always seems to escape the scrutiny of the apologists at this point. According to the New Testament itself, Christians began to "spread the story of the resurrection" *seven weeks* after Jesus' death (Acts chapter 2—the Day of Pentecost). What good would it have done to produce an unrecognizable decayed corpse? Lazarus, we are told, had already started decomposing after a mere four days ("by this time he stinketh")! "Producing the body" would have been a waste of time, since they could never hope to prove whose body it was!

Again, this chapter has not aimed to "disprove" the resurrection. It has simply shown how the evidence, contrary to apologists' claims, *can* be explained in alternate, very plausible ways. Their belief in the value of truth should compel Christians to stop making claims that the evidence is unequivocal if in fact it is not. And what would be lost by such an admission? Probably just excuses for weak faith. "Do you believe because you have seen? Blessed are they who have not seen, and yet have believed" (John 20:29).

At the conclusion of most apologetical arguments for the resurrection we meet with what is essentially an evangelistic appeal to David Hume, as if the philosophical skeptic himself could come back from the grave and repent. Hume wrote: ". . . no testimony is sufficient to establish a miracle, unless the testimony be of such a kind, that its falsehood would be more miraculous than the fact which it endeavors to establish. . . ."[26] The apologists are satisfied that they have so well refuted all alternative explanations for the Easter event that it will now require more faith to deny the resurrection than to believe in it! They have now cornered the skeptic, who they believe must now face the facts and accept this "evidence that demands a verdict." If he doesn't, he will be intellectually dishonest.

It should be obvious by now that I think the poor skeptic still has quite a few loopholes through which to escape if he wishes. But

I would like to make a different point here. It seems to me that I
have heard the mirror-image of this argument before in a very different context. On the issue of biblical inerrancy many of these
same apologists demand precisely the "out" which they deny to the
skeptic.[27] I think I can demonstrate what I have in mind with a
chart:

The Believer in Inerrancy	The Doubter of the Resurrection
We as Evangelicals cannot be too careful in defending our faith in an inerrant scripture.	We as naturalists cannot be too careful in upholding our belief in a closed system of natural causation.
We know that some unbelieving Modernists allege errors to exist in the Bible, such as the order of Peter's denials and the number of cock-crows.	We know that some irrational supernaturalists claim that miracles have occurred, such as the resurrection of Jesus.
If we were to admit the presence of contradictions or errors, we would have no assurance of any sure word from God.	If we were to admit the reality of events like the resurrection, we would have no defense against all kinds of superstition.
How do we meet these allegations? By all means let us propose solutions and harmonizations—e.g., that Peter denied Jesus 6, 8, or 9 times, indeed as many as necessary.	What shall we say to the apologists for Christianity? By all means let us take refuge in alternative explanations, such as the Swoon Theory, the Wrong Tomb Theory, or the Hallucination Theory.
But above all, let us not lose our confidence in the truthful character of our God. Surely this faith should make us stop short of admitting error in His Word. God cannot err.	But if all else fails, let us never abandon our rational commitment to a closed system of cause-and-effect. Science must rule out the possibility of a "resurrection." Miracles just don't happen.
Even if we cannot find any satisfactory way to solve an apparent discrepancy in scripture, let us assure ourselves that one day, even if in heaven, we will be given that solution.	Even if we should have to admit that no alternative explanation accounts for the evidence of Easter morning as well as the so-called resurrection does, let us rationally assure ourselves that one day we will find the answer.

Sometimes, it seems, Evangelicals are not so quick to "demand a
verdict."

Chapter 7

A FALSE TRILEMMA

Once Evangelical apologists feel they have practically proven the resurrection, they attempt to get all the mileage out of it they can. The resurrection itself must be defended anyway. But wouldn't it be helpful to be able to use it as a stepping stone to get an unbeliever to accept a couple of other articles of faith? Like the "deity of Christ," for instance? The apologist goes on to argue that Jesus before his death "claimed to be God" and predicted that his claims would be verified by his resurrection from the dead. "The conclusion? Jesus did rise, and thereby validated his claim to divinity"[1] (Montgomery). Often another similar argument is used in conjunction with this one, though it is logically independent. This is the old "liar, lunatic, or Lord" argument, also known as the "Trilemma." Perhaps the most famous summary of the Trilemma argument comes from C. S. Lewis:

> A man who was merely a man and said the sort of things Jesus said would not be a great moral teacher. He would either be a lunatic—on the level with the man who says he is a poached egg—or else he would be the Devil of Hell. You must make your choice. Either this man was, and is, the Son of God: or else a madman or something worse.[2]

Though I certainly do not want to dissuade anyone from believing in the deity of Christ, simple intellectual honesty compels us to ask how cogent this argument is.

First, it must be said that Jesus' "claims for himself" are not quite as clear as they need to be for this line of reasoning to be compelling. Apologists frequently point to Jesus' exalted "I am" statements in the fourth gospel ("I am the light of the world" [John 8:12], "I am the bread of life [6:35], etc.) as evidence of his self-assessment. Modern biblical scholarship at least makes it a debatable question whether such statements represent the words of the historical Jesus or the inspired theology of John himself. This consideration must weaken the evidential value of such Johannine texts for the question, "What did the historical Jesus say of himself?" Even if these texts do preserve claims Jesus made to be God, this must yet be demonstrated. Since it is itself a matter of debate, it cannot be adduced as unambiguous evidence for something else.

John is the principal but not the only source for Jesus' supposed claims to be God. Recently some apologists have pointed to Ethelbert Stauffer's interpretation of Mark 14:62, to provide another such claim. According to Stauffer, when Jesus answers his accuser's question with the phrase "*ego eimi*," or "I am," he is actually referring to the Jewish liturgical theophany formula "Ani (we) Hu" ("I and he," meaning "I am he"). Thus, Jesus is supposed to be claiming possession of divinity. Stauffer comes to this conclusion from investigating extracanonical literature.[3] This line of argumentation is summarized and applauded by Buell and Hyder[4] and Yamauchi.[5]

All this may be news to the reader, since this is not quite the first impression one receives in reading the text. Isn't it more natural to assume that when Jesus is asked, "Are you the Christ?"

and replies "I am," that he simply means to reply to this question in
the affirmative?   While there is some difficulty in harmonizing the
reply understood in this way with the Matthean-Lucan version "You
say that I am," this latter version is certainly more nearly equivalent to a simple affirmation than to a claim of divinity, as those
apologists read it! Besides Stauffer's suggestion, arrived at by his
own detective work on Jewish literature, would hardly have been
apparent to Mark's audience without explanation.   They even needed
to have simple Jewish dietary laws explained to them (Mark 7:3-4)
for Jesus' words to make sense.   Could they have understood the
complex allusion suggested by Stauffer?

But the high priest tore his robe, as if in response to blasphemy.
Before running off with Stauffer to investigate various extrabiblical
texts, may I suggest that Buell, Hyder, and Yamauchi take a closer
look at the Marcan text in front of them? Jesus claims in the same
breath that he will be "seated on the right hand of Power" (14:62).
I dare say that most readers of this text naturally assume that this
statement was the alleged blasphemy in question.   And I think they
are right.

If one still wants to go in search of extrabiblical corroboration,
it is there to be found. Rabbinic literature refers to a Jewish "binitarian" heresy, whereby some claimed that "There are two Powers
in heaven."   This binitarian heresy was particularly associated with
the idea that one of God's servants should be so highly exalted as
to be enthroned by his side.   According to one rabbinic text, a
scholar suggests that David will occupy a throne next to God. A
colleague reproaches him: "How long will you profane the Shekinah?"
In the late book III Enoch, the exalted Enoch is given the divine
Name and a throne next to God's.   A later redactor tries to tone
this down for fear of binitarianism.[6] What we can see in all this is
that Jesus' claim to be enthroned by God's side could be taken by
hearers as blasphemy even if not intended as a claim to be God.

In the examples just referred to, the binitarian divinity claim was
a conclusion drawn not by the original speaker (or writer), but by
his opponents who feared what *they* saw as the implication of his
words.   We might be justified in reading the "blasphemy" charge in
the Marcan text as one more example of this. My appeal to Jewish
literature merely supports what I believe to be the natural reading
of the Marcan text.   Stauffer's on the other hand serves to interpret the text in a way that is rather less than obvious.   In short,
once again, it is not at all clear that we must reckon with a "claim
to be God."

Reference is often made in this context to certain "indirect claims"
to divine authority made by Jesus.   One wonders, if these claims
are admittedly indirect, why apologists feel so free to use them as
direct and unambiguous evidence!   Surely the favorite is Jesus'
"claim to forgive sins" in Mark 2:1-12.   For instance, Pinnock writes:
"The claims of Jesus were not all direct ones.   His assumption of
the right to pronounce forgiveness shocked the onlookers (Mark
2:7)."[7] John R. W. Stott says that "The claim to deity advanced by
our Lord was made as forcefully by indirect as by direct means. . .
. The first is the claim to *forgive sins*"[8] It is remarkable that apologists find themselves agreeing with the interpretation, if not the
evaluation, of the "bad guys" of the passage, i.e., that Jesus is

claiming to be God. "From this [i.e., the scribes'] response it seems clear that the most obvious interpretation of Jesus' words in Mark 2:5 is that they imply use of *his own* divine authority."[9] Stott agrees that: "the bystanders raised their eyebrows and asked, 'Who is this? What blaspheny is this? Who can forgive sins but God only?' Their questions were correctly worded."[10] Aren't these apologists aware of the New Testament writers' recording of the opponents' misinterpretation of Jesus' words to use it as a springboard to set forth the true interpretation? For instance, do the apologists agree with the scribes that in allowing his disciples to glean wheat, Jesus is "doing what is illegal on the Sabbath" (Mark 2:24)? But at any rate, let us return to the text at hand.

A paralytic is brought to Jesus to be healed. Jesus pronounces that his sins are forgiven and goes on to demonstrate his authority to do this by healing the man. The idea is that the man had been stricken with paralysis for some sins he had committed (cf. John 5:14). For Jesus to have lifted the penalty (i.e., cured the paralysis), he must have been able to absolve the sins that caused it. But is Jesus in effect claiming to be God by doing this, as the scribes think? Not necessarily, any more than Paul and Barnabas are claiming to be Hermes and Zeus by healing the Lycaonian cripple in Acts 14:11. Perhaps the scribes, like the Lycaonians, are jumping to conclusions. Jesus' reply, like that of Paul and Barnabas, may be an attempt to correct the mistaken assumptions of his hearers.

Geza Vermes, in his book *Jesus the Jew* calls attention to a document from Qumran which sheds some light on the religious context of the debate we see in the Marcan passage. In "The Prayer of Nabonidus," the stricken king relates how a human agent (Daniel) cured his ulcers when he "pardoned my sins."[11] Jesus then seems not to have been alone in his belief that human beings ("the son of man") have authority on earth to forgive sins. The scribes in the Marcan passage represent the opposing viewpoint which considered this tantamount to blasphemy whether said by Jesus or other sectarians. It should be noted that in the Matthean version the conclusion of the whole incident is in accord with this understanding. The crowd rejoices, not because Jesus' divine authority has been vindicated, but because "God . . . had given such authority to men" (9:8). Here, as in other passages such as Mark 2:27-28 and Matthew 12:32, "son of man" may be best understood in its generic sense of "man" or "mankind." Jesus' declaration in the Marcan text under consideration ("the son of man has authority on earth to forgive sins") is parallel in ideas to a text from Psalms 115:16. "The heavens are the Lord's, but the earth he has given to the sons of men." Also cf. this hadith of the Prophet Muhammad, "The son of man has no more right than that he should have a house wherein he may live, and a piece of cloth whereby he may hide his nakedness, and a chip of bread, and water."[12] That is, earth is the sphere of man's proper function, where in this case he may even pronounce God's pardon for sin. Notice, incidentally, the "divine passive"— "Your sins *are* forgiven," i.e., "God forgives your sins." Jesus is not exactly saying "I take it upon myself to forgive your sins."

Let us assume, however, that the "Son of Man" reference here was originally meant by Jesus as a messianic self-designation, as is certainly intended at least in Mark's redaction. In this case Jesus

would probably be defending his own private prerogative. Yet this
would still not mean he is "indirectly claiming" to be God. The
scribes may charge him with this, but Jesus' rejoinder could be
understood not as, "You're right! God alone can forgive sins, but
it's OK since I happen to be God." Rather he counters with the
claim that God has delegated authority to someone else, i.e., the
Son of Man, to forgive sins on earth, so that he is not usurping
God's authority. It is *not* "God alone," therefore, who forgives sins.
In a similar manner, Jesus is reported to have delegated to the disciples the authority to forgive sins (John 20:23). Yet I know of no
apologist who understands this to mean the disciples were God!

In this idea of delegated authority we have an important distinction that is conveniently ignored by Evangelical apologists. It is no
secret that in Jewish apocalyptic, the Messiah was, so to speak, the
vice-regent of God. He was to be God's representative on earth,
acting in God's stead. This is quite a different thing from the Messiah *being* God. It seems to me that the arguments appealing to
Jesus' assumption of divine prerogatives (e.g., Jesus' claim one
day to judge the world in Matthew 7:21-23) ignore this crucial distinction.

These exegetical suggestions on passages like Mark 2:1-12 are not
hereby proven to be superior to the interpretation offered by the
apologists. But when passages such as this one admit of several
other viable interpretations, it is illegitimate for apologists to use
them as unambiguous evidence that Jesus "claimed to be God."

Among Jesus' "indirect claims to be God," there is another that
is so indirect as to be almost indetectable. George Carey invites
us to

> Consider the sense of mission [Jesus] so undoubtedly had.
> The Gospels reveal him as under divine constraint. . . . There
> is no hesitation concerning this, no fumbling or uncertainty;
> instead, there is clear direction, even when it entails the
> reality of the cross. Now if Jesus were a man only, . . . we
> would be hard pressed to find a reason for this assurance.[13]

What kind of an "argument" is this? Leaving aside Carey's obvious
neglect of such texts as Mark 14:34-36, this must be judged as an
extreme case of special pleading. When self-assurance and single-
minded zeal become sufficient qualification for Godhood the Trinity
is going to become much more crowded than it already is!

Jesus' "claims for himself" are not quite so unambiguous as they
would have to be to make the Trilemma argument the "open-and-shut
case" it is supposed to be. However most scholars would agree that
there is at least some implicit claim in Jesus' words and acts for
messianic authority, or to be the "eschatological Prophet." This
much could be safely assumed by anyone in debate.

Hardly anyone would suggest that Jesus was a conscious charla-
tan making grandiose claims he himself knew were false. Therefore
we can dismiss the "liar" option and move on to the question of
"lunacy." Apologists argue that most people claiming to be God, or
in our day even to be Jesus Christ himself, are insane and demonstrate it by various other erratic behaviors. They go on to show
that Jesus did not behave insanely, despite his great claims. Thus
he must have been sane and therefore correct in his claims. These

apologists are too quick to ignore some other options. As Albert Schweitzer shows in his dissertation, *The Psychiatric Study of Jesus*, one need not judge Jesus to be paranoid or psychotic even if one doesn't believe in his messiahship or divinity (as Schweitzer himself, strictly speaking, did not). He shows that the analyst needs much more biographical background information than is available on Jesus for such a clinical judgment. He reminds us that what would appear to be delusions from our perspective may seem entirely reasonable in the worldview held by the allegedly insane subject. The Trilemma argument trades on the strangeness to modern ears of claims to saviorhood, messiahship, world-rule, etc. Such claims are so outrageous, it is implied, that the claimant must be either crazy or right. Who else would dare say such things? But in Jesus' day and culture such things were not at all outrageous. They were part of the inherited religious worldview and seemed as real and natural as "the Rapture" does to Evangelicals despite the incredulity of outsiders.

Granted, though most people believed in the Messiah, Son of Man, etc., not everyone would conclude that he himself might be entitled to that status. Jesus did, whereas obviously most did not. But this is unusual in a very different way than implied in the Trilemma argument. It is more analogous to a modern American concluding that he will someday be president of the United States than concluding he is, say, Napoleon.

What about other historical figures who have claimed to be a manifestation of God, the Messiah, or the eschatological Prophet? One may certainly point to some who may have been frauds, though the number might decline if we tried to penetrate hostile propaganda besmirching their reputations (cf. Mark 5:22). Also, certainly some have been mentally ill, e.g., Jim Jones, Charles Manson, and Sabbatai Sevi, who seems to have been manic-depressive. But it is equally true that others such as Muhammad, the Bab, and modern eastern "god-men" like Meher Baba and Sai Baba were apparently neither charlatans nor paranoid psychotics. According to the Trilemma argument, shouldn't their claims also be accepted? I doubt that Evangelical apologists would welcome this prospect.

If the Trilemma argument were valid it would prove too much. The underlying assumption here seems to be that a normal, healthy human psyche cannot sincerely hold the sincere conviction of its own Godhood. The hidden implication of the Trilemma argument seen this way is that Jesus must have been insane even if he was *right*, since the orthodox apologists believe that the incarnate Christ did have a healthy, "fully human" psyche! If a human psyche cannot sanely believe in its own deity, this must apply regardless of the truth or error of that belief. The alternative is to say that Jesus had a qualitatively superhuman psyche, which is however to deny the "full humanity" of Jesus. This is Apollinarianism, a heresy to which most users of the Trilemma argument would probably not want to subscribe. But, again, it is not demonstrable that a grandiose belief in one's own messiahship or divinity is tantamount to insanity as the Trilemma argument alleges.

Parenthetically, one may suspect that part of the fundamentalist hysteria over Martin Scorcese's film *The Last Temptation of Christ* (based on the novel by Nikos Kazantzakis) was due to the clarity

with which it illustrated precisely this point. Though many viewers
(or rather, non-viewers) did not relish the way Jesus was portrayed,
it is hard to deny that the film depicts a strong doctrine of the
incarnation of God in Jesus, attributing to Jesus much stronger
statements to this effect than any to be found in the gospels. The
trouble was that the film depicts the struggle of a genuine flesh-
and-blood man to come to grips with such a shattering truth: Jesus
is shown as the victim of seizures, hallucinations, and moods of
self-reproach, since, at first, as a good Jew he can scarcely take
the inner voices whispering the secret of his own deity as aught
but demonic blasphemy. I say that here we have depicted something of the unseen and distasteful psychological implications of the
Trilemma argument.

The Trilemma argument falsely presents us with a set of compre-
hensive and mutually exclusive alternatives. It cannot prove that
Jesus cannot have been a conscientious but mistaken would-be messiah.

Among the "childish things" a mature Evangelicalism must put
away is what Albert Schweitzer called "the crooked and fragile thinking of Christian apologetics."[14] I conclude the chapter with a
brief tale depicting the apologetical enterprise in its true, childish
colors.

A Christmas Fable

Once upon a Christmas Eve long ago, three precocious children
were sitting around the fireplace. They were waiting for cobwebs
to fill their little heads so they could retire to dreamland until the
morning, when Santa would have made his rounds. The three boys
were named Rudy Bultmann, Johnny Warwick Montgomery, and Franky
Schaeffer. Having exhausted the conversational potential of base-
ball, tricycles and cowboys, their minds turned to theology. One of
them looked at Rudy and said, "Rudolf with your nose so bright,
won't you open our discussion tonight?"

Rudy began, "Friends, as you know, I have been asked to speak
on the subject of Santa Claus. My response is 'Yes, Virginia, there
is a Santa Claus,' but only in *Geschichte*, not in *Historie*, of course.
There are many elements of the traditional Christmas story which
are clearly mythological, and therefore unacceptable to the modern
child. After all, can we really believe that anyone today would wear
a red suit? And flying reindeer—modern zoology and aerodynamics
assure us that this is impossible! And where would Santa get all
those toys? Surely, if he makes them in some North Pole workshop,
he must be infringing on all kinds of patents! No child who has to
go to a toy store and pay for a doll over the counter can possibly
believe in a miraculous appearance of toys beneath the Christmas
tree!

"Indeed, there may well have been a historical 'Saint Nicholas of
Myra,' and he may even have been a charitable fellow. But all this
about a 'Santa Claus' who magically flies around the world giving
presents . . .! Surely this is primitive mythology! All the historian can document is the Christmas Morning Faith of the original
elves. And, of course, what really matters is that Santa flies around
in my heart!"

Johnny quickly became agitated, as he frequently did, and replied, "The trouble with you, Rudy, is that you don't give enough credit to the hard, historical *facts*! Look at the sources for our knowledge of Santa! They're just as good as the documentation for any other historical figure, maybe better! For example, take 'The Night Before Christmas.' It describes Santa's 'belly, which shook when he laughed like a bowl full of jelly.' Obviously, this kind of vivid detail is an internal confirmation of the poem's claim to have been penned by an eyewitness!

"Another thing, Rudy. You operate with an obsolete picture of the universe as a closed system of cause-and-effect. You assume reindeer can't fly just because you've never seen them fly. Why, you've probably never seen any reindeer *period*!

"And how do you explain the *empty plate*? We all know that kids put out a plate of cookies for Santa, and the next morning the cookies are gone! And don't give me that old argument that it was really the parents who ate them! Unless it was Santa himself, the historian can't explain the tremendous change in the Christmas tree! How else could all those presents have gotten there? It would be psychologically impossible for the parents to put them there. Why should they spend hundreds of dollars on those gifts just to perpetuate a myth? If Santa didn't really come it would be much cheaper to expose the deception!"

Franky chimed in, "Well said, Johnny! I can see that Rudy is making an upper-chimney leap. He thinks he'll end up on the roof, but really he'll find himself back down in the fire! All he's gonna get in his stocking is coal! Of course, the decisive argument against Rudy's position is that he can't really live on the basis of it. He inevitably finds himself acting as if Santa does come in space-time history. He wouldn't get up tomorrow morning and go look under the tree if he was consistent with his presuppositions. And besides, if Santa wasn't coming to town, Rudy would have no metaphysical standard to tell him he'd better not pout or cry! Actually, there's a dangerous cultural shift in this very direction. I can prove it by showing the gradual replacement of Santa by other motifs on recent Christmas cards!"

They decided to settle the question by staying up till Santa did or didn't come. So they all found good hiding places and settled down to wait. But, alas, the little fellows soon fell asleep. And the next morning, sure enough, the plate was empty and they all had presents.

Section III
Can
Evangelical Theology
be
Born Again?

"Beloved, now we are the children of God, and it
doth not yet appear what we shall be. . . ."

        --I John 3:2a

"Watch what you say
They'll be calling you a radical,
A liberal, oh fanatical, criminal!"

        --Supertramp,
           "The Logical Song"

"He was drifting free, open and light-sensitive
and susceptible. He remained a religious man, a
true believer cut loose from one system of faith
and looking for another that would more nearly
suit his experience of the world and would offer
him religious legitimacy as well."

        --Peter Goldman,
          The Death and Life of Malcolm X

Chapter 8

BIBLICAL VENTRILOQUISM

Carl F. H. Henry and others have called for creativity on the part of Evangelical theologians. Up to now, it seems, these theologians have occupied themselves chiefly with criticism of other theological views. (Interestingly, this is not least true of Henry himself.) But now, we are told, Evangelicals must begin to offer creative alternatives. The outsider must wonder just what kind of theological creativity these Evangelicals can have in mind. Most of their criticisms of other positions are aimed at Liberal theologians' creativity or innovativeness. Instead of creativity, faithfulness in handing on "the faith once and for all delivered to the saints" is prized by Evangelicals. If "faithfulness" in the sense of repetition is valued so by Evangelicals, what creativity could one expect from their theologians but creative new *criticisms* of other positions? And this is exactly what we do find in, e.g., David F. Wells's *The Search for Salvation* or Gundry and Johnson's collection *Tensions in Contemporory Theology*.

Often Evangelicals can be heard to lament indignantly the fact that while they are open-minded enough to study Liberal texts, Liberals do not read Evangelical works. I believe that this is a pretty accurate perception. It is an unfortunate one, yet an understandable one. It seems to me that by and large Evangelical critiques of Liberal theology are not only repetitive and predictable, but also ineffective for various reasons. A Liberal will not be too far off if he concludes, "once you've read one, you've read 'em all," and then decides to read no further. Yet it need not be so. Reading the perceptive and constructive criticisms of outsiders would have to be beneficial to any position. I hope to point out a few dead ends in Evangelical polemics which often prevent Evangelicals from leveling really significant and helpful criticisms. In what follows, I do not mean to suggest that all Evangelical writers are prey to these errors, or that there is no important and cogent criticism being offered in their literature. I only wish to indicate a few false leads which presently prevent Evangelical theological critiques from being as helpful and to the point as they might be.

What is the function of Evangelical critiques? Though they may have resulted from an Evangelical scholar's serious interaction with Liberal theology, I believe that they come to function as excuses for most readers *not* to take Liberal theology seriously. One gets this feeling from the stereotyped and derivative way these arguments are often rehearsed in Evangelical literature. I get the impression that, e.g., conservative seminarians read these stock arguments and take them as a license henceforth either to ignore Liberal theologians, or to read them only to refute them. No one can know whether those Evangelical thinkers who originated these criticisms intended them to function this way. And if they do so function, this fact alone does not reflect on their cogency. They might be very fine arguments. But they often serve as reflexive defense mechanisms to protect the Evangelical position, in much the same way as the social avoidance tactics of Chapter 2 and the apologetical devices of Chapters 5-7.

Consequently, much of the argument of the next two chapters aims at persuading the Evangelical reader to take a second look at Liberal theology. It may deserve more of a sympathetic hearing than he has been led to think. The present chapter will inevitably have implications for Evangelical theological methodology. (In it I scrutinize the Evangelical doctrine of scripture, since once articulated this doctrine is itself supposed to disqualify Liberal theology.) But in general my purpose here is not so much to criticize Evangelical theology as it is to clear away the obstacles which prevent serious attention to other views.

Evangelical theologians point to the Bible, the inspired Word of God, as the guarantor of their theological opinions. Whereas Liberal theological views have nothing to build on but the "sinking sands" of human opinion, the Evangelical can appeal to the Bible. His, we are to believe, is no mere human opinion. Thus Liberal theologians are ruled out of court on principle since they do not operate "in a scriptural manner."

What seems to go unnoticed in this argument is that the decision to believe in this propositional authority of the Bible is little more "objective" or self-evident than a preference for any other view of theological authority. When someone raises this point, apologists reply with a host of arguments for their view. Of course, this very response is a tacit admission that their choice of "biblical authority" is but one more debatable human opinion! Trying desperately to escape the circle of human subjectivity, Evangelicals claim that they unlike Liberals are only taking seriously "the Bible's own witness to itself" as verbally-inspired and infallible. These remarks are representative:

> What the Bible teaches about its own inspiration is a matter *purely of Divine testimony*, and our business is simply to receive the testimony. . . . (Arthur W. Pink)[1]

> . . . if [the advocates of "Biblical Theology," e.g., G. Ernest Wright] were consistent in reading the Bible "from within" and receiving what its authors were concerned to teach, they would be led to the doctrine of Scripture which we have expounded. . . . (J. I. Packer)[2]

This argument is circular at three strategic points. First, let us grant for the sake of argument that biblical texts do "teach" such an estimate of themselves. How does one know to take this self-claim with the particular kind of seriousness advocated by Evangelicals? There are other ways of taking biblical texts seriously besides parroting their literal, propositional sense. David H. Kelsey demonstrates this in his ground-breaking work *The Uses of Scripture in Recent Theology*. One has not really said anything when he claims that "the Bible is authoritative for my theology." Even demythologizing Liberals sincerely make this claim. The question is a hermeneutical one: granted that the Bible is normative, precisely *how* is that norm to be applied? Normative symbols? Normative propositions? Normative linguistic "deep structures"? The choice of *how* one takes the Bible as normative is a theological decision made prior to one's opening of the Bible. Kelsey shows this to be true no less of Warfield than of Bultmann.[3] One only need "take seriously the biblical witness in the particular way Evangelicals do if one already reads biblical texts such as II Timothy 3:16 from an Evangelical viewpoint!   By contrast, a Neo-Orthodox or Liberal theologian may have a doctrine of scriptural authority which logically leads him to bracket the literal, propositional reference of a text (supposedly) teaching verbal inspiration.   Only if one *already holds* an Evangelical view of scripture does the literal claim of the texts seem to decide the issue!   Once one opts for such a view of the authority of texts, one is free to decide issues like the "pre- versus post-tribulation Rapture" on this basis.   But if the issue to be decided is the view of scripture itself, then quoting texts to decide the issue is clearly begging the question.

The second concentric circle of the Evangelical argument is closely related to the first.   I call this the fallacy of the false monolith. Evangelical apologists beg the questions of the unity and boundaries of the canon when they argue in terms of the claims of "the Bible," i.e., one book in which claims made in one section automatically apply to all others.   There is no such self-conscious unity.   Such unity-uniformity is imposed from without by the Evangelical reader's doctrine of scripture.   (Please note the difference between the notion of structural unity here, i.e., the Bible as one book with sixty-six chapters, and that of *doctrinal* unity, i.e., the absence of contradictions between the thought of various biblical writers.   The latter question will concern us soon enough.)   If the prophet Jeremiah claims "this is the Word of the Lord," is he referring also, e.g., to II Chronicles, or only to his own words?   To assume the former one must also assume the canonical unity of the Bible as we know it.   And, again, this is what is supposedly being proven.

The third ring in our theological circus concerns the exegesis of several texts in which the Bible is held to claim its own inspiration and infallibility.   Once the "false monolith" is removed from consideration, it becomes apparent that several biblical writings are left on their own with no claim for inspiration at all, e.g., Proverbs, Samuel, Kings, Acts.   Where we do find "claims for inspiration" in biblical texts, they are usually misapplied.   Usually, they have nothing whatever to say about the production of inspired *texts*, which of course is the whole point at issue.   For instance, there is an enormous number of passages in the Old Testament where a prophet announces that he is about to speak "the Word of the Lord."   But do such statements say anything at all about the anonymous persons who at unknown dates recorded and compiled the prophets' oracles? Obviously not.   There is no claim in these texts for an inspired preservation of the prophetic *books* from error or falsification. These claims for prophetic inspiration simply do not refer to the later recording and editorial processes from which our biblical *texts* resulted.   And remember, the Evangelical apologist is arguing precisely for the inspiration of the *text*.

A similar fallacy occurs in the oft-heard argument that Jesus "authorized" the writing of inspired New Testament books in advance.[4]   The passage usually in mind here is John 16:13a: "But when he, the Spirit of truth, comes, he will guide you [the disciples] into all truth."   Notice, however, that this passage says nothing specifically about Jesus' hearers going on to write a set of inspired texts.   Even if it did, there would still be trouble, since

most of the New Testament documents are not written by the original
twelve disciples. Tradition ascribes Matthew, I and II Peter, I, II,
and III John, the fourth gospel, and the Revelation to three of the
original twelve. But anyone at all conversant with current New
Testament scholarship (as the apologists certainly must be) knows
that these ascriptions are matters of serious debate. I am not assuming the traditional ascriptions to be in error; I only point out
that these apologists could at the most say that John 16:13a *probably*, or *possibly*, "authorizes" the inspiration of some New Testament literature. This would be a rather feeble argument. Furthermore, the protest that Mark, Luke, and the writer to the Hebrews
are "authorized associates"[5] of the twelve is obviously no argument
at all. Even the apologists can produce no saying of Jesus authorizing apprentices to write canonical books.

In all the above, it was not my intention to cast doubt on the
inspiration of biblical books. I do not even deny that there are
occasional claims by an individual writer that his own writing is
inspired (e.g., I Corinthians 14:37).[6] I am merely calling the
apologists' bluff that all they are doing is to affirm the view of
scripture "claimed by scripture for itself."

There is a slightly different form of this argument that deserves
mention. Here it is contended that we can at least reconstruct and
abide by the attitude toward (Old Testament) scripture held by
Jesus and the apostles (or the early church). By saying "We hold
Jesus' view of scripture," the Evangelical apologists really mean,
"Jesus held *our* view of scripture." Did he? The theological apologists produce texts like "Scripture cannot be broken" (John 10:35),
or "It is easier for heaven and earth to disappear than for the least
stroke of a pen to drop out of the Law" (Luke 16:17). Even Liberals, who do not themselves hold such a view of scripture, are supposed to agree that Jesus believed scripture to be inerrant and
inspired. The favorite Liberal to quote on this point is Bultmann,
in *Jesus and the Word*:

> Jesus agreed always with the scribes of his time in accept-
> ing without question the authority of the (Old Testament)
> Law. . . . Jesus did not attack the Law, but assumed its
> authority and interpreted it.[7]

So far, Bultmann sounds amazingly like John R. W. Stott or J. I.
Packer! Isn't it odd that Evangelicals stop quoting Bultmann where
they do? For instance why are we not told that Bultmann's historical judgment is that Jesus'

> . . . interpretation often did violence to the original meaning
> of the Law, that Jesus' own course of action on occasion was
> opposed to the Law. . . . [And] in contrast to the scribal
> assumption that all passages of Scripture are equally binding
> and that apparent contradictions are to be reconciled, Jesus
> sets one passage against another.[8]

Ulrich Wilkens and Ernst Käsemann are only two of many other
New Testament historians and exegetes who deny that Jesus' attitude
toward scripture was purely one of obedient submission. Instead,
they argue, Jesus felt free to set aside the demands of scripture on
his own authority. Evangelicals themselves are not entirely unaware

of this attitude of Jesus. In fact in debates on the "deity of Christ" they constantly appeal to Jesus' sovereignty over the Law to prove that he claimed divine authority for himself! So depending on which point they are arguing at the moment, Evangelicals seem to attribute to Jesus two different attitudes toward scripture. But Evangelicals are hardly faithful to either one.

First, insofar as Jesus did abide by the authority of the Old Testament scriptures, he seemed to include adherence to Old Testament laws as well. This is certainly the plain sense of a passage often quoted by Evangelicals in this connection:

> Do not think that I have come to abolish the Law or the Prophets; I have not come to abolish them but to fulfill them. I tell you the truth, until heaven and earth disappear, not the smallest letter, not the least stroke of a pen, will by any means disappear from the Law until everything is accomplished. Anyone who breaks one of the least of these commandments and teaches others to do the same will be called least in the kingdom of heaven, but whoever practices and teaches these commands will be called great in the kingdom of heaven (Matthew 5:17-19 NIV).

Yet those who, in obedience to such a text observe Old Testament laws (e.g., Seventh Day Adventists), are stigmatized by Evangelicals as heretics! Will the real adherent of Jesus' view of scripture please stand up?

When some Evangelicals emulate Jesus' freedom to set aside one biblical text in favor of the "weightier matters of the Law," they fare no better. In his treatment of the divorce question (Mark 10:2-9), Jesus sets aside one Pentateuchal passage (Deuteronomy 24:1-4) with another (Genesis 1:27; 2:24). Virginia Mollencott and Paul Jewett use the same hermeneutical device on the issue of equality for women, setting aside I Timothy 2:12 with Galatians 3:28. Are their fellow Evangelicals happy about this? Far from it! Surely Jesus himself would have merited a chapter in some first-century *Battle for the Torah!*

There is yet another area in which Evangelicals conspicuously decline to affirm Jesus' and the apostles' view of scripture. Studies like Richard Longenecker's *Biblical Exegesis in the Apostolic Period* make it clear that Jesus and early Christians made abundant use of rabbinical techniques such as *midrash*, *raz pesher*, and allegorizing in their exegesis. Very often these devices had little to do with the plain intent of the biblical writer, as even a casual glance at the Qumran commentaries or the first chapters of Matthew will show. Yet Evangelicals claim to espouse the grammatico-historical method, formulated in the Reformation to avoid such uncontrollable allegorizing and spiritualizing of texts. Surely these two would be unequally yoked together! This irony becomes painfully apparent in the frequent Evangelical citing of two New Testament passages:

> Now about the dead rising—have you not read in the book of Moses, in the account of the bush, how God said to him, "I *am* [i.e., not *was*] the God of Abraham, the God of Isaac, and the God of Jacob"? He is not the God of the dead, but of the living (Mark 12:26-27).

The promises were spoken to Abraham and to his seed. The Scripture does not say "and to seeds," meaning many people, but "and to your seed," meaning one person, who is Christ (Galatians 3:16).

These texts are cited as proof that Jesus and Paul believed in strictly verbal inspiration. They must have, so the argument runs, since they based the weight of entire theological arguments on the mere tense of a verb or number of a noun. Perhaps so, but do Evangelicals really wish to swallow this kind of fanciful exegesis? In both cases the "exegetical" argument has left the plain sense of the Old Testament passage far behind! Can one consistently accept Jesus' and Paul's view of inspiration, and then reject the manner of using scripture that followed from it? It is not clear that only one of these things and not both would constitute a "view of scripture."

Apparent Contradictions are the Worst Kind

For most Evangelicals the Bible is a harmonious source book for doctrine. It yields "propositions" representative of "didactic thought models" (Pinnock) which when put together coherently form a normative system of doctrine.

Theology renders explicit in orderly doctrines the truth implicit in the Word of God. It expresses logically the truths which are set forth chronologically in the Bible. . . . All the data of scripture are relevant data, the raw material of theological models. . . . The exegesis of Scripture thus has *absolute priority* over all systems. Systems which fail to fit the data are to be dismantled. A faulty theological system is one which cannot satisfy the biblical evidence. . . . (Pinnock).[9]

The focus on scripture's authority here seems to be on the statements appearing in an inspired *text*. This is evidenced by the very term "propositional revelation," as well as by the distinction sometimes drawn to the effect that a biblical writer is infallible only when he writes, not otherwise. This is a parallel to the infallibility of the Pope speaking *ex cathedra*, and for obviously similar apologetical reasons. Instead of gifted or inspired personalities, the important thing for the Evangelical is the inspired text. Otherwise, the endless haranguing about the alleged fact and nature of "plenary, verbal" inspiration as opposed to "conceptual" or some other kind of inspiration would make no sense.

The locus of authority in the text is also to be distinguished from a focus on the subject matter of the text. For example, Gerhard Maier deplores the distinction first made by Semler between the text of scripture and the Word of God.[10] Instead, the Word of God should be identified with the text of scripture. Evangelicals ceaselessly protested the Neo-Orthodox claim that the Bible "contained" or "became" the Word of God. No, they said, the text *is* the revealed "Word of God written." "What scripture says, God says."

With this estimation of the scriptural text, hermeneutics would seem to consist of little more than exegesis. To be believed a statement need only appear in the text, at least theoretically. The recognition of theological disunity in the Bible would be absolutely fatal to such an understanding. Two "inspired" but contradictory statements would neutralize each other and would take the criterion of authority (i.e., the presence of a statement in the text) with them. "If all inspiration guarantees us is that we get viewpoints that are contradictory, which ones are we to believe and how are we to know who is right and who is wrong?" (Lindsell).[11] This is why all "apparent contradictions" are harmonized. "As for the principle of harmony, this . . . is dictated by the doctrine of inspiration, which tells us that the Scriptures are the products of a single divine mind." "Scripture should not be set against Scripture. . . . The expectation for this principle is the expectation that the teaching of the God of truth will prove to be consistent with itself" (Packer).[12] "Scripture is in agreement with itself. God who is eternal truth does not contradict Himself" (Pinnock).[13] "Inasmuch as all Scripture is the product of a single divine mind, interpretation must stay within the bounds of the analogy of Scripture and eschew hypotheses that would correct one Biblical passage by another. . . ." (Chicago Statement on Biblical Inerrancy).[14] "[Our] utter trust in Scripture—in all that it teaches—must govern the interpreter's practice, thus eliminating in principle any interpretation which sees the biblical texts as . . . self-contradictory" (Montgomery).[15] "We would assert . . . that there is no disagreement [e.g.] between Paul and James, and that such a principle of theological diversity destroys the doctrine of inspiration completely" (Ranald MacAulay and Jerram Barrs).[16]

Evangelical theologians profess to use the grammatico-historical method in discovering the straightforward meaning of texts since it is this "plain sense" of all texts that is to be believed. Yet it is obvious from the above statements that they are not free to do so. "Less clear" (i.e., theologically troublesome) texts may require "broader interpretation" (Montgomery) in the light of "more clear" texts. Evangelicals point out that if one recognized a "real contradiction" between two texts, both could not be believed, and an extra-biblical criterion of some sort would have to be employed in order to decide which one to believe. They think they avoid this trap by hiding behind "apparent" contradictions. Yet ironically it is just *this* kind of contradiction which must destroy a notion of biblical authority based on the "apparent" or "plain" sense of the text! The moment one admits that the "apparent" meaning of Text A cannot be accepted since it would conflict with Text B, one has surrendered the criterion of biblical authority, i.e., that the plain sense of any and all texts is normative. Thus "apparent contradictions" are actually fatal to the Evangelical schema, whereas "real contradictions" (whatever that would mean) are irrelevant!

A couple of brief examples are in order. If one turns to the New Testament for guidance on the question of divorce, he finds Mark allowing no excuse for divorce (Mark 10:11). But Matthew is a bit more lenient, allowing one legitimate pretext, i.e., adultery (Matthew 19:9). Well, it *looks* like these two texts are in conflict. But surely the *real* meaning of one of them lies deeper than the surface meaning! Perhaps a less obvious meaning would make one passage echo the teaching of the other! All right, but wasn't it supposed to be the "apparent sense" of both that was normative? And how are you going to decide which text's "apparently contradictory" meaning is to harmonize into the other's "plain sense"? If you choose Matthew's version, you negate Mark's, since it cannot be correct to say there

is no legitimate excuse for divorce if it turns out there is one good
excuse after all. (And note that Matthew realized this and changed
the wording of the scribal question accordingly!)

Another example would be the question of "mountain-moving faith."
Pentecostals such as Kenneth Hagin take as normative the plain meaning of Mark 11:24. *Any* request will be granted. Calmer Evangelicals remind their brethren that I John 5:14 adds a qualification:
God will only answer requests that are "according to his will" anyway. The two texts do not agree. The blanket promise of Mark
11:24 would change in meaning completely if this "catch 22" were
intended. Non-Pentecostals assume in effect that Mark (and Jesus)
really did have this "God's will" qualification in mind—it just isn't
apparent. Uh—oh! Then the normative "real meaning" of the Marcan passage is *not* the "*apparent* sense"! How do we know? Because we prefer the apparent sense of I John 5:14 with its level-
headed common sense.

The Evangelicals end up doing exactly what they criticize Käsemann and others for doing; they harmonize one text into another
instead of believing both. They do so on the basis of doctrinal
preference:

> A passage of Holy Scripture is to be taken as true in its
> natural, literal sense unless . . . an article of faith estab-
> lished elsewhere in Scripture requires a broader understand-
> ing of the text. (Montgomery)[17]

One could ask for no better example of a "canon within the canon"!

As they often do, Evangelicals here adopt an all-or-nothing stance.
If the Bible is not in complete agreement, it might as well be in
complete disagreement. The mirror image of their position is that
of Walter Kaufmann:

> . . . if [theologians] must offer a single message, they simply
> have to gerrymander [the Bible]; and it stands to reason that
> different theologians will come up with different messages. If
> they were to be fair . . . they would have to admit that there
> is no single message; that there are many different views. . .
> .[18]

Kaufmann and Evangelicals agree that without a uniform message
"from cover to cover," any theological use made of the Bible would
be completely arbitrary. However, the attempted solution of Evangelicals turns out to be no more adequate than the "dead ends"
they decry.

> In spite of all . . . apparent evidence to the contrary,
> one can maintain with confidence that the Bible has one mes-
> sage, speaks with one voice, tells one story, unfolds one plan
> of salvation, has one view of itself. . . ."

But as the same writer admits, "This may be easier said than demonstrated. . . ." (John H. Gerstner)[19]

The Evangelical claim is that their doctrine of scripture gives
them virtual immunity from subjectivism and qualitative superiority
over Liberal theologies. Yet the doctrine only serves to lengthen
the line of defense. Not only is their doctrine of scripture not
self-evidently the only proper option; in addition it falls prey to

fatal self-contradictions. One must sacrifice some texts to defend the authority of *all* texts! Thus it is the peculiar bane of this doctrine of scripture that, in order to defend it, one must betray it!

About now some readers may be protesting, "But surely not all Evangelicals employ this model of biblical authority! What about Theologian A, or Exegete B?" I hope that by this, such a reader does not intend to throw Pinnock, Packer, Montgomery, et al., to the wolves, claiming that they do not represent "true Evangelicalism." No, it must be admitted that the writers dealt with in this chapter are influential spokesmen representing many if not most Evangelicals. Bickering about who are the "real Evangelicals" only confuses the issue. My objective is to critique one particular model of scriptural authority. As a matter of fact, it happens to be the most common one among Evangelicals, and it is quite often used by its adherents as a yardstick with which to disqualify Liberal theologies.

But there is a new trend among some Evangelical theologians. Of late there has been a shift toward Barthian Neo-Orthodoxy, at least on the scripture question, among some Evangelicals, such as G. C. Berkouwer and Donald G. Bloesch. Karl Barth had maintained that the Bible itself is not the Word of God but rather contains or becomes the Word insofar as it witnesses to Jesus Christ, the true and unequivocal Word of God. Berkouwer's important work *Holy Scripture* is moving in the same direction. Much of his book is taken up with demonstrating how the traditional predicates of scripture ("infallibility," "perspicuity," etc.) really refer to the salvific message of scripture, not all the incidentals. Similarly Bloesch in his *Essentials of Evangelical Theology*, announces that "Jesus Christ and the message about him constitute the material norm of our faith. . . . The Bible is authoritative because it points beyond itself to the . . . living and transcendent Word of God."[20]

Critics sympathetic to Barth, Colin Brown for one, warned their fellow Evangelicals not to be overly upset at Barth's doctrine of scripture. Even though it was theoretically inadequate (i.e., non-Evangelical), in practice Barth used scripture texts in much the same way he would if he had believed in verbal inspiration. "O happy fault!" Bloesch pointed out this very inconsistency in an earlier book: "In practice Barth seems to take for granted the essential reliability and trustworthiness of Scripture, but in principle he allows for errors even in the matters of theological judgment"[21] (*The Evangelical Renaissance*). The point is that Brown, Bloesch, and others saw an *inconsistency* here: though Barth used scripture as an Evangelical would, his doctrine of scripture could not justify such a use, since Barth held scripture to be infallible only regarding the rudimentary gospel message. Interestingly, now some of these same writers have moved in a Barthian direction, and, ironically, they are becoming guilty of the very same contradiction!

Bloesch himself now writes that "not all Scripture attests equally to the incarnation and atoning work of Jesus Christ, to the Gospel of reconciliation and redemption, which is the formal norm of Scripture."[22] He even calls this "formal norm" a "canon within the canon."[23] The implications for the secondary elements are clear:

. . . not only the historical and cultural perspective of the biblical writers was limited but also their theological and ethical ideas. It is only when their testimony is related to and refined by the self-revelation of Jesus Christ that it has the force of infallible authority.[24]

What is the result of this fact for the theological use of the Bible? "It is inadmissible to treat the Bible as though it were a sourcebook of revealed truths that can be drawn out of Scripture by deductive or inductive logic."[25] Yet, shades of Barth, this is precisely how Bloesch goes on to use the Bible! Citing texts from this and that corner of scripture, Bloesch maps out, e.g., the relations between heaven, hell, sheol, paradise, and the millenium. He could never press the Bible for such detailed information if he didn't consider it some kind of metaphysical encyclopedia, the very notion which (if language means anything) he has disavowed! The fact that Bloesch fails to accept the implications of his new approach to scripture is doubly odd since he had pointed out this very inconsistency in Barth!

Those Evangelicals who look to theologians like Berkouwer and Bloesch to deliver them from the headaches of the Packer-Montgomery model must not imagine that their accustomed use of scripture (to settle secondary points of doctrine) can remain unchanged. In the final chapter I will note the views of some Evangelicals who have begun to face the implications of a new model of biblical authority.

Chapter 9

THEOLOGICAL RHETORIC

In the last chapter we saw the ineffectiveness of the Evangelical attempt to disqualify Liberal theology as "unscriptural." We noted that, contra J. I. Packer and company, it is not self-evident that the only way to take scripture seriously is to construe it as a set of "propositions and logical analyses, factual assertions and deductions, embodying direct teaching from God."[1] In view of these conclusions, what do the condemnations of other views as "unscriptural" finally amount to? Since the measuring-stick is conformity to Evangelical doctrine, the Evangelical critics wind up merely saying, "Your view is different from our view." This is no news, but logically it is no real criticism either! What remains to be seen is just why a non-Evangelical theology is for that reason a bad thing.

Evangelical theological criticism usually skirts this crucial criterial question. A second important criticism makes much the same mistake. This is the charge that Liberal theology is to be rejected insofar as it subordinates biblical truth to culturally-determined thought forms. The Bible is demythologized by Liberals, who then make biblical symbols into a sort of figurehead or set of illustrations for a philosophy derived from contemporary thought. Tillich, Bultmann, Ogden and others are usually cited as examples here. Liberal theology, following modern cultural trends, is said to evacuate salvation of its supernatural biblical meaning by reducing it to existentialist "authentic existence" or Marxist "political liberation."

Evangelicals will not sit still for this. As we have seen, the Bible is valued for its "propositional revelation," its "didactic thought-models."[2] David F. Wells is quick to denounce the enterprise of demythologizing biblical ideas:

> To scrap the mythological garb is, in fact, to evacuate Christianity of its saving content. For what is discarded is not, as Bultmann imagines, secondary and peripheral, but primary and central. . . . Where the biblical outlook violates the assumptions of modern man it is these assumptions which need to be depicted as mythological.[3]

Clark Pinnock echoes the same indignation. He rejects Liberal theology because it sacrifices scriptural truth to modernity. It exalts the word of man above the word of God.[4] But does any Liberal theologian think he is doing this? Of course not. Liberals believe themselves to be in continuity with the biblical writers who articulated their faith (or God's revelation) in the available thought-forms of their day. They hold that we must do the same with the categories of our day if we are to make the gospel intelligible and available to our contemporaries.

Evangelicals and Liberals are agreed that revelation appeared in our history in time-bound forms. The difference is this: Evangelicals believe that the revelation is essentially unchanging in its *concepts*. What changes from culture to culture is the bare words of language. The cross-cultural task is merely one of translation. Liberals believe that the revelation is of a more general character, e.g., of a "divine-" or "depth-dimension" of reality. The concepts

with which this revelation is articulated in the Bible are culturally
relative and time-bound, and thus dispensable.   Here, the cross-
cultural task is demythologization.[5]   Carl F. H. Henry sees this difference in just these terms.   He contends that "the message of the
Bible is a call not to the task of demythologization but of translation."[6]

These are certainly two very different notions, and it would serve
no purpose to obscure this fact. But it is not self-evident that one
is superior to the other. The Evangelical critics of Liberal theology
have not shown *why* their choice is preferable.   They *seem* to have
done this when they use loaded rhetoric like this:

> Liberal theology seeks to accommodate the classical Chris-
> tian message to the spirit of the times. . . . If God's speak-
> ing can be fitted into man's thinking, it will be fitted; if it
> can't, it will be eliminated . . . I don't think I'm giving a
> Fundamentalist reading of Liberal theology.   I'm getting it
> from . . . what these people *say* they are doing. (Pinnock)[7]

This criticism seems to assume that Liberals know as well as Evangelicals that biblical thought-forms are "God's speaking" but reject
them anyway!   It would be hard to deny the inadequacy of a theology which actually intended to negate what it believed to be God's
revelation!   But of course Liberals do not intend this! Pinnock is
only able to make it look as if they do by subconsciously projecting
his evaluation of biblical "thought-models" (i.e., as divinely normative) onto the Liberal rejection of those thought-models. Obviously
Liberals do not believe these thought-forms to be divinely revealed
or they would not dispense with them! Pinnock needs to show *why*
the biblical thought-forms should be considered divinely normative
and indispensable.   If he could do this, he would have an effective
argument, i.e., "For such-and-such reasons, Liberals turn out actually to be dispensing with God's word, though they do not intend
to."   This would be much superior to mere rhetoric like "Liberals
make it their business to negate the revelation of God."

The insistence of Pinnock and others that biblical "thought-models" are normative is, ironically, being challenged from elsewhere
within their own camp.   Missiologists who must come face to face
with the question of cross-cultural communication are not quite as
sure as Pinnock that biblical thought-forms are irreplaceable.   In
Christianity in Culture, Charles Kraft says that different worldviews
are a stubborn fact of life.   And if one wants to communicate divine
truth, he had better be willing to reconceptualize that truth according to the worldview and thought-forms of his audience, just as God
himself did in his revelations to the writers of the Bible! He calls
this "dynamic-equivalence theologizing."[8]

Often Evangelical "critiques" of Liberal theology are no critiques
at all; they only amount to saying "we don't see things the same
way."   A real critique would furnish some criteria for deciding which
viewpoint is more satisfactory.   In his booklet, *Keep Yourselves
from Idols*, J. I. Packer takes John A. T. Robinson to task for the
views presented in his famous book *Honest to God*:

> This teaching does not stand [on its own]; it is not mean-
> ingful unless it leans on something else. . . . Dr. Robinson
> talks glowingly about love being perfectly revealed in Jesus,

but it is not clear what that can mean when the biblical meaning of the cross is denied. . . . It thus appears that Robin-
sonianism is a parasite which lives off the very thing it pro-
fesses to reject—[it is] a theological bankrupt, that can only
keep in business by illegitimately transferring orthodox Christian capital to its own account.[9]

This is a cogent argument, pointing out a structural deficiency
or internal contradiction *within* the opposing theological system.   A
good way to check if a critique is in principle cogent is to ask if it
would make sense if applied self-critically by a Liberal theologian to
his own system.   We find exactly the same kind of argument as
Packer used, applied by Dennis Nineham to his fellow-contributors
to *The Myth of God Incarnate*:

> So long as the doctrine of the incarnation was taken as a
> statement of an objective metaphysical fact, that Jesus was
> literally divine, then the unique perfection of his humanity
> was a legitimate deduction from the fact of its hypostatic con-
> junction with divinity . . . [but in modern Christological re-
> formulations] the perfection of Jesus is being used . . . as a
> starting-point for an alternative conceptualization or symboli-
> zation. . . . In that case, it is difficult, at any rate at first
> sight, to see how the claim for the perfection of Jesus' human-
> ity could be supported. . . .[10]

There is a great difference between this argument and that put
forth by Pinnock, Wells, and others, that Liberals exalt the word of
man over (what Evangelicals believe to be) the word of God, i.e.,
biblical thought-forms.   The latter argument could never be leveled
self-critically by a Liberal; he would not be inconsistent in dispensing with biblical thought-forms if he didn't regard them as divinely
normative.   Now, the Evangelical may in fact be right—perhaps in
reality Liberals do turn out to be downplaying God's normative word.
But this is what needs to be proven; the mere assumption that Liberals are downplaying divine truth is no argument that they are
doing this.
     Here we need to call another bluff.   It has to do with a serious
confusion between contemporary thought-forms and worldviews on
the one hand, and the *Zeitgeist*, or "spirit of the age," on the other.
Liberals are said to "capitulate" to modernity in disobedience to
Paul's admonition to affirm the "foolishness of the cross" *against*
"the wisdom of this age."   But this is too superficial a reading both
of Liberal theology and the relevant Pauline passage, I Corinthians
1:18-25.   "Worldly values" are the target of Paul in his attack on
the wisdom of this age, not "world*views*" as such.   According to the
context, the cross is a stumbling block for those Jews who reject
faith in favor of stubborn, sign-seeking unbelief (cf. John 4:48;
Matthew 16:4).   It is foolishness to those Greeks who scorn moral
repentance in favor of haughty gnostic intellectualism.   Ironically,
to demand the acceptance of an alien worldview's thought-forms as a
condition for faith (as Pinnock and company want to do) comes dis-
turbingly close to gnosticism, with its saving cosmological secrets!
At any rate, no Liberal theologian intends that Christian theology,
to be modern, must accept "the ways of the world," i.e., hedonism,
aggression, pride, avarice, self-aggrandizement, etc.

Evangelical apologists are able to score a cheap victory by making this implicit false equation between modernity and worldliness. This confusion obscures an important fact. Liberal theologians do adopt modern thought-forms so as to make faith intelligible. But they proclaim that faith in opposition to the current *Zeitgeist* which is no more sympathetic to the gospel than that of Paul's day. Bultmann wanted to clear the *false* stumbling block of mythology out of the way so modern man would not turn away without facing the *real* "scandal of the cross," justification by grace alone. Schleiermacher adopted modern thought-forms (in his case, a Kantian anthropocentrism) only so as to challenge the assumptions of his culture which "despised religion."

The Liberal theological movement that came closest to the Evangelical stereotype was the short-lived and extremist "Death of God," or secular, theology. Following some of Bonhoeffer's later writings, these thinkers sought to find a non-religious interpretation of Christian faith. They even went so far as to suggest that man must solve his problems standing on his own two feet, without help from God. Man was thought to have "come of age"; he should live without God, and this according to God's will! Altizer could even say that "theology is now called to listen fully to the world, even if such a listening demands a turning away from the church's witness to Christ."[11] Yet even here, it should be kept in mind, the aim was to answer Bonhoeffer's question, "How can Christ become the Lord even of those with no religion?" So even in this extreme form of Liberal theological "contextualization," the motive was, so to speak, evangelistic. On the whole, Liberals seem just as sensitive to the danger of cultural accommodation as Evangelicals are. For instance, even radical theologian Fritz Buri can warn that if it is not careful, theology "might assimilate revelation to the world and the world becomes revelation."[12] In other words, accommodation to the world is what Liberals want to *avoid*, not what they aim to accomplish! Again, Buri and company may in fact wind up doing what they seek to avoid. This is not unusual among human beings. Most Evangelicals will admit that their theology, too, has sometimes lapsed into cultural accommodation. But it is sheer caricature to charge that Liberal theology actually makes such accommodation its goal. Liberals join Evangelicals in challenging the values and self-sufficient assumptions of modern man. The two camps differ in their choice of ancient or modern thought-forms.

Many Evangelical writers take it as a telltale sign of Liberal theology's futility that its reconstructions have no staying power. They often quote Dean Inge's remark that the thinker who marries the spirit of the age will soon find himself a widower. In the words of Kenneth Hamilton, "The disadvantage of founding a theology upon relevance is that it may suddenly become irrelevant and die."[13] Pinnock laments that "increasingly we are being confronted with a theology in motion. A doctrine is 'true' for one generation, not for the next. Yesterday's error becomes today's truth."[14] Such critics have little trouble demonstrating that in the history of recent theology, one Liberal reconstruction follows another in rapid-fire succession. This very fact once stated is supposed to demonstrate the weakness of the whole approach. But why? Evangelicals seem to see the theological task as that of articulating an ever-valid credo or system. They project this desired goal onto the Liberal endeavor and then, inevitably, pronounce it a failure. If they themselves were in the position of creating a new theology for the modern world, they as Evangelicals would see themselves as providing a creed that could stand across the ages, unlike the old one which must have been flawed, else it would not have needed replacement. They assume the Liberal's task would be that of providing a better candidate for a timeless theology, one that will not again need replacement.

But Liberals do not see things this way. In the very nature of the case, no theology could be eternally valid. Theology today needs reformulation not so much because modern thought is definitive, superior to all other possible worldviews, but because man's concepts and ideas must always change with the passage of history. Bultmann admits that "no world-view of yesterday or today or tomorrow is definitive."[15] In Peter Berger's terms, the relativizers have relativized themselves as well. H. Richard Niebuhr plainly states: "A critical historical theology cannot, to be sure, prescribe what form religious life must take in all places and all times beyond the limits of its own historical system."[16] Thus it comes as no surprise to Liberal theologians that their formulations are sooner or later superseded. It is supposed to happen that way. The Liberal theologian wants only to come up with a theology adequate to express faith for people of his time. So why do Evangelicals see the transitoriness of Liberal theology as a disproof of its validity? Simply because they assume everyone should share their agenda, i.e., the construction of a permanent orthodoxy. And they believe that they already have such a theology and that no reconstruction is necessary.

A similar criticism is that Liberal theology can produce no compelling consensus even among its own theorists. Hamilton complains:

> It sounds plausible to argue that the Christian Gospel cannot get home to modern man unless it is translated into terms meaningful to him in his cultural situation. But the trouble is that different interpreters of the present-day situation advance conflicting reports.[17]

Pinnock agrees that this makes modern theology "disreputable and chaotic."[18] Evangelical critics do not seem to notice that their own theology is but one more competing option; does the lack of universal acceptance of Evangelical theology make it, too, a false option?

Why is it that Evangelicals see such diversity or disunity as another disconfirmation of Liberal thought? Again, they are assuming the propriety of the Evangelical goal, i.e., to have one universally valid creed, an unequivocal propositional theology. But this is not the way Liberals seek "catholicity" in theology. Rather than demanding that everyone assent to the same formulation of faith, they seek to enable different people to formulate the one faith in ways natural to them. They do not feel that one particular worldview or philosophy, traditional supernaturalism, should be made into a shibboleth for Christian faith. Thus Bultmann proposes a translation of the gospel message that existentialists can accept. Van Buren provides a version for empiricists. The fact that the option of each will not be workable or acceptable for all, does not disqualify it for those who can accept it.

The commitment here is more tentative: one devotes himself
sufficiently to a point of view to give perhaps a good many
years of his life to determining what is contained or implied
in it, while simultaneously recognizing that there are other
ways of doing theology, other "experiments" being carried on
that are worth observing and learning from. . . . A theologian with such a pluralistic and experimental orientation will
rejoice precisely in the diversity and openness of the current theological scene because of his conviction that it is only
through the strife of perspectives and systems that some new
truth, beyond all the currently struggling partial insights,
may be won. (Gordon D. Kaufman)[19]

What is needed is a pluralistic framework, since honest minds
differ; and to tie faith to one conceptual worldview would bar many
from faith.   One gets the feeling that some conservatives would
rather not recognize that non-supernaturalists have sincere and
intelligent convictions.   If they did, how could they be morally cul-
pable for not accepting supernaturalism?   For instance, Kenneth
Hamilton's choice of words betrays such an assumption.   He depicts
Liberal theologians as "happening" to "favor" particular philosophies
because of their "tastes."[20] The reader is sure to pick up the
insinuation.   Francis Schaeffer, however, is not content merely to
insinuate.   He baldly declares that Liberal theologians "did not accept their own form of naturalism because they were forced to do so
by the facts.   They did so to conform, and liberal theology has
been conforming ever since."[21]

Basically, Evangelicals assume that one mark of a "true theology"
is that its propositions are valid for all men everywhere.   Central
to the Liberal enterprise, however, is avowed pluralism.   People in
different cultures, or even in different intellectual subcultures (Berger's "plausibility structures") within the same culture, must have
the right to conceptualize (theologize) faith in their own terms.
Surely this ought to be evident from the current interest in "contextualization," especially among black, feminist, Latin American,
and African theologians.

Liberal theology is being criticized not for failing to meet its *own*
goals (though certainly it may do this) but for failing to meet *Evangelical* goals!   Liberalism is again being criticized simply for not
being Evangelicalism.   Cogent criticism would demonstrate just why
the Evangelical approach is preferable.   And there are critiques
which attempt to do this.   The interested reader should invest his
time with the latter and not draw conclusions too quickly on the
basis of the former.

If Miracles are Possible, are Legends Impossible?

One often hears conservative Evangelical New Testament scholars
and apologists (it is sometimes difficult to distinguish them) make
the claim that the only reason biblical critics consider a miracle story
to be a legend is that the critics approach the text with the dogmatic "philosophical presupposition" that miracles simply cannot occur.

Dissatisfaction with the traditional view of revelation was
not created by the rise of Biblical criticism.   Criticism was

born out of its denial. For in its modern form, criticism is for the most part grounded upon naturalistic presuppositions which reflect scepticism in the supernatural content and preparation of the Bible. (Clark H. Pinnock)[22]

By the same token, if the supernatural really occurred in history, criticism cannot disprove it. Its naturalistic presuppositions require that it interpret the supernatural as legend, mythology. (George E. Ladd)[23]

Whether you can accept them [i.e., miracles] depends not primarily on the evidence, but on your view of the limits of possibility. (R. T. France)[24]

In attempting to be objective or "scientific," many recent scholars have used only naturalistic concepts. The idea that God actively controls the course of nature and history doesn't even enter their minds. They assume, then, that divine interventions cannot be part of legitimate historical interpretations. We cannot say Jesus really rose from the dead; the resurrection traditions must have developed over time as the early believers experienced a dynamic (but only human) new faith. (John Duff)[25]

It is not surprising therefore that the historical evidence for miracles and the supernatural is sometimes held to be inadequate. For unless the mind is at least genuinely willing to accept the possibility that such events occurred, no amount of historical evidence will be sufficient to convince. (Kenneth G. Howkins)[26]

No doubt all these writers have in mind these words from Rudolf Bultmann's essay "Is Exegesis without Presuppositions Possible?":

The historical method includes the presupposition that history is a unity in the sense of a closed continuum of effects in which individual events are connected by the succession of cause and effect. . . . This closedness means that the continuum of historical happenings cannot be rent by the interference of supernatural transcendent powers and that therefore there is no "miracle" in this sense of the word.[27]

From the context it is not quite clear whether Bultmann intends these words to mean that no miracles are possible metaphysically or simply that the historian cannot render accounts of miracles "probable" as apologists would like to do. But whatever Bultmann means to assert, let us grant that some critics do declare all miracle stories legendary because they reject the supernatural *a priori*.

Having established, at least asserted, this, our scholars/apologists appear to believe they have settled the question of miracles. If this purely *a priori* consideration of naturalism vs. supernaturalism is the only issue, then all the biblical miracle stories stand or fall together. If we bracket the "naturalistic presupposition," all the miracles stand, and we need trouble ourselves as to their historicity no more. That someone might still want to pick and choose seems perverse to C. S. Lewis. He marvels at and pities "a theology . . . which either denies the miraculous altogether or, more strangely, after swallowing the camel of the Resurrection strains at

such gnats as the feeding of the multitude."[28]   Again, "I can understand the man who denies the miraculous altogether; but what
is one to make of the people who admit some miracles but deny the
Virgin Birth?"[29] These words clearly imply that once miracles are
deemed possible there is no reason for doubting any of them.

But continued doubts as to particular miracle stories are not
really so puzzling: a critic may reject some miracle stories as legendary, and not others, with no inconsistency at all for the simple
reason that even if one holds miracles to be possible, one need not
hold legends to be *impossible!*   There are other factors, literary
and historiographical ones, that might lead a critic to conclude that
even though miracles can happen, it does not appear that in this or
that case they did.   I would like to look briefly at four such factors to make clear how they do not presuppose any across-the-board
rejection of the supernatural.   When we have done so, the conser-
vative/apologetic charge with which we began may appear in a surprising new light.

The first criterion for identifying possible legends, and the most
controversial, is the principle of analogy, classically formulated by
Ernst Troeltsch and recently reformulated and championed by Antony
Flew and Van A. Harvey.[30] The main point here is that the historian (including the biblical critic) must use the standards of today's
observed and documented experience as his criterion for what may
be viewed as "probably" having happened in the past. Without this,
there is no safeguard at all against unrelenting credulity. Why not
accept Papias's claim that after the betrayal of Jesus, Judas Iscar-
iot's head swelled up to such grotesque proportions that Judas could
not make it through a pass through which a wagon could easily drive,
and that he began to urinate worms?

If on the principle of analogy critics have often discounted biblical "nature miracles" (like Jesus walking on the sea) as having no
analogy in present-day experience, let it be noted that it works
both ways.   In the various charismatic movements of our day and of
recent history we have seen enough paranormal events paralleling
some of the biblical miracles as to render the latter historically "probable," however one wishes to explain them. It is difficult to deny
that faith healings and exorcisms occur today (e.g., in the Pentecostal movement), so why consider the stories of Jesus' healings and
exorcisms legendary? Even Bultmann does not:

> There can be no doubt that Jesus did the kind of deeds
> which were miracles to his mind and to the minds of his con-
> temporaries, that is, deeds which were attributed to a super-
> natural, divine cause; undoubtedly he healed the sick and
> cast out demons.[31]

Even details of the exorcism stories are paralleled in modern reports
(though these tend to be anecdotal and hearsay in nature). John
Nevius, a missionary in China, reports that after an exorcism

> an extraordinary commotion occurred among the fowls, which
> rushed and flew about in great consternation without any ap-
> parent cause. . . . After awhile they cowered up in the cor-
> ner of the yard in a state of fright. The swine also belonging
> to the family, more than a dozen in number, occupying a large

pen . . . nearby, were put into a singular state of agitation
rushing about the enclosure, running over each other and
trying to scramble up the walls.[32] (cf. Mark 5:11-13.)

Rudolf Otto clearly understood that the principle of analogy worked
both ways.

> But from the point of view of the history of religion it
> would be a mistake to pass over the entire class of charismatic
> phenomena [in the gospel records] in a modern spirit of skep-
> ticism . . . simply because the matters do not appeal to our
> taste. . . . Our task is to ask what kinds of actual occur-
> rences are typically found in a charismatic milieu, in order in
> this way to gain a criterion for what actually happens; . . .
> in order then to apply it . . . to early records.[33]

On this basis Otto recognizes not only Jesus' healings and exorcisms
as historical, but also his prophecies and direct knowledge of what
people were thinking.

Surprising as it might sound to some, we may even suggest a
biblical basis for the use of analogy in evaluating biblical miracle
stories. Surely the teaching of the New Testament is that the same
Spirit that energized Jesus of Nazareth remains active in Christians,
with the result that "he who believes in me will also do the works
that I do; and greater works than these will he do, because I go to
the Father" (John 14:12). Oral Roberts took this seriously and began his healing ministry this way:

> How could I get up and preach about Jesus making the
> lame to walk, the dumb to talk, the deaf to hear, the blind to
> see, the leper to be cleansed, and the dead raised to life and
> then let it all be treated as something in the past, something
> irrelevant to our life and time? How could I talk about the
> Bible being in the NOW? I began to be consumed with a pas-
> sion either to have a ministry like Jesus or to get out of the
> ministry. What good did it do to tell about events that weren't
> happening in this world, in the now?[34]

Roberts, then, as all Pentecostals, did not want to be Bultmann's
"modern man," but rather wanted to close the gap between New
Testament times and our own. We must assume the presence of at
least a mustard seed's weight of faith in those who minister in Christ's
name today expecting miracles, yet what Pentecostal healer has walked
on water, cured insanity at a word, raised the dead, or restored
visibly maimed limbs? Shall we believe God is capriciously withhold-
ing some of the Christ-like works of power promised in John 14:12,
or ought we not rather to conclude that God works today as he did
then, that no one ever did such miracles as do not occur today, and
that instead those stories are legends conveying spiritual truth in
their own unique way?

But forget the principle of analogy; to some readers the very
phrase reeks so strongly of Hume and Bultmann that they cannot
consider it in an unprejudiced way. Let us consider a second factor that has nothing to do with analogy *or* with the denial of miracles. If, when we compare two versions of a story, the second
known to be a retelling of the first, and find that the second has
more of a miraculous element, we may reasonably conclude we have

legendary (or midrashic or whatever) embellishment. The tale has
grown in the telling.   This sort of comparison is common in extra-
biblical research and no one holds that it cannot properly indicate
legend formation there.[35] When biblical scholars apply the same
method to the Bible it in no way implies a wholesale rejection of
miracles.

For instance, let us suppose that Mark's account of Jesus walking
on the sea (6:45-51) is an accurate account of a real event. When
we read Matthew's retelling of the incident (14:22-33) suddenly it
seems that Peter, too, walked on the waves. It is hard to imagine
that if this really happened Mark could possibly have omitted it. On
the other hand, Matthew's motivation for expanding the story is not
far to seek: Peter functions as the prototype of all disciples. When
he takes his eyes off Jesus, he begins to sink.   Even so, let us
"keep our eyes fixed on Jesus, the pioneer and perfector of our
faith" (Hebrews 12:2).   One may well believe Jesus walked on water
but doubt that Peter did.   The same sort of analysis has been applied to Matthew's detachment of guards at the tomb (Matthew 27:62-
66; 28:4, 11-15) and Luke's story of Jesus restoring Malchus's sev-
ered ear in the garden (Luke 22:50-51), both unknown in Mark's
earlier version, the source of Matthew and Luke.

Third, though we believe miracles can and do happen, we might
find certain conceptual or chronological problems in a particular
story that would lead us to classify it as a legend. One example
might be the feeding of the four thousand with seven loaves (Mark
8:1-9).   Let us assume that the previously told miraculous feeding
of the five thousand with five loaves (Mark 6:35-44) actually occurred. This makes it not less difficult but more to believe that it
happened again as recorded in chapter 8, because each time the
disciples are said to be equally astonished when Jesus announces his
intention to feed the vast crowd. One can understand the disciples'
astonishment the first time, but the second? How dense can they
have been?   The suggestion is attractive that one of these stories is
simply a second version of the other, with a few details and numbers altered.

An Old Testament example of a miracle story whose conceptual
difficulties imply its legendary character is that of Samson's killing
the thousand Philistine soldiers with the jawbone of an ass (Judges
15:14-17).   Are we to imagine the thousand Philistines lining up to
be killed one by one? No one, no matter how supernaturally strong,
could resist and overcome the simultaneous onslaught of a thousand
men. The same difficulty occurs in the case of the seventy men of
Bethshemesh who dared peer inside the Ark of the Covenant and
died (I Samuel 6:19-21):   how many could have looked inside at
once?   Did the rest clear away their fellows' corpses and then take
their turn to look, knowing the same fate must await them? In the
case of the Samson story, there is even more reason to believe we
have a legend. It concludes with the note "and that place was called
Ramath-lehi," that is "the Hill of the Jawbone," a name easily understood as originally deriving from the topography of the place, but
here reinterpreted with the aid of an exciting etymological legend.
No one is saying that God could not miraculously endow someone
with superhuman power (or that he could not miraculously destroy
those who look at forbidden things) but the difficulties of the stories

as stories properly lead us to doubt that God did these things as
reported in Judges and II Samuel.

Fourth, when a biblical miracle story is strikingly similar to extrabiblical stories which no one would deny are legends, we may
justly ask if we have found a legend in the Bible. The miraculous
birth of Jesus and the attendant phenomena are very similar to the
miraculous birth stories of, e.g., Alexander the Great and the Buddha, both of whom were begotten on their mothers by supernatural
agencies. Stars and other supernatural signs herald the birth of
various ancient heroes, as do attempts by wicked tyrants to destroy
the holy newborn. Indeed God could have and may have sent Jesus
into human history via the virgin birth, but looking at the evidence
of comparative myth and legend, neither would it be strange if we
were dealing with a pious and meaningful legend. To suggest that
the birth story is legendary is a plausible though admittedly un-
provable way of understanding the story; it is not some kind of
desperate expedient forced upon a stubborn disbeliever in the miraculous.

Sometimes a biblical story may simply read like a legend. We feel
we are no longer on terra firma. Of course this is subjective, but
not completely so. In fact those who defend the complete historical
veracity of the gospels often appeal to just such a subjective judgment by C. S. Lewis who "pulled rank" as a literary critic.

> If he [the biblical critic] tells me that something in a Gos-
> pel is legend or romance, I want to know how many legends
> and romances he has read, how well his palate is trained in
> detecting them by the flavour. . . . I have been reading
> poems, romances, vision-literature, legends, myths, all my
> life. I know what they are like. I know that not one of them
> is like this [i.e., like John 7:53-8:11].[36]

But how about the gospel tale of the coin in the fish's mouth
(Matthew 17:24-27)? Not only may it strike the palate as decidedly
legendary in flavor, but one may even compare it to another of the
same vintage:

> Joseph-who-honors-the-Sabbath had in his vicinity a certain
> Gentile who owned much property. Soothsayers told him,
> "Joseph-who-honors-the-Sabbath will consume all your prop-
> erty." So he went, sold all his property, and bought a pre-
> cious stone with the proceeds, which he set in his turban.
> As he was crossing a bridge the wind blew it off and cast it
> into the water, and a fish swallowed it. [Subsequently] it
> [the fish] was hauled up and brought [to market] on the Sab-
> bath eve towards sunset. "Who will buy now?" cried they.
> "Go and take them to Joseph-who-honors-the-Sabbath," they
> were told, "as he is accustomed to buy." So they took it to
> him. He bought it, opened it, found the jewel therein, and
> sold it for thirteen roomfuls of gold denarii. A certain old
> man met him and said, "He who lends to the Sabbath, the
> Sabbath repays him." (b. Shabbath, 119a.)

It appears, then, that even a confirmed believer in the possibility
of miracles may conclude that this or that miracle story in the Bible
is a legend. None of the factors we surveyed had a thing to do

with any "naturalistic presuppositions." Rather all stemmed from
careful scrutiny of the text itself.   And it is hard to imagine that
the conservative scholars with whom we began do not have sufficient
familiarity with the works of biblical critics to realize that most of
their arguments against miracle-historicity are in fact of this kind.
How then do we account for the rehearsal of the charge that one will
reject *any* miracles only if one approaches the text with certain dogmatic presuppositions?   Do these conservatives/apologists in fact believe that if one grants the possibility of miracles one is thereby
committed to believe every recorded miracle story ever told?   In
other words, if you believe miracles are possible, must you believe
too that the formation of legends is *impossible*? Of course not: these
scholars have no trouble recognizing the legendary nature of extra-
biblical miracle stories.[37]   It is only every miracle story in the
Bible that is to be believed unless one holds those nefarious
"presuppositions."   Now we might ask: just what *a priori* principle
would make this difference, that to hold it or not dictates whether
one will accept the biblical miracle stories *in toto*?   Clearly it would
have to be not the blanket denial of the miraculous, but the
fundamentalist doctrine of verbal inspiration, whereby every word,
every story in the Bible is to be taken as inerrant.   What our
conservatives are really objecting to is that the standpoint of critical
scholars does not require implicit belief in every Bible story.
Whether critics hold "naturalistic presuppositions" is not really the
issue, as we have seen.   The sin of critics is that they do *not*
approach the text *with* a presupposition, the presupposition that
the Bible is inerrant.   Only so could one's rejection of the critics'
position entitle one to accept all biblical miracle stories with no
further problems.   As the history of exegesis has shown, to
approach the text with a belief that errors (or legends) cannot occur
there is just as arbitrary and procrustean a procedure as to
approach it with the assumption that miracles cannot happen.   God
save us from both.

Demythologizing the Supernatural

I have just tried to explain how Bultmann's description of the
nature of historical-critical research does *not* depend on philosophical or theological presuppositions and that the Liberal disinclination
to believe in miracles is a separate question.   Now I want to explore
the Evangelical objection to the theological decision made by Liberals
to demythologize, or desupernaturalize, Christian faith.
Clark Pinnock claims that the real watershed between Evangelical
theology (or "classical Christianity") and Liberal theology ("Satan's
lie"!), is the issue of demythologizing.   He is much clearer on this
issue than is another current Evangelical spokesman, Donald G.
Bloesch who between the covers of a single book invites us to recognize the presence of myth in scripture yet warns us not to demythologize![38] But perhaps the most straightforward of all is elder
statesman Carl F. H. Henry.   In his magisterial work *God, Revelation and Authority*, Henry writes:

> Christian revelation is nullified unless the crucifixion and
> resurrection of Jesus Christ belong to the same history that

includes the death of Julius Caesar and of Adolf Hitler. The Christian must either believe that the great redemptive events belong to the realm of history or forfeit his faith.[39]

I believe this statement to be typical of Evangelical writing on the subject. Evangelical theologians and apologists believe that the non-occurrence of the redemptive miracles of the biblical story would prove fatal for faith. And the Neo-Orthodox relegation of these events to a nonfactual realm of "meta-history" (*Geschichte*) seems to them merely an unsuccessful cop-out. Why do we find this tenacious connection of theological reality to the historically miraculous?

What we are seeing here is a confusion of two logically quite distinct things—the supernatural on the one hand, and the sacred on the other. By "supernatural," I mean paranormal, the occurrence of events apparently from without the normal sequences of cause-and-effect. "Miracles" are events that are supernatural. By "sacred," I mean that sometimes less than obvious higher dimension of reality to which man appeals for meaning and wholeness. It is the "Holy," the "Other," the complementary opposite to our feeling of creatureliness. It is the divine side of things.

Evangelicals seem not to make this distinction; the sacred is practically identified with the supernatural. There would be no meaning without miracle. We find this often-hidden assumption articulated in Francis Schaeffer's famous "line of despair" theory. According to this schema, man lost the possibility of finding meaning for life when he began to think that the world of history, nature, and reason was thoroughly explainable on its own terms, without recourse to the supernaturally-imparted information of the Bible, and without the causal hypothesis of miraculous intervention, e.g., in the creation of life. Huston Smith makes a similar point in his book *Forgotten Truth*, where he says that the error of "scientism" is the foolish assumption that the mundane level of reality which admittedly can be adequately explained by science, is the *only* level of reality. The difference between Smith and Schaeffer is that Schaeffer denies that *any* level of reality is fully accountable with the scientific method. If there were even such a limited realm of adequacy for the scientific method, then "scientism" would be correct! There would be no reason to postulate any other realm, a realm of transcendent meaning. To proceed to postulate such a realm of meaning would then be an irrational "upper-story leap." All this is tantamount to saying that unless the realm of mundane reality is *penetrated on the same level* by supernatural events (e.g., biblical miracles or the inspiration of the Bible itself), there is no sacred realm of meaning at all, only despair. The supernatural and the sacred have been practically identified.

We find a close parallel to this thinking in John Warwick Montgomery. He trains the guns of analytic philosophy on Neo-Orthodoxy, with its referral of miracles to the land of "meta-history."

> If, for example, the claim is made that Christ rose from the dead, but in the suprahistorical realm of *Geschichte*, not in the empirical realm of *Historie*, one has every right to ask: "What precisely do you *mean* by the realm of *Geschichte* and how do you know anything—much less a resurrection—goes on there?" A supra-experiential realm is *ex hypothesi*, untest-

able, and therefore . . . irrelevant as a theological concept.

> The historicity of the Resurrection [and] the facticity of
> the Biblical miracles . . . must be sustained, or the God of
> Scripture will fade away into a misty transcendence . . . and
> eventually disappear.[40]

Again, we find the notion that without the occurrence of paranormal
events in history, there is no real realm of meaning, no real God.
God "fades away into a misty transcendence." For Schaeffer, too,
the God of Liberal theology "is no more than a mist."[41] For Kenneth Howkins, he "is not the living God."[42] Thus the existence
of the sacred is practically identified with, or even reduced to,
the existence of the supernatural.

Why should the existence or occurrence of the supernatural imply
the sacred, or convey meaning? For example, how would the mere
fact that a superpowerful "supreme being" caused paranormal events
on earth differ in principle from the concept of "Chariots of the
Gods"? What is the difference between this and the notion that "God
drives a flying saucer"? Where would meaning or sacrality enter the
picture? This is quite a relevant question to pose to Evangelical
theologians, especially Schaeffer. He claims that modern theology
has no real basis outside experience for believing in the reality of
love.

> On the other hand, the [Evangelical] Christian does have
> the adequate universal he needs in order to be able to dis-
> cuss the meaning of love. . . . [The] Trinity was before the
> creation of everything else and . . . love existed between the
> persons of the Trinity before the foundation of the world.[43]

But one must ask just how the fact that superhuman beings experienced love chronologically before we did provides any kind of ontological grounding for their love? Why do not the persons of the
Trinity in turn seek for some ontological grounding for their love?
Similarly, Schaeffer holds that in Evangelical theology "Man has true
[i.e., ontological] guilt." Why? "Because man is guilty before the
Law-giver of the universe. . . ."[44] But why is the will or character of a being, even a supreme one, ontologically determinative of
right and wrong?

In short, the mere existence or activity of superhuman entities
in itself says nothing about ontological questions of meaning. And
though such a being might be feared for its power, why should it
be worshipped as sacred? As Tillich put it in his booklet *Biblical
Religion and the Search for Ultimate Reality*, "each of the biblical
symbols drives inescapably to an ontological question."[45] In other
words the supernatural itself cannot bear the weight of questions of
meaning. The existence and occurrence of the supernatural is only
religiously significant when *the supernatural mediates the sacred*. In
itself, it need not do so, but if it does then a "miracle" (literally,
"work of power") becomes a "sign" pointing to the sacred.

The question now becomes, "If the supernatural does not have to
imply the sacred, must the sacred imply the supernatural?" Liberals
seem to think that one can have the sacred without the supernatural,
without the occurrence of miracles in history. Evangelicals disagree.
How do Evangelicals imagine miracles to communicate meaning? The

answer to this question becomes apparent when we recall the Evangelical attacks on the "Biblical Theology Movement" led by G. Ernest Wright and others. In this controversy Evangelicals like Carl F. H. Henry, Bernard Ramm, and J. I. Packer maintained that in God's "mighty acts in history" he revealed himself, not only in the bare events, but also as interpreted in the inspired scriptural commentary on the events. Thus, miraculous acts mediate the sacred by revealing the character of God. And such revelation is always effectual—people are changed, transformed by their knowledge of God (cf. II Peter 2:20a). Such a revelation of God can come through natural as well as supernatural means, as when God demonstrated his justice in allowing Assyria to conquer Israel.

But are not Liberal theologians able to say very nearly the same thing even when they demythologize? As we have just seen, the real issue is that historical events reveal God *whether these events are miraculous or not.* Demythologizing, or desupernaturalizing, does not stop Liberal theologians from speaking of "acts of God in history" which reveal his character:

. . . what is meant when we say that God acts *in* history is primarily that there are certain distinctively human words and deeds in which his characteristic action as Creator and Redeemer is appropriately represented or revealed. We mean that there are some human actions, some specific attempts to express the ultimate truth of our existence through symbolic words and deeds, that are vastly more than merely human actions. Because through them nothing less than the transcendent action of God himself is re-presented, they are also acts of God, that is, they *are* acts of God analogously to the way in which our outer acts *are* our acts insofar as they re-present our own characteristic decisions as selves or persons. (Schubert Ogden)[46]

Talking of God's activity is, then, to be understood as a way of speaking about those events within the natural order or within human history in which God's purpose finds clear expression or special opportunity. (Maurice Wiles)[47]

I am not trying to deceive the reader into thinking there are no real differences between Evangelical and Liberal positions at this point. I merely mean to point out that *to demythologize is not to dehistoricize,* as is often supposed. In both kinds of theology, events in history become "discernment situations" (Ian Ramsey) in which is disclosed a transforming knowledge of God. Let me illustrate this with regard to the most controversial item on the demythologizing agenda, namely the resurrection of Jesus. Evangelicals believe that God's love and power were revealed on Easter Morning in the miracle of the bodily resurrection of Jesus. Liberals such as Rudolf Bultmann and Gordon Kaufman believe that God's love and power were revealed on Easter Morning in the formation of the disciples' resurrection-faith, even though Jesus did not rise bodily. These two notions are different, but both agree that Easter was the *historical occasion* of the act of God in raising Jesus, whether "to the right hand of God," or "into the kerygma." In both cases we are talking about *what happened* in history.

So the sacred could be mediated in history without the supernat-

ural.   This being the case, it is not evident that disbelief in the
literally miraculous would spell the end of Christian faith.   Conversely, belief in the miraculous in and of itself goes very little
distance in helping to answer questions of meaning and the sacred.
Evangelical critics might do well to devote some thought to whether,
in their zeal for the supernatural, they are doing justice to the
reality of the sacred in its own right.   While the analysis in this
section has by no means militated against a theological belief in the
paranormal and miraculous, it has suggested that this question be
discussed in a different, less charged, context.   The question of
God's transcendence and revelation does not stand or fall with it.

The Failure to Develop a Post-Modern Position

I began Section III with the question of creativity in Evangelical
theology.   I said I suspected that we should look for mainly new
criticisms of other theological positions.   And in view of the inadequacy of the arguments reviewed in the last two chapters, some new
ones are certainly in order!   But it would not be fair to leave it at
this.   The critical efforts of Evangelical theologians do have a positive goal in mind.   They seek to fill a gap created by the perceived
bankruptcy of Liberal theology.   Wells and Pinnock in the preface to
their book *Toward a Theology for the Future* make their purpose
clear.   Ever since Liberalism yielded to the "Neo-Orthodox consensus," and the latter gave way to Process theism, Liberation theology, the "God is Dead" movement, etc., it has been impossible to
keep the players straight without a scorecard.   Wells and Pinnock
see this as an undesirable situation.

> Contemporary theology has drifted into a dangerous cul-de-
> sac.   The situation demands that a vigorous restatement of
> historic belief emerges which will offer a convincing and cred-
> ible way out.   Evangelical scholarship intends to do this, set-
> ting as its main goal nothing less than the recapturing of
> leadership in theological research.[48]

Triumphalism aside, it would certainly be in everyone's best interests for Evangelicals to make the best possible showing for their
theology.   Evangelical theologians are acutely aware of having been
left behind in current theological debate, and they want a piece of
the action.   They at least seem to realize that if they are to shed
their "backwater" image, they must begin to engage the same issues
that occupy mainstream theologians.   Yet there is no thought that
interaction with these issues might cause some modification of the
Evangelical position.   What is envisioned is a "postliberal" position.
Pinnock predicts that

> our evangelical alternative will be clearly seen to be, not pre-
> liberal (as if we wished to pretend that nothing of importance
> had happened in theology since Luther and Calvin!) but post-
> liberal, a proposal which self-consciously turns away from the
> deficiencies of liberal thought and aligns itself in a fresh way
> with the historic faith of the church.[49]

There is a problem of credibility here.   Thomas Oden, whose priorities on this question are closely parallel to Pinnock, makes an

important point. He distinguishes

> between two types of orthodoxy: *pre-* and *post*modern. Both
> are schooled in the same scriptural and patristic texts, and
> both celebrate and embody the same Christ, but one has jour-
> neyed through and dwelled in modernity, while the other has
> not.[50]

Though Pinnock et al. want to be "postliberal" or "postmodern,"
they show no evidence of having made this journey. For instance,
J. I. Packer warns that unless Evangelicals concern themselves with
current issues of hermeneutics, "we shall be forced to remain (where
we have long been!) on the edge of the modern Protestant debate
about Holy Scripture. . . ."[51] Yet Packer goes on merely to
reiterate the old scholastic system of harmonization and inerrancy,
the collapse of which gave rise to the whole "modern debate" in
the first place! Similarly, some Evangelical writers have tried to
"transcend" the "propositional" vs. "personal" revelation debate
by suggesting that no one need worry—though the Bible is
propositional revelation it also conveys personal encounter with God
himself. The point has been completely missed. This "either-or"
situation arose only because biblical criticism made the notion of
propositional revelation seem untenable (cf. Chapter 8). Before
this everyone had agreed that personal encounter with God was
included in propositional revelation. Liberals and Neo-Orthodox
thinkers did not claim that propositional revelation was logically
nonsensical (as Francis Schaeffer seems to assume). Rather it
seemed that biblical criticism made it look as if whether or not such
revelation were possible, in fact it had not occurred. These
theologians then *limited* the meaning of revelation to personal
encounter as a salvage maneuver. The Evangelical "answer" here
is simply to ignore the problem and return to the pre-critical
understanding.
Another example of such theological sleight of hand occurs in
Donald Bloesch's *Essentials of Evangelical Theology*. Bloesch pretends to settle the famous "Jesus of history-Christ of faith" debate:

> Against both strands of liberalism we contend that the church
> must begin neither with the Jesus of history [cf. Harnack]
> nor the Christ of faith [cf. Bultmann] but with the historical
> Jesus Christ of the Scriptures whose identity can only be
> perceived by faith. We further maintain that the picture that
> faith gives is identical with the true perception of the his-
> torical reality of Jesus.[52]

Though professing to accept the "solid gains" of historical criticism,
Bloesch acts as if the historical Jesus problem doesn't exist. This
is not quite the same as solving it! He goes on deftly to camou-
flage yet another Christological rift: "We reject both a Christology
from below [cf. Küng, Sobrino, Schillebeeckx] and one from above
[cf. Barth, Kaspar] and affirm instead a Christology of the center."[53] The context makes it clear that Bloesch in fact advocates
an incarnational Christology "from above." The fact that he won't
simply admit it makes one wonder if he even understands the issue.
What seems to be happening here is *not* an attempt to encounter
modernity and formulate a truly postmodern position. Rather Evan-

gelicals try to leapfrog modernity and repristinate precritical positions. They say they are willing to struggle with modernity as long as they can continue to believe exactly what they already do believe! If the conclusion is drawn before the process starts, it is no wonder that all that results is apologetics for traditional (premodern) Evangelicalism! A genuine postliberal Evangelicalism is going to have to be willing to undergo real changes. We might expect that such a postmodern version will have *continuity but not identity* with the preliberal ancestor. At least a few Evangelicals have dared to think in this direction. In the next chapter, I will try to chart the prospects for a genuinely postmodern Evangelicalism.

Chapter 10

TOWARD A REALLY NEW EVANGELICALISM

Never has Evangelical biblical scholarship been so mercilessly run through the wringers as it was in James Barr's *Fundamentalism* (1977). Many of his reviewers criticized Barr for not offering any alternative to what he tore down. This was not entirely a fair criticism since Barr's earlier work *The Bible in the Modern World* in large measure fills such a gap. Though this criticism of Barr may have been largely an attempt to sidestep the force of his criticisms, there is a valid point here. Unless an alternative is offered, how else may readers be expected to respond to a radical critique of their opinions and beliefs? So what have I to offer, after all my criticisms? I haven't kept readers completely in the dark up to now; in various chapters I have already sketched alternatives being espoused or explored by what I have dubbed "soft-line" or "left-wing" Evangelicals. I have also suggested some new correctives of my own (for instance in Chapter 4). Here I want to tie it all together with some hints at a framework for a really new Evangelicalism.

And, let's not kid ourselves; that's what it's going to take—a *really* new Evangelicalism. As much as I sincerely appreciate the advances of the "Neo-Evangelicalism" christened by pioneer Harold J. Ockenga, and the "Young Evangelicalism" promoted by commentator Richard Quebedeaux, I am afraid that each is still only a kind of "piecemeal fundamentalism." I could not agree more with James Barr's assessment:

> Has evangelicalism succeeded in developing a conceptual framework recognizable, distinct from a strict fundamentalist one? If evangelicals, in departing from a strict fundamentalist position, continue to take that position as the base line for their thinking, and fail to construct a theology governed on quite other principles, fundamentalism will continue to be the governing force in their minds.[1]

What we need is a new theological methodology. This is the only way for Evangelicals to make good their promise of a postmodern position. However, perhaps to the disappointment of some readers, I will not attempt to provide such a new theology here. There are two good reasons for this reticence.

First of all, any such suggestions would involve the construction of a whole new system correcting all the abuses I have outlined so far in this book. But I recognize that some readers will agree with only parts and not the whole of my preceding analysis. (And they are quite free to pick and choose since few of the points made were logically interdependent.) Thus if I outlined a new methodology or theology it would not match the problems as some readers see them.

Second, before any genuinely new Evangelical methodology can be constructed, there has to be a theoretical path-clearing. I must show what room there is in Evangelicalism for such a new way of doing things. Put another way, I must give some idea of how Evangelicalism could survive such major changes in more than name only. Once I have cleared the ground in this way (if it can be done!), and shown *how* a new theological method may be "plugged in," the reader will be free to adopt any particular one that seems to him most adequate to meet the problems he sees. My suggested framework thus may be used no matter how conservative or liberal one wishes to be in his theological adjustments. What I hope to provide is a framework for a truly postmodern Evangelicalism.

I have thought long and repeatedly over an essay by Richard Mouw of Calvin College. Entitled "New Alignments," this piece was written in reflection upon the ecumenical "Hartford Appeal for Theological Affirmation" issued in 1974. Mouw considers the relationship of different varieties of Evangelicalism between themselves and with other segments of American Protestantism. Eventually he raises this provocative question:

> What, finally, does the evangelical label come to? For many of us, it comes down to the fact that there are basic elements in the evangelical understanding of the Christian message and life style that we cherish and do not find adequately treated in nonevangelical Christian groups: the sense that Christianity is a *message* . . . that must be verbally articulated to those who do not profess Jesus Christ as Lord; an emphasis on the need for a "personal relationship" with Jesus Christ as Savior and Lord of one's life; a set of basic *attitudes* toward the Holy Scriptures, which are typified by certain devotional patterns and regular references in Christian discussion to what "the Bible says."[2]

I want to draw a distinction that Mouw most likely does not intend to make. It seems to me that these three factors have more to do with *style* than with content. In short, the distinctive thing about Evangelicalism is *the shape and style* of religion it promotes. Several different kinds of theological content could be "plugged in" with integrity. The work of this final chapter will be to illustrate this point with reference to Mouw's aptly-drawn list of Evangelical distinctives. It is this style which will form the continuity between postmodern Evangelicalism and its heritage.

We may paraphrase Mouw's first distinctive in this way: "Christianity as a message to be proclaimed." This is the issue of evangelism, and especially the use of "personal evangelism," the sharing of faith person-to-person, or "soul-winning." In evangelism, as traditionally understood, the stakes are indeed high. There is an urgency to "fulfill the Great Commission in our generation." Why? Because every day "millions are passing into a Christless eternity." In other words, nonbelievers are going to wind up damned to hellfire. You may not be able to prevent it, but at least you can do your best to "snatch them as brands from the burning." If you had a cure for cancer, would you keep it to yourself? If you saw a house on fire, would you calmly proceed on your way without trying to warn and save those within?

How does anything I have said in this book bear on this issue? In Chapter 2, I discussed the severe "us vs. them" perception of reality which lies at the heart of such a view of evangelism, salvation, and damnation. I hinted that increased personal contact with outsiders tends to modify or question the plausibility of such an airtight separation of sheep and goats. This is particularly true in the context of theological dialogue. Recently, some Evangelicals have begun dialogues not only with other kinds of Christians, but even with members of other religions. I mentioned Marvin Wilson of Gordon College and the book *Evangelicals and Jews in Conversation*. In an NBC "First Estate" telecast, Wilson and Rabbi James Rudin (two editors of this volume) agreed that Jews and Evangelicals should "witness" to each other by demonstrating the vitality of their faith in producing good social and family life. Similarly "Young Evangelical" Richard Quebedeaux, during an Evangelical dialogue with Moonies at the Unification Theological Seminary, spoke glowingly of the "agape love" in evidence there. It's going to be increasingly difficult to look into the face of a non-Christian whose love and piety is patently as real as one's own, and to tell him he's going to hell. It was this kind of face-to-face encounter that moved Paul Tillich and Wilfred Cantwell Smith to modify their theological exclusivism: "An existential contact with outstanding representatives of non-Christian religions forces one into the acknowledgment that God is not far from them, that there is a universal revelation." (Tillich)[3]

> . . . except at the cost of insensitivity or delinquence, it is morally not possible actually to go out into the world and say to devout, intelligent, fellow human beings: "We are saved and you are damned. . . ." . . . so far as actual observation goes, the evidence would seem overwhelming that in fact individual Buddhists, Hindus, Muslims, and others have known, and do know God. I personally have friends from these communities whom it seems to me preposterous to think about in any other way. (Smith)[4]

Insofar as real listening dialogue increases (not just "listening" so as to be better able to refute), sensitive Evangelicals are going to reject their habit of writing off the religious (or other authentic human) experience of non-Christians as "counterfeit." They will begin to feel the embarrassment of the scribes who absurdly charged that Jesus cast out demons only by the power of Beelzebub. The fruits of the Spirit are manifest as such wherever they appear. Take the example of Bill Lane Doulos, a contributor to *Sojourners*. He describes how his exposure to the Catholic Worker Movement helped him tear down

> the wall erected by doctrine. Those who believe are in; all others are out. Some are going to heaven, some to hell. A lot of us evangelicals have never quite learned to accept this wall that has been built around the orthodox camp. Some of us have had the good fortune to see Jesus bulldozing his way through the cherished creed of his religious culture, and of our own.[5]

A great deal is made, especially in so-called "presuppositionalist" apologetics, of what is sometimes called the "empirical fit" argument. It is an essentially common-sense pragmatic argument that questions the adequacy of a worldview based on how it translates into everyday experience. "In the clear light of day," does philosophy X really account for our existential reality? It is on this basis that Os Guiness, in *The Dust of Death*, is able to write off all of Eastern thought in relatively few sentences. He feels (whether rightly or not) that the Eastern idea of the illusory character of the world

does not sufficiently take into account the existential depth of grief,
love, etc.   Similarly, Francis Schaeffer takes secular humanism to
task because its presuppositions simply cannot justify the meaning
found in life as lived by secular humanists and everyone else.   While
recognizing some weaknesses in Schaeffer's use of it, I do not think
this is basically a bad argument.

The only trouble is that the same line of reasoning leads one to
doubt seriously a belief certainly held by Guiness, Schaeffer, and
company.   My years of experience in Evangelicalism have shown me
the practical results of a belief in the damnation of "the unregener-
ate."   There arises a kind of invisible wall between "us" and "them"
that cripples, even destroys, gut-level human solidarity, a reality I
found I finally could no longer deny.   Recall what I said in Chapter
2 about strictly defining and limiting one's contact with "the unsaved."   Such an elitism is inevitable with such a belief, and "in
the clear light of day" I find that it just doesn't ring true.   To get
the feel of this, take a look at the in-group consciousness of any
"cult" such as the Children of God or Jehovah's Witnesses.   Aren't
Evangelicals really doing the same thing?   In their book Snapping:
America's Epidemic of Sudden Personality Change, Flo Conway and
Jim Siegelman note that

> the Evangelical movement shares many characteristics with
> religious cults and mass therapies. . . . There were [Evan-
> gelical] individuals who, at the end of what we thought was
> an open and genuine discussion, declared flatly that we would
> be condemned to Hell for the opinions we expressed and the
> beliefs we held.[7]

I do not think that the "saved-damned" schema is adequate to human
experience.   It does not survive the test of "empirical fit," as far
as I am concerned.

What would become of "Christianity as a message to be proclaimed"
in our hypothetical postmodern Evangelicalism?   I do not think evangelism would be undermined in the least, though some of the guilt-
motivated pressure would be relaxed.   The key is to see that "fire
insurance" was never supposed to be the only motivation for evangelism and the missionary enterprise.   Of course all evangelists and
missiologists realize this; they just have a tendency to ignore the
fact in arguments about Universalism.   "But, if everyone is going
to heaven anyway, what is the point of the Great Commission?" They
hope to defend belief in damnation by the commonly agreed-upon
propriety of evangelism.   But there is a logically quite separate
reason for evangelism.   The evangelist or missionary is concerned to
spread faith in, and glorification of, Jesus Christ as Lord.   Even if
one held with some Barthians that the objective work of Christ avails
for the salvation of all people regardless of their subjective response,
this motive for evangelism would remain.   For the sake of "the glory
of his name" (as the Lausanne Covenant puts it), shouldn't all people be invited to confess his Lordship, even if they will not be damned
otherwise?   To say that apart from the threat of hellfire, no purpose
remains for evangelism is surely a sign of man-centered rather than
"God-centered evangelism," in the phrase of one Reformed tract.

I would be willing to go farther still.   Suppose one wanted to
recognize the legitimacy and truth of all the great world religions

(and there are theologically coherent ways of doing this—see for instance Tillich's *Christianity and the Encounter of the World Religions*, or Raymond Panikkar's *The Unknown Christ of Hinduism*). Would there still be a place for evangelism? Would Christianity still be "a message to be proclaimed"? Of course it would. One must only realize that evangelistic zeal does not depend on the logical syllogism "if my religion is true, his must be false." Rather, I should think the genuine desire to evangelize arises from the felt benefits deriving from one's commitment to Christ, i.e., "Christ has done so much for me that I want to share him with others." This is what the term "witnessing" implies. This motivation should remain untouched even if the witness allows that others to whom he speaks also might have something to which they could bear witness. Again, the two facts are logically independent. If the Jew or humanist is already happily experiencing what you would call the fruits of the Spirit through his own faith, so be it. Picture it like a testimony meeting where two Christians testify to different blessings they have received from God in the past week. To rejoice in your own blessing, do you need to deny the other person's blessing? Conversely, to receive encouragement or admonition from your testimony, must your friend renounce the different blessing God has given him? That doesn't lessen the fact that Jesus Christ has given you, and can give others, abundant life.

And the pressure would be off. No more worrying, "how can I work Christ into this conversation?" Things would now have the freedom to happen naturally and authentically. I realize that many Evangelicals with a conventional belief in hell and damnation do not subject themselves to this kind of guilty agitation anyway. Yet I cannot help but wonder if, with their belief, they should. Alan Watts contends that,

> . . . it is quite obvious to the canny observer that most Christians . . . do not believe in Christianity. If they did, they would be screaming in the streets, taking daily full-page advertisements in the newspapers, and subscribing for the most hair-raising television programs every night of the week. Even Jehovah's Witnesses are polite and genteel in their door-to-door propaganda. Nobody, save perhaps a few obscure fanatics, is *really* bothered by the idea that . . . [most] people are sinners and unbelievers, and will probably go to hell. So what? Let God worry about that one![8]

What kind of belief is it that if taken seriously would make one into a fanatic? The reconstruction I am proposing (note, in various possible versions) would still leave Evangelicals with "Christianity as a message to be proclaimed." All I am suggesting is (in the words of Bill Bright) "sharing Christ in the power of the Holy Spirit and [maybe for the first time] leaving the results to God."

I have already discussed at some length Mouw's second Evangelical distinctive, a piety centered on "a personal relationship with Christ." I will not rehearse that discussion here except to point out an important implication. Remember that the real truth of "personal relationship" language was to stress the personal or existential nature of one's commitment to Christ, not that one necessarily knows Jesus Christ as an individual person analogous to ourselves. If this

is so, there is more room to recognize the genuine commitment to
Christ of people who do not happen to use the "personal relationship" language of the Evangelical tradition.

Turning to the related issue of Born Again experience and coping
mechanisms, I have already sketched the contours of a "soft religious line." It meant basically the putting away of a childish dependence on a God conceived animistically in terms of a primitive
worldview. The mature Born Again Christian does not demand the
life of faith be problem-free, or that all problems have pat religious
answers. The "soft-line" Evangelical will swallow hard and admit
the ambiguity of life and its decisions. He will try to do God's will,
but will have done with complicated schemes of divination which
look for God under every bush. He will stop cruelly kidding himself
by "praising the Lord" for tragedy, repressing grief, and giddily
refusing to take responsibility for his own life. Christian faith will
inform all decisions and priorities, but life will be lived for the sake
of its own beauty and meaning, to which Christ has opened the
Christian's eyes. But we mustn't overlook the problem which seemed
to cast doubt on the legitimacy of the soft religious line as an Evangelical option. It seemed at various points not to comport with the
strictly fundamentalist view of the Bible allegedly maintained by
Evangelicals, i.e., that all biblical texts are authoritative in a literal,
propositional sense for the Christian's "practice" including his understanding of life and man. It is to this question we turn in conclusion.

Mouw lists as the third element implied in the Evangelical label,
"a set of basic *attitudes* toward the Holy Scriptures, which are typ-
ified by certain devotional patterns and regular references in Christian discussion to what 'the Bible says.'" Mouw's description here
is splendidly clear and helpful in its delineation of what is at stake,
namely attitudes. More light is shed on this situation by Gerald T.
Sheppard in an essay entitled "Biblical Hermeneutics: The Academic
Language of Evangelical Identity." Sheppard points out how words
such as "inerrancy" and "infallibility" serve chiefly as shibboleths
or passwords to "the social contract at the heart of the evangelical
identity."[9] The real theological "battle for the Bible" is being fought
over questions or theories of intentionality, e.g., whether the inerrant truth of texts is intended (by God) to include the historical or
cosmological trappings of the text, or only the religious point of it.
I will soon return to this important question. For now let me point
out that what is common to all factions involved is a set of "connotation words" (Francis Schaeffer's term) which set the Evangelical
style and *attitude* toward the Bible. What is being debated is the
most appropriate theological content of connotation words like "inerrancy" and "infallibility." Here is the style/content dichotomy I am
advocating.

I argue in this final section that one can maintain those attitudes
and connotation-words concerning scripture, and thus maintain (postmodern) Evangelical identity, even if one changes considerably the
theological content. Again, keep in mind that the content could be
changed in any of several ways as seems most appropriate to the
reader. I want to take a few stock pieces of Evangelical scripture-
jargon and examine first their traditional meaning, and then make
some suggestions for new theological content, in some cases already

being put forth by Evangelicals themselves.

First let us consider the matter of "reverence for scripture." What often infuriates conservatives about historical-critical study of the Bible is the critical axiom that the Bible must be studied like any other book. Actually, with their espousal of the anti-allegorical grammatico-historical method, Evangelicals are not so far from this axiom themselves. The real red flag is the careless language often used by critical scholars which seems to infer a casual, or even disdainful, attitude toward the Bible. This it seems to me is an objection postmodern Evangelicals would have to maintain if they are to keep the Evangelical style. The Bible must remain a cherished object at the center of any Evangelical style of faith.

But what is the *content* attached to this objection by traditional conservatives? They say that we must never criticize the Word of God (i.e., question the historical accuracy of its statements); rather we must allow it to criticize us. This stance is increasingly meeting rejection by younger Evangelical scholars who see that there is a pious confusion between two meanings of "criticism" here. Even historical criticism, they feel, may be carried on in a spirit of reverence. It is no different in kind from textual criticism or even exegesis. All such "criticism" is only a matter of trying to come to grips with the religious message of the text. This kind of "criticism" is quite a different thing from *moral* criticism which "biblical critics" too may humbly accept from the Word of God, better understood through their labors. Thus the "reverence" required by an "Evangelical style" would not affect the method of biblical study as it has done traditionally. By way of example, David M. Scholer points out how in dealing with the chronological difficulty in Acts 7:16, Liberal Ernst Haenchen says Stephen has "confused" two Old Testament texts, while conservative F. F. Bruce says Stephen has "telescoped" the two passages. Notice that the only difference here is the negative or positive connotation of the descriptive word used. The critical solution is the same.

"Verbal inspiration" is another term indispensable to Evangelical Bible-talk. I think it would be fair to say that this phrase was originally intended to anchor theological thought in the text of the Bible by pointing to the origin of the particular statements of the text in the providence of God. During the Fundamentalist-Modernist Controversy, the term became a banner of resistance to the idea that the Bible being merely a human book serves as but a repository of greater and lesser religious ideas. The doctrinal content of "verbal inspiration" was that these words and the statements formed by them correspond almost pictorially to divine realities. Their propositional sense was literally true. Verbal inspiration as traditionally understood seems to make the Bible a revelation of information. It is the guarantee of the textual vehicle of propositional revelation.

In my opinion, this view is no longer viable. Contradictions in the Bible make meaningless the idea that biblical texts render inspired statements in this literal, propositional sense. Remember, the admission of precisely "apparent" contradictions nullifies this theory since according to it, the verbally inspired propositions are located in the "apparent" or "plain" sense of the text, i.e., exactly that sense which in one passage contradicts that of the other. But in rejecting this, one is not rejecting all meaning of the term "verbal

inspiration." In discussions of "verbal" vs. "content" inspiration
models, Henry, Packer, and others pointed out that if a statement
is in any sense inspired, the words themselves must participate in
the inspiration, since one has no other access to the statement's
meaning except via its wording. This seems true enough, as even
James Barr admits.[10] It is important to note that "verbal inspiration" thus understood does not mean that the inspired point could
not have been put into other, equivalent words, but that the point
as we find it expressed in these words is inspired. But please
note that such a recognition of the words, i.e., the text as is,
also does not logically imply that inspiration guarantees the presence
of pictorially accurate informational propositions. Alternatively,
what *could* a really postmodern Evangelical theology make of verbal
inspiration?

The point of departure is the centrality of the text, rather than
of some pre-textual or post-textual reality. First, it means remov-
ing the "fence around the Torah," the obscuring of the Bible with
doctrines of the Bible. Paul Holmer says,

> For one thing, there is far too much said about the Bible,
> almost as if the Bible cannot speak for itself and show one
> the Savior without sundry helps. . . . strangely enough,
> theories about dispensations, inspiration, authorship, and a
> lot else, begin to intervene. It almost looks as if a chief
> piece of theology, a kind of knowledge of God, has to be made
> up by evangelicals to get the business moving. And soon the
> fireworks are not in the gospels and epistles but in the evan-
> gelical spokesmen's scheme about the book.[11]

Closely related to this evasion of the text is that which makes the
biblical text primarily "Exhibit A" for a theological system which
itself is the real source of instruction and comfort. No, a really
new Evangelical understanding would make the biblical text itself
the place of the divine-human encounter. For an example of such
nondoctrinal encounter with the Bible, see Walter Wink's *The Bible
in Human Transformation.*

Verbal inspiration meaning the centrality of the text would also
mean the end of the apologetical "quest for the Evangelical Jesus"
which concentrates on proving that "the picture [of Jesus] that
faith gives is identical with the true perception of the historical
reality of Jesus." (Bloesch)[12] The texts containing statements attributed to Jesus are supposed to be worthless if Jesus didn't actually say them: ". . . how can you believe in Christ as the Bread
of Life without believing in a historical basis to John's Gospel?"
(Charles Caldwell Ryrie)[13] Yet why couldn't one be Evangelical if
he believed such texts, though not spoken by the historical Jesus,
were inspired by the Holy Spirit? And since on my theory, what is
distinctly Evangelical is primarily a matter of style, I suggest that
one *could* hold to an extremely Liberal skepticism about the historical Jesus, yet still treasure the gospel texts about Jesus as the
place where one encounters "the Numinous," or one's "Ultimate Concern," or whatever. My point is not that one could consistently
hold no other view within the authentic Evangelical style.

In the preceding paragraphs, I have maintained that Evangelicals
themselves continually, and almost on principle, relativize the text

of the Bible. Of course this is just what they damn form-critics for
doing.   But the most flagrant, yet least obvious, way in which conservatives relativize the text is harmonizing.   Trying to harmonize
two divergent texts takes one or both with less than full seriousness.   For instance, two variant accounts of the same event are
harmonized by the postulation of a composite sequence of events
which, if it really happened, would account for the details of both
texts, *though actually suggested by neither*.   Harold Lindsell's incredible suggestion of six denials of Jesus by Peter is only an extreme example of all such harmonizations.   Reading either text by
itself would not yield the harmonization's sequence of events, yet
the harmonization henceforth governs the reading of each text!   No,
a postmodern Evangelical insistence on verbal inspiration will seek to
learn from both texts (remembering that revelatory propositions are
not the only thing one might learn), instead of silencing one or
both of them.   Basically, then, "verbal inspiration" understood in a
postmodern way means the centrality of the *text*, not of some particular theological system, hermeneutic, theory of religious authority,
or reconstruction of underlying events.   Any of several options
could be entertained on these logically separate matters.
      What may be said about inerrancy?   The traditional content
"plugged into" this connotation word is that all biblical statements
are factually correct, whether they touch on matters of theology,
science, history, or geography.   This seems plain enough, though
even the most conservative inerrantists have a way of obscuring the
terms of the discussion, as in the recent "Chicago Statement on
Biblical Inerrancy" in which the definition propounded in one para-
graph seems to contradict that assumed in the next.
      But what if one finds (as many do) this definition unacceptable?
Should the word be dropped, or is it considered definitive enough
of the Evangelical style of regarding scripture to be salvaged with
a new theological content?   Clark Pinnock, in his more recent writings, is representative of much newer Evangelical thinking here:

> Inerrancy when applied to Scripture is relative to the scope,
> purpose, and genre of each passage. . . . [This is a] quali-
> fication, according to which one could fairly say that the Bible
> *contains* errors but *teaches* none, or that inerrancy refers to
> the *subjects* rather than all the *terms* of Scripture or to the
> *teaching* rather than to all the components utilised in its for-
> mulation.[14]

In slightly different terms, Daniel Fuller (who may be said to have
sparked this whole debate) speaks of the inerrancy of revelational
as opposed to nonrevelational material in scripture.   The latter would
include matters of history, geography, cosmology, etc.
      How do these limited-inerrantists know to draw the line where
they do, at religious material?   Would-be biblicists still, they maintain that scripture itself mandates such a plumbline.   "The Biblical
writers make it clear that their purpose was to report the happenings and meaning of the redemptive acts of God in history so that
men might be made wise unto salvation." (Fuller)[15]   Reference is
usually made to passages like II Timothy 3:15-16, where the biblical
writer describes the usefulness of scripture for (religious) instruction.   Yet such passages do *not* say that the other (e.g., geograph-

ical, cosmological, chronological) assertions of scripture need *not* be
believed.   Why do limited inerrantists feel compelled to take seriously the literal propositional sense of I Timothy 3:15-16 (as far as it
goes), but *not* of passages making historical and other factual statements?   I suggest that they do so on grounds quite different from
the biblicism they think to espouse.

In his famous essay "Is Exegesis without Presuppositions Possible?" Rudolf Bultmann pointed out the inevitability (and propriety)
of the "hermeneutical circle" in which the exegete stands. What he
learns from the Bible (or any other text) depends on the "pre-
understanding," or type of concern, with which he approaches the
text.   In other words, what does the exegete want to know when he
comes to the Bible?   Everyone agrees that his concern is one of
human existence and its possibilities, or in other words "What must
I do to be saved?"   Even the strictest inerrantist will admit this,
since his defense of all biblical statements is admittedly intended as
a safeguard for the possibility of getting a reliable biblical answer
to this question.   What Bultmann (and the advocates of the New
Hermeneutic) conclude from this is that details tangential to this
saving purpose (e.g., historical and cosmological information) may
be safely disregarded.   This is what limited inerrantists have done
implicitly in their particular limitation.   What concerns them is revelational material, so the rest can be dropped as at least potentially
"errant."

Strict inerrantist R. C. Sproul is clear in his perception of this
point:

> The . . . "norm" of Scripture is reduced *de facto* to that
> content relating to faith and practice. This immediately raises
> the hermeneutical question concerning what parts of Scripture
> deal with faith. . . . [The] principle of the reduction of canon
> to matters of "faith" is precisely the chief operative in Bult-
> mann's hermeneutic. Bultmann thinks we must clear away the
> prescientific and faulty historical "husk" of Scripture to get
> to the viable kernel of "faith."[16]

To approach this from a slightly different angle, let us focus on
Pinnock's talk about the writers' intention. When the emphasis is
shifted in this manner a change occurs which is probably more significant than the limited inerrantists realize. As James Barr points
out, belief directed to the *intent* of the writer is thus directed to
an internal, mental referent rather than an external, factual referent.   To be consistent, one must now ask *not*, "Did Jesus really
walk on water?" but rather, "What is the theological point Mark
intended us to get by including (or inventing!) this story?"[17] Why
could not *any* historical account, even the resurrection itself, be
included at least potentially, among the errors "contained but not
taught" in scripture? Why not demythologize? Sproul is exactly
right.   It is on the basis of this distinction that Bultmann is able
to dispense with the bodily resurrection of Jesus. It is a legend,
but so what? Its normative "intent" is the message that in the kerygma we are offered a new possibility of existence.

No limited-inerrantist Evangelical wishes to go quite this far:

> To be sure, God revealed himself in the events of redemptive
> history—e.g., the Fall, the Flood, the call of Abraham, the

Exodus . . . and many others; if some aspect of these events which is an essential of revelation, did not happen, then it would destroy the truth of Scripture just as much as if historical reasoning should show that Jesus did not rise from the dead.. (Fuller)[18]

Now the viability of an Evangelical theology is dependent upon the basic historicality of the Bible story. . . . (Goldingay)[19]

(But of course even Bultmann admitted that the factual *das* of the existence of Jesus was necessary for theology, even if we had no *was*, or specific content data about Jesus.)   Why do these limited inerrantists draw a line even *here*?

It will no doubt be used as a *reductio ad absurdum* argument against such a view that nothing in their doctrine of inerrancy would stop them in principle from admitting that the resurrection, or even the existence, of Jesus is a dispensable historical "term" rather than an indispensable inerrant "subject" in Pinnock's terms.   This objective misses a crucial point, but makes one as well.   First, one's doctrine of inerrancy is not the only theological reason one might have to affirm the historical reality of some biblical events.   A line might be drawn on such matters on other bases than a doctrine of scripture.   One might decide that the logic of the Christian system as a whole (rather than a doctrine of scripture) demands the historicity of a few key events such as the incarnation and resurrection, leaving most other matters up for grabs.   (Belief in the doctrine of inerrancy is itself an example of making assertions about matters of historical fact on the basis of the perceived demands of faith.   I suggest that faith might demand a more modest list of assertions.)   But the corollary of all this is that if for various reasons one did *not* feel that faith demanded even, say, the historicity of the resurrection, a postmodern doctrine of inerrancy could accommodate even this view!   "Inerrancy of intention" does logically allow for demythologizing.

Limited-inerrantists have bought themselves considerable critical freedom, though most are too squeamish to make much use of it. This is why so many of their "critical scholars" turn out to be "maximal conservatives" (as James Barr calls them), using criticism to defend traditional positions on dating, authorship, and historicity held out of nostalgia more than anything else.   John Goldingay has seen the implication of limited inerrancy (though I do not believe he uses this exact term for it), and suggests that Evangelicals should at least consider using "radical criticism."

What does all this have to say about a postmodern Evangelical understanding of the connotation-word "inerrancy"?   As formulated by Fuller, Pinnock, and others, "inerrancy" need denote only some kind of assent to the "intended teaching" of the biblical writers. Inerrancy itself thus dictates *absolutely nothing* about the factual or historical elements of the text!   Again, please note, postmodern Evangelical reworking of the term does not logically necessitate the most radical theological position; rather it can accommodate even such a position, though one might have good theological reasons for "plugging in" a rather conservative content as most limited-inerrantist Evangelicals do.   But in either case, one would be genuinely Evangelical.

Lastly, we come to consider the question of canonical unity in the Bible. Traditionally, "canon" has implied for Evangelical theology a content to this effect: the sixty-six books of the Bible provide us with a uniform though multifaceted set of teachings with which to govern faith and life. This understanding at least theoretically allowed one to say "the Bible says" on any question, i.e., there was a single, authoritative biblical doctrine or ethical principle to be obeyed/applied. Remember, Mouw included the phrase "the Bible says" as a key feature characterizing the Evangelical attitude toward scripture.

The starting point for making room for new theological contents for terms like "the Bible says" is well presented in a position statement by New Testament scholar David M. Scholer:

> My confession that the scripture is the Word of God involves a commitment to the unity of scripture. Such unity, however, must be expressed in terms and relationships which are fully honest to contextual exegesis and which do not impose a false concept of unity on the scripture. . . . the scripture texts themselves [must] define the unity of the canon in the midst of the historical and theological diversity expressed there.[20]

In other words, this unity must come at the end, not the beginning of the exegetical process.

What if exegesis discloses real ethical and theological differences between biblical writers? If the reader is not persuaded that this is the case, then he need not make much of a change in what it means for him to say "the Bible says." But, if like myself and several recent Evangelical biblical scholars you do see real disunity in the Bible, there is a new kind of content that may be applied to the Evangelical connotation-phrase "the Bible says." The Bible could be said to canonize a plurality of opinions, any of which would therefore be legitimate for Christians to hold today. It is in this sense that one could assent to the "inerrancy" (i.e., in this context, the "theological legitimacy") of all passages whether they agree or not.

Now instead of being a rule of faith, the canon is a rule of faiths. Because of the authorizing role of the biblical canon, various positions arising from any of its diverse strands may be considered legitimate. Thus the Bible forms one roof under which various types of Christian faith may live as one happy family. Here we meet with another issue very important to the re-thinking of Evangelical hermeneutics. Must a hermeneutical model, to be authoritative, ensure uniformity of conclusions? Evangelicals seem to assume that it must (though in fact none ever has). But again, this bears consideration.

As might be expected, this basic approach admits of some variation. John Goldingay maintains that there is a basic religious message in the Bible which finds different expression in different situations. He gives the Paul vs. James problem as an example here. Each expression is legitimate as a theological norm for modern Christians, who should align themselves with the idiom most appropriate to their situation. Thus far Goldingay seems to be admitting no real disunity, but the logic of his position indicates that even a formulation of how one is justified (i.e., by faith alone, or not) is an only relatively valid theological datum.

Goldingay points out that

> . . . if the varying messages did reflect "irreconcilable the-ological contradictions" [Käsemann] then it is difficult to see how the whole could be inspired and infallible. [Still,] This does not . . . imply that every message is equally near to the heart of divine truth. . . . sometimes we will be able to estab-lish some hierarchy amongst the various expressions of the will of God.[21]

He illustrates this with Matthew's secondary "except for *porneia*" qualification of Jesus' divorce prohibition, and with the emergence of "early catholicism" as an ossification of earlier Christian dynamism. It would be interesting to see just how far Goldingay would be will-ing to go relativizing theological expressions, e.g., of Christology, in the New Testament. Are some of them only relatively adequate, and thus not literally true? At any rate, Goldingay sees all these "situational responses" as inspired and authorized as legitimate by virtue of their presence in the New Testament.

Moving a bit more toward the left, we come to James D. G. Dunn. He frankly admits that there is no one orthodoxy present in the early Christianity represented in the New Testament, with the clear result that there can be none today either. Instead we find in the New Testament a rather narrow "unifying center," i.e., "Jesus-the-man-now-exalted" which amounts to "the conviction that in Jesus we still have a paradigm for man's relationship to God and man's rela-tionship to man . . . (whether in these or alternative words). . ."[22] Dunn seems to skirt the issue of the nature of religious language, but he appears by such an admission to have moved in an obviously Liberal direction. This is even more obvious when he says that all New Testament theological models, earlier ones as well as later de-velopments, are valid. Since they do not agree (as he himself points out), they cannot all be true in any literal fashion. So Dunn does not seem to mean that one should hold such positions as literal "di-dactic thought models" or "propositions."

But Dunn is not canonizing the bare principle of diversity. Dunn says that the fact of a unifying center in the New Testament also serves to circumscribe the circumference of legitimate diversity. No theology could claim the New Testament's blessing that did not hold to the unifying center. But theology is not simply restricted to parroting those options actually spelled out in the canon. Diversity there provides a precedent for creativity in theology today. Dunn claims that

> The more we believe that the Spirit of God inspired the writers of the New Testament to speak the Word of God to people of the . . . first century A.D., reinterpreting faith and lifestyle diversely to diverse circumstances the more ac-ceptance of the New Testament canon requires us to be open to the Spirit to reinterpret in similar or equivalent ways in the twentieth century.[23]

Thus, Dunn seems willing to allow that we may come up with new models for our day:

If the New Testament canon does not support the sole legitimacy of only one of the subsequent developments (Catholic
orthodoxy), neither does it restrict legitimacy only to the
developments which are actually enshrined within its pages.[24]

Yet the New Testament models are the "original traditions," on which
all other developments must be "variations," and with which they
must be in "primary dialogue."[25]
    Admittedly this is quite a different picture from that of tradition-
al Evangelicalism, where the phrase "the Bible says" was expected
to end with only one option. But I am not as certain that the suggestion of Dunn and Goldingay differs all that much from what has
actually been happening in Evangelical hermeneutics all along. Indeed it is a well-known embarrassment that a doctrine of scripture
thought to be the one sure guardian against doctrinal error has
been unable to ensure exegetical agreement on any single issue!
Holding to the same doctrine of scripture, conservative exegetes opt
for Calvinism or Arminianism, Covenant or Dispensational theology,
pre- or post-tribulationism, pre- or amillennialism, infant or adult
baptism, etc. So much for the "perspicuity of scripture"! Yet
Evangelicals already tolerate many of these differences, even admitting that the ambiguity of scripture allows for a variety of conclusions on "nonessentials." This is in effect to make virtue of necessity; the fact that scripture is ambiguous at a certain point means
that such a point *must* be nonessential, since scripture would certainly clarify an essential matter. By definition, then, nothing left
unclear in the Bible could be essential.
    I submit that "the existence of ambiguity in the canon giving rise
to a legitimate espousal of diverse opinions among Christians" is not
qualitatively different from "the existence of diverse opinions in the
canon which are legitimately reflected by diverse opinions among
Christians." And if it turned out that this diversity of opinions
concerned vital issues like Christology, would this issue not automatically become a "nonessential" as to the precise formulation one
held? I believe this will have to be admitted as long as we are talking about what a doctrine of scripture would demand. Again, I will
agree that logically separate theological reasons might (but might
not) move one to press for one particular Christology as normative.
But this would be a different question, not decided by one's doctrine of scripture. Once again I am pointing out the diversity of
possible contents of Evangelical connotation words.
    Now one might qualify this model along the lines suggested by
John Goldingay or Charles Kraft, i.e., that some of these canonized
options are more or less close to the heart of divine truth. But, it
seems to me, what one could not do and remain an Evangelical would
be to deem some of the various New Testament opinions as being so
radically contradictory that some must be rejected. This would be
the point of division between the kind of view represented by Dunn
and Goldingay, and the famous "canon within the canon" approach
of Käsemann. (Incidentally, Dunn also uses the term "canon within
the canon," but not in the same sense.)[26]
    I mentioned in my discussion of both Dunn and Goldingay that
their model of the canon raises the issue of religious language. For
instance, if Mark's Christology apparently without pre-existence is

as sufficient a doctrinal view as John's Christology of the Incarnate Word, can both of them be true in any literal, propositional sense? I believe that Dunn's and Goldingay's views tend logically toward the idea that the New Testament doctrinal data represent symbols, not pictures. Though they are informative in the sense of helpfully articulating something about God, they are not propositionally descriptive of him. This is obviously very analogous to Paul Tillich's view that the Bible renders symbols which participate in the Holy but are not identical to it, which reveal the divine Mystery but do not make it less mysterious.

Here again Evangelicals already have a conceptual base from which to approach this understanding. Francis Schaeffer indicates that our concepts of God are "truly true" though admittedly not "exhaustively true." What I am suggesting is along the same general lines, though my proposal would involve more relativization or deliteralization than Schaeffer has in mind. Keep in mind also that the less severe one judged the differences between biblical writers to be, the less their various formulations would have to be relativized.

In the final analysis, then, in the context of a really new, postmodern Evangelicalism, one could definitely go on saying "the Bible says," but there might be a few ways to end the sentence. There would also be a bit of room left for the guidance of the Holy Spirit, which is not after all particularly un-Evangelical.

Throughout this book I have criticized several important elements of the Born Again Christianity in which I have spent many years. In place of these inadequacies I have sought to suggest new ways of being Evangelical. Mainly this involved the development of a framework according to which Evangelical identity hinges more on a style than a particular theological content. Though this style certainly fits well with traditional Evangelical theology and spirituality, it is not inseparable from these. It could accommodate a spectrum of other theologies and spiritualities. Thus this study may be seen as a first preparatory step to a really new, postmodern Evangelicalism, or even to several postmodern Evangelicalisms.

It is the irony of religious union movements (e.g., the Plymouth Brethren, the Unification Church, the Baha'i Faith) that their platform for reconciliation becomes merely the ideology of one more new sect. But I am not so naive, at least on this point. It is quite obvious to me that most Evangelicals will not accept my agenda for a "really new Evangelicalism." But the viability of the proposal does not depend on its universal acceptance. Remember, I have stressed pluralism throughout. Thus my purpose will be accomplished if I have demonstrated to those few(?) disillusioned individuals ready to leave Evangelical faith, that there is still hope. Their Evangelical identity can be redeemed, "born again," if they want it.

In many ways, what all this amounts to is a return to earth, a renunciation of the Promethean superiority to which Evangelical rhetoric often lays claim. It means an admission that "Born Again Christians" are not supposed to be problem-free, always "victorious." They don't have all the answers, or even the means to get all of them. They're not the enlightened elect, outside of whose magic circle everyone is damned and in darkness. Their beliefs are not so unambiguously compelling as to make everyone else an intellectually dishonest bigot.   They are in fact only people, people who have faith in Jesus Christ, and they are not unique even in this. A really new Evangelicalism will realize these things and take them into theological consideration.

In the words of my title, what all of this means is going "beyond born again."   The equivocal character of the phrase has probably not been lost on the reader.   Do I intend that "born again" is one of the "childish things" to be "put away"?   One might face the problems I have set forth and decide to seek an entirely different form of faith.   Then perhaps one goes beyond born again in the sense of repudiation.   I don't think this would be so terrible.   I am not trying to prescribe an Evangelicalism which still considers itself "the only true faith."   I am only trying to outline an option for those who see the need for sweeping changes yet wish to maintain their identity as Evangelicals.   In this latter case, going beyond born again means that the born again experience must be put behind one's self as any starting point must be.   The "childish things," in this case, are the psychologically immature "hard religious line," the elitist exclusivism, the self-contradictory version of biblical author- ity, and the manipulative apologetics.   Isn't it time for something better?

"Therefore let us leave the elementary teachings about Christ and go on to maturity" (Hebrews 5:1, NIV).

FOOTNOTE REFERENCES

Introduction

[1]Malcolm Boyd, *Christian, Its Meanings in an Age of Future Shock* (New York: Hawthorn Books, 1975), p. 70.

[2]Clark H. Pinnock, *Biblical Revelation—The Foundation of Christian Theology* (Chicago: Moody Press, 1976), p. 14.

[3]Carl F. H. Henry, *Frontiers in Modern Theology* (Chicago: Moody Press, 1968), pp. 152-153.

Chapter 1

[1]Larry Norman, "The Great American Novel" (Strawbed Music, 1972).

[2]Frank and Ida Mae Hammond, *Pigs in the Parlor, A Practical Guide to Deliverance* (Kirkwood, MO: Impact Books, 1973), p. 18.

[3]Bill Bright, *How to Walk in the Spirit* ([n.p.] Campus Crusade for Christ, 1971), p. 35.

[4]L. Gilbert Little, *Nervous Christians* (Chicago: Moody Press, 1956), p. 12.

[5]Jay Adams, *Christ and Your Problems* (Nutley, NJ: Presbyterian & Reformed Publishing Co., 1971), p. 18.

[6]Ronald M. Enroth, Edward E. Ericson, Jr., and C. Breckinridge Peters, *The Jesus People* (Grand Rapids: Eerdmans, 1972), p. 162.

[7]Daniel B. Stevick, *Beyond Fundamentalism* (Richmond, VA: John Knox Press, 1964), p. 188; see also Keith Miller and Bruce Larson, *The Edge of Adventure* (Waco, TX: Word Books, 1977), pp. 171.

[8]Bill Bright, *How to Experience God's Love and Forgiveness* ([n.p.] Campus Crusade for Christ, 1971), pp. 6, 14-16.

[9]Tim LaHaye, *Ten Steps to Victory over Depression* (Grand Rapids: Zondervan, 1974), p. 18.

[10]John R. Rice, *When a Christian Sins* (Chicago: Moody Press, 1954), p. 41.

[11]Jay Adams, *The Use of the Scriptures in Counseling* (Grand Rapids: Baker Book House, 1976), p. 12.

[12]Little, p. 18; cf. also e.g., pp. 25, 64.

[13]R. B. Thieme, *Satanic Plot* (Houston, TX: Berachah Church, 1971), p. 10.

[14]Don Basham, *Deliver Us from Evil* (New York: Bantam Books, 1977), pp. 105, 108; see also Pat Brooks, *Using Your Spiritual Authority* (Monroeville, PA: Banner, 1973), pp. 67-69, 74; see also Frank and Ida Mae Hammond, pp. 113ff.

[15]Rice, p. 120.

[16]Rice, pp. 122-123.

[17]Thieme, p. 21.

[18]Vernon Grounds, *Emotional Problems and the Gospel* (Grand Rapids: Zondervan, 1976), p. 102; see also Phillip J. Swihart, *How to Live with Your Feelings* (Downers Grove, IL: IVP [Inter Varsity Press], 1977), p. 56.

[19]Phillip J. Swihart, p. 56; also see Merlin R. Carothers, *Bringing Heaven into Hell* (Old Tappan, NJ: Fleming H. Revell Co., 1976), p. 65.

[20]Peter Gillquist, *Handbook for Spiritual Survival* (Grand Rapids: Zondervan, 1975), p. 82.

[21]Jay Adams, *What do You do When You Become Depressed?* (Nutley, NJ: Presbyterian & Reformed Publishing Co., 1975), n.p.

[22]Grounds, pp. 27ff.

[23]Adams, *Use of the Scriptures*, pp. 4, 5, 6.

[24]Grounds, p. 18.

[25]Bill Gothard, *Institute in Basic Youth Conflicts* (Seminar Syllabus) (LaGrange, IL: Institute in Basic Youth Conflicts, [n.d.]), n.p.

[26]Thieme, p. 9.

[27]George W. Dollar, *A History of Fundamentalism in America* (Greenville, SC: Bob Jones University Press, 1973), p. 269.

[28]Little, p. 71.

[29]Walter J. Hollenweger, *The Pentecostals* (Minneapolis: Augsburg Publishing House, 1973), p. 380.

[30]Sigmund Freud, *New Introductory Lectures on Psychoanalysis*, quoted in James D. Mallory, *The Kink and I* (Wheaton, IL: Victor Books, 1975), p. 67.

[31]Gillquist, pp. 36, 47.

[32]Quoted in Wilfred Bockelman, *Gothard, the Man and His Ministry: An Evaluation* (Santa Barbara: Quill Publications, 1976), p. 93.

[33]Larry Norman, "Reader's Digest" (Strawbed Music, 1972).

[34]Mary Douglas, "Primitive Thought-Worlds," in Roland Robertson (ed.), *Sociology of Religion* (Baltimore: Penguin Books, 1969) pp. 79-99.

[35]Merlin R. Carothers, *Prison to Praise* (Plainfield, NJ: Logos International, 1971), p. 66.

[36]Carothers, *Bringing Heaven*, p. 90.

[37]Frances Gardner Hunter, *Praise The Lord Anyway* (New York: Family Library, 1973), pp. 29-31.

[38]Quoted in Bockelman, *Gothard*, p. 117.

[39]Eli S. Chesen, *Religion May Be Hazardous to Your Health* (New York: Macmillan Publishing Co., 1974), p. 102.

[40]Merlin R. Carothers, *Power in Praise* (Plainfield, NJ: Logos International, 1972), p. 79.

[41]Ibid., p. 104.

[42]Carothers, *Prison to Praise*, p. 68.

[43]Carothers, *Power in Praise*, p. 108.

[44]Gillquist, p. 88.

[45]LaHaye, p. 15.

[46]Quoted in Bockelman, *Gothard*, p. 117.

[47]John P. Kildahl, *The Psychology of Speaking in Tongues* (New York: Harper & Row, 1972), p. 50.

[48]Adams, *Use of the Scriptures*, p. 37.

[49]Little, pp. 50, 89.

[50]Gothard, n.p.

[51]Mabel Williamson, *"Have We No Right?"* (Chicago: Moody Press, 1957), (cover blurb).

[52]Swihart, p. 12.

[53]Gothard, n.p.

[54]Rice, pp. 11, 110.

[55]Carothers, *Bringing Heaven*, pp. 62, 38.

[56]Adams, *What do You do?*, p. 10.

[57]Gillquist, p. 57.

[58]Kenneth E. Hagin, *Authority of the Believer* (Tulsa, OK: Kenneth Hagin Evangelistic Assn., 1975), p. 21.

[59]Kenneth E. Hagin, *What Faith Is* (Tulsa, OK: Kenneth Hagin Evangelistic Assn., 1976); also "Practicing Faith" (taped lecture); see also Carothers, *Prison to Praise*, p. 68.

[60]Frank and Ida Mae Hammond, p. 10.

[61]Thieme, p. 7.

[62]Swihart, p. 13.

[63]Frank and Ida Mae Hammond, pp. 113ff.

[64]See list of safeguards in Brooks, p. 98; see also Basham, p. 148.

[65]Carothers, *Bringing Heaven*, p. 93.

[66]Gillquist, p. 45.

[67]Rice, pp. 35ff; see also Gillquist, p. 45.

[68]Gothard, n.p.

[69]Gothard, n.p.; see also Carothers, *Bringing Heaven*, p. 100.

[70]Brooks, p. 45.

[71]Carothers, *Bringing Heaven*, p. 90.

[72]Carothers, *Bringing Heaven*, p. 103.

[73]Carothers, *Power in Praise*, p. 84.

[74]Bright, *How to Walk in the Spirit*, p. 42.

[75]Carothers, *Bringing Heaven*, p. 77.

[76]Gillquist, pp. 102-103.

[77]Rice, pp. 122-123.

[78]Gordon W. Allport, *The Individual and His Religion* (New York: Macmillan Publishing Co., 1974), p. 62.

[79]Paul Tillich, *Dynamics of Faith* (New York: Harper & Row, 1958), p. 106.

[80]Chesen, p. 27.

[81]"The New Rebel Cry: Jesus is Coming!," *Time* (June 21, 1971), p. 63.

[82]Kildahl, p. 60.

[83]Quoted in Bockelman, *Gothard*, pp. 140-141.

[84]O. Quentin Hyder, *The Christian's Handbook of Psychiatry* (Old Tappan, NJ: Fleming H. Revell Co., 1974), p. 153.

[85]Bruce Larson, *No Longer Strangers* (Waco, TX: Word Books, 1974), p. 118; see also Miller and Bruce Larson, p. 182.

[86]Bruce Larson, p. 117.

[87]Miller and Bruce Larson, pp. 121, 180, 193.

[88]Bruce Larson, pp. 22ff.

[89]Keith Miller, *The Becomers* (Waco, TX: Word Books, 1977), n.p.

[90]Hyder, p. 158.

[91]Mallory, pp. 71-72.

[92]Bruce Larson, p. 94.

[93]Hyder, p. 186.

[94]Gary Collins, *How to Be a People Helper* (Santa Ana, CA: Vision House, 1976), p. 170.

[95]Mallory, p. 75.

[96]Yves Congar quoted in John A. T. Robinson, *Honest to God* (Philadelphia: Westminster Press, 1963), p. 137.

[97]Miller and Bruce Larson, pp. 189-190; see also Cecil Osborne, *The Art of Understanding Yourself* (Grand Rapids: Zondervan, 1976), p. 20; see also Mallory, p. 55.

[98]Bruce Larson, p. 73.

[99]Osborne, p. 16.

[100]Miller and Bruce Larson, p. 190.

[101]Bruce Larson, pp. 51, 55.

[102]Swihart, pp. 21, 36, 45.

[103]Tim LaHaye, *Transformed Temperaments* (Wheaton, IL: Tyndale House, 1974), p. 18.

[104]Van A. Harvey, *The Historian and the Believer* (New York: Macmillan Co., 1972), pp. 187-194.

[105]Little, p. 102.

[106]Collins, p. 170; see also Bockelman, p. 53.

[107]Joseph Fletcher, *Situation Ethics, the New Morality* (Philadelphia: Westminster Press, 1966), p. 158.

[108]Abraham Maslow, *Religions, Values, and Peak-Experiences* (New York: Viking Press, 1974), p. 52; cf. also Allport, p. 3.

[109]"Obey Thy Husband," *Time* (May 20, 1974), p. 64.

[110]J. Rinzema, *The Sexual Revolution* (Grand Rapids: Eerdmans, 1974), p. 105.

[111]Fletcher, p. 60.

[112]Chesen, p. 84.

[113]Donald G. Bloesch, *The Evangelical Renaissance* (Grand Rapids: Eerdmans, 1973), p. 56.

[114]James Barr, *The Bible and the Modern World* (New York: Harper & Row, 1973), p. 142.

[115]Charles H. Kraft, *Christianity in Culture: A Study in Dynamic Biblical Theologizing in Cross-Cultural Perspective* (Maryknoll: Orbis Books, 1979), Ch. 7, "Supracultural Meanings via Cultural Forms," pp. 116-146, especially pp. 131-143.

Chapter 2

[1]See Peter L. Berger and Thomas Luckmann, *The Social Construction of Reality* (Garden City, NY: Doubleday & Co., 1967).

[2]Robert S. Ellwood, *One Way: The Jesus Movement and Its Meaning* (Englewood Cliffs, NJ: Prentice-Hall, 1973), p. 31.

[3]"Counting Souls," *Time* (October 4, 1976), p. 75.

[4]James Barr, *Fundamentalism* (London: SCM Press, 1977), p. 104.

[5]Bob Larson, *Rock & Roll, the Devil's Diversion* (McCook, NE: Bob Larson, 1970), pp. 159, 155, 159.

[6]Frank Garlock, *The Big Beat, a Rock Blast* (Greenville, SC: Bob Jones University Press, 1971), p. 26.

[7]Francis A. Schaeffer, *Art & the Bible* (Downers Grove, IL: IVP, 1977), p. 43.

[8]Bockelman, p. 93.

[9]Kenneth G. Howkins, *The Challenge of Religious Studies* (Downers Grove, IL: IVP, 1973), pp. 3, 5.

[10]Leon Festinger, Henry W. Riecken, and Stanley Schachter,

When Prophecy Fails (New York: Harper & Row, 1964), p. 28.

[11]Ellwood, p. 34.

[12]John Lofland, *Doomsday Cult, A Study of Conversion, Proselytization, and Maintenance of Faith* (Englewood Cliffs, NJ: Prentice-Hall, 1966), pp. 209, 208.

[13]Francis A. Schaeffer, *Escape from Reason* (Downers Grove, IL: IVP, 1977), pp. 82, 61, 66.

[14]James W. Sire, *The Universe Next Door: A Basic Worldview Catalog* (Downers Grove, IL: IVP, 1977), p. 14.

[15]Os Guiness, *The Dust of Death* (Downers Grove: IVP, 1973), p. 317.

[16]Walter R. Martin, *The Kingdom of the Cults* (Minneapolis: Bethany Fellowship, 1974), pp. 25-26.

[17]James Bjornstad, *Twentieth Century Prophecy* (New York: Pyramid Books, 1970), pp. 120, 256.

[18]John Weldon and Zola Levitt, *UFO's, What on Earth is Happening?* (New York: Bantam Books, 1976), p. 144.

[19]Berger and Luckmann, p. 103.

[20]Ellwood, p. 31.

[21]Arthur Wallis, in Preface to Frank Bartleman, *Another Wave Rolls In!* (Northridge, CA: Voice Publications, 1970), p. 5.

[22]Francis A. Schaeffer, *How Should We Then Live?* (Old Tappan, NJ: Fleming H. Revell Co., 1976), p. 13.

[23]Robert M. Price, "The Return of the Navel: The 'Omphalos' Argument in Contemporary Creationism," *Creation/Evolution*, Fall, 1980; "Old-Time Religion and the New Physics," *Creation/Evolution*, Summer, 1982; "Scientific Creationism and the Science of Creative Intelligence," *Creation/Evolution*, Winter 1982; "Creationism and Fundamentalist Apologetics: Two Branches of the Same Tree," *Creation/Evolution*, Fall, 1984.
Really, any issue of this journal contains abundant and detailed refutations of the so-called Creation Science and its fraudulent claims. In fact, it's like shooting fish in a barrel.

[24]Jan Vansina, *Oral Tradition as History* (Madison: University of Wisconsin Press, 1985), pp. 117-118.

[25]Ralph Martin, *Unless the Lord Build the House: The Church and the New Pentecost* (Notre Dame: Ave Maria Press, 1977), p. 11.

[26]David F. Wright, "James Barr on 'Fundamentalism'—a Review Article," *Themelios* (Fall, 1978), p. 88.

Chapter 3

[1]See John Warwick Montgomery, *Principalities and Powers: A New Look at the World of the Occult* (Minneapolis: Bethany Fellowship, 1975), pp. 168-170.

[2]See *Demon Experience [A Compilation]* (Wheaton, IL: Tyndale

House, 1972) for examples.

3Peter L. Berger, *A Rumor of Angels, Modern Society and the Rediscovery of the Supernatural* (Garden City: Doubleday, 1970), p. 42.

4John Warwick Montgomery (ed.), *Demon Possession* (Minneapolis: Bethany Fellowship, 1976), pp. 260-261.

Chapter 4

1Richard J. Coleman, *Issues of Theological Warfare, Evangelicals and Liberals* (Grand Rapids: Eerdmans, 1974), p. 44.

2Wilhelm Herrmann, *The Communion of the Christian with God* (Philadelphia: Fortress Press, 1971), p. 283.

3I owe the analogy of the "imaginary playmate" to Jeff Gregg, a student of psychology.

4Herrmann, p. 281.

5C. S. Lewis, *The Screwtape Letters* (New York: Macmillan Co., 1970), pp. 21-22.

6See Chapter 12, "Claims to 'Know' Christ," in Don Cupitt, *Christ and the Hiddenness of God* (Philadelphia: Westminster Press, 1971), pp. 184-197.

7Miles J. Stanford, *The Green Letters* (Grand Rapids: Zondervan, 1976), p. 37. This book is also current under the title *Principles of Spiritual Growth.*

8Watchman Nee, *The Normal Christian Life* (Wheaton: Tyndale House, and Fort Washington: Christian Literature Crusade, 1983), pp. 181-182.

9Stanford, p. 36.

10Johannes Weiss, *Jesus' Proclamation of the Kingdom of God* (Philadelphia: Fortress Press, 1971), pp. 74-76.

11Rudolf Bultmann, *Theology of the New Testament*, vol. 1 (New York: Charles Scribner's Sons, 1951), p. 332.

12Claude Levi-Strauss, *Structural Anthropology* (Garden City: Doubleday, 1967), Chapter X, "The Effectiveness of Symbols," pp. 181-201.

13Nee, p. 75.

Chapter 5

1Clark H. Pinnock, *Set Forth Your Case* (Chicago: Moody Press, 1978), p. 99.

2Josh McDowell, *More Evidence That Demands a Verdict* ([n.p.]: Campus Crusade for Christ International, 1975), p. 205.

3John Warwick Montgomery, *History & Christianity* (Downers Grove, IL: IVP, 1974), p. 37.

4A. H. McNeile, *An Introduction to the Study of the New Testa-*

ment, second edition revised by C. S. C. Williams (Oxford at the Clarendon Press, 1953), p. 54.

[5]F. F. Bruce, *Tradition: Old and New* (Grand Rapids: Zondervan, 1970), p. 41; Jon A. Buell and O. Quentin Hyder, *Jesus: God, Ghost or Guru?* (Grand Rapids: Zondervan, 1978), pp. 70-71.

[6]Gershom Scholem, *Sabbatai Sevi, the Mystical Messiah* (Princeton: Princeton University Press, 1973), pp. 252, 265.

[7]Ibid., pp. 390, 535, 375, 605.

[8]Gershom Scholem, *Major Trends in Jewish Mysticism* (New York: Schocken Books, 1973), pp. 82, 99.

[9]Vittorio Lanternari, *The Religions of the Oppressed. A Study of Modern Messianic Cults* (New York: New American Library, 1965), pp. 25-26ff; see also G. C. Oosthuizen, *Post-Christianity in Africa* (Grand Rapids: Eerdmans, 1968), p. 40; see also Marie-Louise Martin, *Kimbangu, An African Prophet and his Church* (Grand Rapids: Eerdmans, 1976), pp. 73-75.

[10]Robert A. Moore and Robert M. Price, "Branham's Legacy," forthcoming in *Pneuma: The Journal of the Society for Pentecostal Studies*; see also C. Douglas Weaver, *The Healer-Prophet, William Marrion Branham: A Study of the Prophetic in American Pentecostalism* (Macon: Mercer University Press, 1987), p. 156.

[11]Ed Sanders, *The Family* (New York: Avon Books, 1972), p. 133.

[12]Montgomery, *History & Christianity*, p. 32.

[13]Ibid., p. 37.

[14]Edwin M. Yamauchi, *Jesus, Zoroaster, Socrates, Buddha, Muhammad* (Downers Grove: IVP, 1977), p. 9.

[15]Wilbur Smith, *Have You Considered Him? A Brief for Christianity* (Downers Grove: IVP, 1972), pp. 5-6.

[16]Edwin M. Yamauchi, "A Secret Gospel of Jesus as 'Magus'? A Review of Some of the Recent Works of Morton Smith," *Christian Scholars Review*, Vol. 4, No. 3, 1975, p. 248.

[17]Yamauchi, *Jesus, Zoroaster*, p. 13.

[18]F. F. Bruce, *The New Testament Documents: Are They Reliable?* (Grand Rapids: Eerdmans, 1972), p. 45.

[19]Scholem, *Sabbatai Sevi*, p. 252.

[20]Hippolyte Delehaye, *The Legends of the Saints* (Notre Dame: University of Notre Dame Press, 1961), pp. 16-17.

[21]Bruce, *New Testament Documents*, p. 46.

[22]Scholem, *Sabbatai Sevi*, p. 612.

[23]See Leon Festinger, Henry W. Riecken, and Stanley Schachter, *When Prophecy Fails. A Social and Psychological Study of a Modern Group that Predicted the Destruction of the World* (New York: Harper & Row, 1976).

[24]Scholem, *Sabbatai Sevi*, p. 215.

[25]Ibid., p. 411.

[26]Henry Ansgar Kelly, *The Devil, Demonology and Witchcraft: The Development of Christian Belief in Evil Spirits* (Garden City: Doubleday, 1974), p. 95.

[27]Haim Shaked, *The Life of the Sudanese Mahdi* (New Brunswick: Transaction Books, 1978), pp. 60-61.

[28]Lucian, *The Death of Peregrinus*, sections 37-43, Lionel Casson (ed. and trans.), *Selected Satires of Lucian* (New York: W. W. Norton & Co., 1968), pp. 379-380.

[29]David F. Hall, Susan J. McFeaters, and Elizabeth F. Loftus, "Alterations in Recollections of Unusual and Unexpected Events," *Journal of Scientific Exploration*, Vol. 1, Sampler, 1987, p. 2.

[30]Bruce, *New Testament Documents*, p. 46.

[31]F. F. Bruce, *Paul and Jesus* (Grand Rapids: Eerdmans, 1974), p. 70.

[32]I. Howard Marshall, *I Believe in the Historical Jesus* (Grand Rapids: Eerdmans, 1977), p. 195; see also Montgomery, *History and Christianity*, pp. 37-38.

[33]Vincent Taylor, *The Formation of the Gospel Tradition* (London: Macmillan & Co., 1957), p. 41.

[34]Robert D. Smith, *Comparative Miracles* (St. Louis, MO: B. Herder Book Co., 1965), pp. 131-132.

[35]Vansina, pp. 129-130.

[36]George Eldon Ladd, *The New Testament and Criticism* (Grand Rapids: Eerdmans, 1978), pp. 153, 163.

Chapter 6

[1]J. N. D. Anderson, *The Evidence for the Resurrection* (Downers Grove: IVP, 1974), p. 9.

[2]Ibid.

[3]John Warwick Montgomery, *Where is History Going?* (Grand Rapids: Zondervan, 1972), p. 82.

[4]Michael Green, "Jesus in the New Testament," in Green (ed.), *The Truth of God Incarnate* (Grand Rapids: Eerdmans, 1977), p. 36.

[5]Anderson, *Evidence*, p. 11.

[6]The most convenient place to find this text is in David L. Dungan and David R. Cartlidge, *Sourcebook of Texts for the Comparative Study of the Gospels* (Missoula, MT: Scholars Press, 1974), p. 155.

[7]Ibid., pp. 295-296.

[8]Anderson, *Evidence*, p. 10.

[9]Ibid., p. 19.

[10]John R. W. Stott, *Basic Christianity* (Grand Rapids: Eerdmans, 1959), p. 51; also F. F. Bruce quotes A. T. Olmstead (*Jesus in the Light of History*, 1942, p. 248) to the same effect: "the narrative of the empty tomb in chapter xx is 'told by an undoubted eyewitness —full of life, and lacking any detail to which the sceptic might take justifiable objection'" (Bruce, *New Testament Documents*, p. 49).

[11]Dungan and Cartlidge, p. 157.

[12]Mary R. Lefkowitz and Maureen B. Fant (eds.), *Women's Life in Greece and Rome* (Baltimore: John Hopkins University Press, 1982), p. 122.

[13]Anderson, *Evidence*, p. 21.

[14]Ibid.

[15]Scholem, *Sabbatai Sevi*, pp. 417, 446.

[16]Gershom Scholem, *Kabbalah* (New York: Quadrangle/New York Times Book Co., 1973), p. 274.

[17]The Acts of Peter, translated by Wilhelm Schneemelcher, in W. Schneemelcher and Edgar Hennecke (eds.), *New Testament Apocrypha, Volume II* (Philadelphia: Westminster Press, 1965), p. 304.

[18]George Barton Cutten, *The Psychological Phenomena of Christianity* (New York: Charles Scribner's Sons, 1908), pp. 65-66.

[19]Pinnock, *Set Forth Your Case*, p. 97.

[20]C. S. Lewis, *Miracles* (New York: Macmillan Co., 1974), p. 153.

[21]Dungan and Cartlidge, pp. 51, 52, 61, 278-279.

[22]Anderson, *Evidence*, p. 26.

[23]Frank Morison, *Who Moved the Stone?* (Grand Rapids: Zondervan, 1978), p. 132.

[24]George Eldon Ladd, *I Believe in the Resurrection of Jesus* (Grand Rapids: Eerdmans, 1975), p. 23.

[25]Michael Green, *Man Alive!* (Downers Grove: IVP, 1967), p. 38.

[26]David Hume, *On Religion* (New York: Meridian Books, 1964), p. 211.

[27]See, for instance, Reuben Archer Torrey, *Difficulties in the Bible* (Chicago: Moody Press, n.d.), p. 25; Harold Lindsell, *The Battle for the Bible* (Grand Rapids: Zondervan, 1976), p. 183.

Chapter 7

[1]Montgomery, *History & Christianity*, p. 78.

[2]C. S. Lewis, *Mere Christianity* (New York: Macmillan Co., 1977), p. 56.

[3]Ethelbert Stauffer, *Jesus and His Story* (New York: Alfred A. Knopf, 1960), pp. 183-184, cited in H. J. Schoeps, *Paul, the Theology of the Apostle in the Light of Jewish Religious History* (Phila-

delphia: Westminster Press, 1961), p. 161; cited by Edwin M. Yamauchi, "Passover Plot or Easter Triumph? A Critical Review of H. Schonfield's Recent Theory," Appendix A to John Warwick Montgomery (ed.), *Christianity For the Tough-Minded* (Minneapolis: Bethany Fellowship, 1973), pp. 267-268.

[4]Jon A. Buell and O. Quentin Hyder, *Jesus: God, Ghost or Guru?* (Grand Rapids: Zondervan, 1978), pp. 34-36.

[5]Edwin M. Yamauchi, "Passover Plot or Easter Triumph?" in Montgomery, *Christianity for the Tough-Minded*, pp. 267-268.

[6]For the definitive discussion of Jewish binitarian heresies, see Alan F. Segal, *Two Powers in Heaven, Early Rabbinic Reports About Christianity and Gnosticism* (Leiden: E. J. Brill, 1977).

[7]Pinnock, *Set Forth Your Case*, p. 89.

[8]Stott, *Basic Christianity*, 1959, p. 28.

[9]John R. W. Stott, *Basic Christianity* (Downers Grove: IVP, 1978), p. 23.

[10]Stott, *Basic Christianity*, 1959, p. 28.

[11]Geza Vermes, *Jesus the Jew, A Historian's View of the Gospels* (Glasgow: Fontana/Collins, 1977), pp. 67-69.

[12]Mirza Abul-Fazi (ed.), *Sayings of the Prophet Muhammad* (New Delhi: Award Publishing House, 1980), p. 35.

[13]George Carey, *God Incarnate* (Downers Grove: IVP, 1978), p. 14.

[14]Albert Schweitzer, *Out of My Life and Thought* (New York: Meridian Books, 1963), p. 186.

Chapter 8

[1]Arthur W. Pink, *The Divine Inspiration of the Bible* (Grand Rapids: Guardian Press, 1976), p. 96.

[2]J. I. Packer, *'Fundamentalism' and the Word of God* (Grand Rapids: Eerdmans, 1960), p. 152.

[3]David H. Kelsey, *The Uses of Scripture in Recent Theology* (Philadelphia: Fortress Press, 1975), pp. 17-24.

[4]John R. W. Stott, *The Authority of the Bible* (Downers Grove, IL: IVP, 1974), p. 23; see also Jacob A. O. Preus, *It is Written* (St. Louis: Concordia Publishing House, 1971), pp. 45-46; see also Edward J. Carnell, *The Case for Orthodox Theology* (Philadelphia: Westminster Press, 1959), p. 44.

[5]Stott, *Authority of the Bible*, p. 27.

[6]Though even here care must be taken not to read one's doctrine into such passages, as in an amazing piece of exegetical ventriloquism from the *New Scofield Reference Bible*. In a note on Luke 1:3 ("It seemed good to me also having had perfect understanding of all things from the very first, to write unto thee in order, most excellent Theophilus. . . ."), the editors throw context

to the wind and announce: "'From the very first' is from the Greek *anothen* and would be better rendered 'from above.' . . . Luke's use of *anothen* is an affirmation that his knowledge of these things . . . was confirmed by revelation" (p. 1075).

[7]Rudolf Bultmann, *Jesus and the Word* (New York: Charles Scribner's Sons, 1958), pp. 61-62.

[8]Ibid., pp. 62-63, 74-75.

[9]Pinnock, *Biblical Revelation*, p. 135.

[10]Gerhard Maier, *The End of the Historical-Critical Method* (St. Louis: Concordia Publishing House, 1977), p. 15.

[11]Lindsell, p. 181.

[12]James I. Packer, "Hermeneutics and Biblical Authority," in *Themelios* (Autumn 1975), pp. 3-12.

[13]Pinnock, *Biblical Revelation*, p. 213.

[14]"The Chicago Statement on Biblical Inerrancy," prepared by the International Council on Biblical Inerrancy, 1978. (Mimeographed.)

[15]John Warwick Montgomery, "The Fuzzification of Biblical Inerrancy," in Montgomery, *Faith Founded on Fact* (New York: Thomas Nelson, 1978), p. 225.

[16]Ranald MacAulay and Jerram Barrs, *Being Human: The Nature of Spiritual Experience* (Downers Grove: IVP, 1978), p. 212.

[17]Montgomery, *Faith Founded on Fact*, p. 225.

[18]Walter Kaufmann, *The Faith of a Heretic* (Garden City, NY: Doubleday, 1963), p. 116.

[19]John H. Gerstner, "The Message of the Word," in Merrill C. Tenney (ed.), *The Bible—The Living Word of Revelation* (Grand Rapids: Zondervan, 1976), p. 170.

[20]Donald G. Bloesch, *Essentials of Evangelical Theology*, Vol. 1 (New York: Harper & Row, 1978), pp. 62-63.

[21]Bloesch, *Evangelical Renaissance*, p. 93.

[22]Bloesch, *Essentials*, p. 55.

[23]Ibid., p. 63

[24]Ibid., p. 68.

[25]Ibid., p. 69.

Chapter 9

[1]J. I. Packer, *Keep Yourselves from Idols* (Grand Rapids: Eerdmans, 1965), p. 17.

[2]Clark H. Pinnock, "Evangelical Theology and the Liberal Experiment" (Forum Tapes and Theological Students Fellowship). (Tape)

[3]David F. Wells, *The Search for Salvation* (Downers Grove, IL: IVP, 1978), p. 91.

[4]Pinnock, "Evangelical Theology and the Liberal Experiment."

[5]On this question, see the helpful discussion in Coleman, pp. 73-104.

[6]Carl F. H. Henry, *God, Revelation, and Authority*, Vol. 1, p. 49.

[7]Pinnock, "Evangelical Theology and the Liberal Experiment."

[8]Kraft, *Christianity in Culture*, Chapter 15, "Dynamic-Equivalence Theologizing," pp. 291-312.

[9]Packer, *Keep Yourself From Idols*, pp. 11, 12.

[10]Dennis Nineham, "Epilogue," in John Hick (ed.), *The Myth of God Incarnate* (Philadelphia: Westminster Press, 1977), p. 188.

[11]Thomas J. J. Altizer, *The Gospel of Christian Atheism* (Philadelphia: Westminster Press, 1966), p. 10.

[12]Fritz Buri, *How Can We Still Speak Responsibly of God?* (Philadelphia: Fortress Press, 1968), p. 3.

[13]Kenneth Hamilton, *Revolt Against Heaven* (Grand Rapids: Eerdmans, 1965), p. 91.

[14]Pinnock, *Biblical Revelation*, p. 29.

[15]Rudolf Bultmann, *Jesus Christ and Mythology* (New York: Charles Scribner's Sons, 1958), p. 37.

[16]H. Richard Niebuhr, *The Meaning of Revelation* (New York: Macmillan Co., 1974), p. 13.

[17]Hamilton, p. 15.

[18]Pinnock, *Biblical Revelation*, p. 109.

[19]Gordon D. Kaufman, *God the Problem* (Cambridge: Harvard University Press, 1973), pp. 6-7.

[20]Hamilton, pp. 176-177.

[21]Francis A. Schaeffer, *The Church Before the Watching World* (Downers Grove: IVP, 1971), p. 12.

[22]Clark H. Pinnock, *A Defense of Biblical Infallibility* (n.p.: Presbyterian & Reformed Publishing Co., 1975), p. 7.

[23]Ladd, *New Testament and Criticism*, p. 159.

[24]R. T. France, *I Came to Set the Earth on Fire* (Downers Grove: IVP, 1976), p. 33.

[25]John Duff, "Religion Courses: Take 'em and leave 'em (with your faith intact)," *His*, December 1982, p. 6.

[26]Howkins, p. 44.

[27]Rudolf Bultmann, "Is Exegesis Without Presuppositions Possible?" in Schubert M. Ogden (ed.), *Existence and Faith: The Shorter Writings of Rudolf Bultmann* (New York: Meridian Books, 1964), pp. 291, 292.

[28]C. S. Lewis, "Modern Theology and Biblical Criticism" in C. S. Lewis, *Christian Reflections* (Grand Rapids: Eerdmans, 1980), p. 153.

[29]C. S. Lewis, "Miracles" in C. S. Lewis, *God in the Dock* (Grand Rapids: Eerdmans, 1973), p. 31.

[30]Antony Flew, *God and Philosophy* (New York: Dell Publishing Co., 1966), Chapter 7, "Miracle and History," pp. 140-158; Van A. Harvey, *Historian and Believer*.

[31]Bultmann, *Jesus and the Word*, p. 173.

[32]John Nevius, *Demon Possession* (Grand Rapids: Kregel Publications, 1968), p. 344.

[33]Rudolf Otto, *The Kingdom of God and the Son of Man* (Boston: Starr King Press, 1957), pp. 333-334.

[34]Oral Roberts, *The Call* (New York: Avon Books, 1973), pp. 37-38.

[35]See for examples Gershom Scholem, *Sabbatai Sevi, The Mystical Messiah*, p. 411; Henry Ansgar Kelly, pp. 94-95; Andrew D. White, *A History of the Warfare of Science with Theology in Christendom* (New York: George Braziller, 1955), Vol. II, pp. 5-22.

[36]Lewis, "Modern Theology and Biblical Criticism," pp. 154, 155.

[37]The zeal and ingenuity of conservative evangelical scholars in dismantling the miracles and exploding the scriptures of non-Christian and extra-biblical traditions is worthy of the most skeptical gospel critic. See Benjamin Breckenridge Warfield, *Counterfeit Miracles* (London: Banner of Truth Trust, 1972); George W. Peters, *Indonesia Revival, Focus on Timor* (Grand Rapids: Zondervan, 1973), Chapter 4, "The Miracle Phenomena of the Revival," pp. 57-85; Yamauchi, *Jesus, Zoroaster, Socrates, Buddha, Muhammad*; Gordon Fraser, *What Does the Book of Mormon Teach?* (Chicago: Moody Press, 1964). One exception might be John Warwick Montgomery, *Principalities and Powers*, where against the modern anti-supernaturalist bias, Montgomery defends not only the biblical miracles but also other phenomena including leprechauns, werewolves, and alchemy. He comes closer than anyone else to arguing that legends are impossible.

[38]Bloesch, *Essentials*, p. 78.

[39]Henry, *God, Revelation, and Authority*, Vol. 2, p. 289.

[40]John Warwick Montgomery, *The Suicide of Christian Theology* (Minneapolis: Bethany Fellowship, 1975), pp. 331, 106.

[41]Francis A. Schaeffer, *The God Who is There* (Downers Grove: IVP, 1977), p. 79.

[42]Howkins, p. 41.

[43]Schaeffer, *The God Who is There*, p. 47.

[44]Ibid., p. 105.

[45]Paul Tillich, *Biblical Religion and the Search for Ultimate Reality* (Chicago: University of Chicago Press, 1972), p. vii.

[46]Schubert M. Ogden, *The Reality of God* (New York: Harper & Row, 1977), p. 184.

[47]Maurice Wiles, *The Remaking of Christian Theology* (Philadelphia: Westminster, 1978), p. 38.

[48]Clark H. Pinnock and David F. Wells, "Preface," in Pinnock and Wells (eds.), *Toward a Theology for the Future*, p. 7.

[49]Clark H. Pinnock, "Prospects for Systematic Theology," in *Toward a Theology for the Future*, p. 96.

[50]Thomas C. Oden, *Agenda for Theology* (New York: Harper & Row, 1979), p. 50.

[51]Packer, "Hermeneutics and Biblical Authority," p. 3.

[52]Bloesch, *Essentials*, Vol. 1, p. 121.

[53]Ibid., p. 139.

Chapter 10

[1]Barr, *Fundamentalism*, pp. vi-vii ("Preface to the American Edition").

[2]Richard Mouw, "New Alignments," in Peter L. Berger and Richard John Neuhaus, *Against the World For the World* (New York: Seabury Press, 1976), pp. 109-110.
Richard Quebedeaux has essentially the same list of the distinguishing marks of Evangelicalism in his *The Young Evangelicals* (New York: Harper & Row, 1974): "(1) the complete reliability and final authority of Scripture in matters of faith and practice; (2) the necessity of a *personal* faith in Jesus Christ as Savior from sin and consequent commitment to him as Lord; and (3) the urgency of seeking actively the conversion of sinners to Christ" (p. 4).

[3]Paul Tillich, *The Theology of Culture* (New York: Oxford University Press, 1977), p. 170.

[4]Wilfred Cantwell Smith, *The Faith of Other Men* (New York: New American Library, 1965), pp. 119, 123.

[5]Bill Lane Doulos, "Mere Orthodoxy," in *Sojourners* (December 1976), p. 25.

[6]See two very instructive works of sympathetic criticism: Clark H. Pinnock, "Schaefferism as a World View," in *Sojourners* (July 1977), pp. 32-35; and Thomas V. Morris, *Francis Schaeffer's Apologetics: A Critique* (Chicago: Moody Press, 1976).

[7]Flo Conway and Jim Siegelman, *Snapping: America's Epidemic of Sudden Personality Change* (New York: J. B. Lippincott, 1978), pp. 44-45.

[8]Alan Watts, *Beyond Theology* (New York: Vintage Books, 1973), p. 83.

[9]Gerald T. Sheppard, "Biblical Hermeneutics: The Academic Language of Evangelical Identity," in *Union Seminary Quarterly Review* (Winter 1977), p. 84.

[10]Barr gives some interesting hints about the contours of a "modern doctrine of verbal inspiration" in both *Fundamentalism* (pp. 293-296) and *The Bible in the Modern World* (pp. 178-179).

[11]Paul Holmer, in David F. Wells and John P. Woodbridge (eds.), *The Evangelicals* (New York: Abingdon Press, 1975), pp. 72-73.

[12]Bloesch, *Essentials*, p. 121.

[13]Charles Caldwell Ryrie, *Neo-Orthodoxy* (Chicago: Moody Press, 1969), p. 49.

[14]Clark Pinnock, "The Inerrancy Debate Among the Evangelicals" (Vancouver, BC, [n.d.]). (Mimeographed.)

[15]Daniel Fuller, "The Nature of Biblical Inerrancy," in *The Journal of the American Scientific Affiliation* (June 1972), p. 47.

[16]R. C. Sproul, in James Montgomery Boice (ed.). *The Foundation of Biblical Authority* (Grand Rapids: Zondervan, 1978), p. 115.

[17]Barr, *The Bible and the Modern World*, pp. 173-174.

[18]Fuller, "The Nature of Biblical Inerrancy," p. 50.

[19]John Goldingay, "Inspiration, Infallibility and Criticism," in *The Churchman* (January-March 1976), p. 20.

[20]David M. Scholer, "The Authority and Character of Scripture: A Brief Statement of Position," 1978, p. 2. (Mimeographed.)

[21]Goldingay, p. 15.

[22]James D. G. Dunn, *Unity and Diversity in the New Testament* (Philadelphia: Westminster Press, 1977), p. 376.

[23]Ibid., p. 381   [24]Ibid.   [25]Ibid., p. 383.

[26]Does Paul Jewett of Fuller Seminary violate my canon criterion for Evangelicalism in his book *Man as Male and Female* (Grand Rapids: Eerdmans, 1975)? He invited much criticism for rejecting Pauline statements on women in favor of what he considered to be the chief Pauline thrust on the question—Galatians 3:28. Jewett has claimed that instead of "breaking the analogy of scripture" himself, it was Paul who broke it with his subordinationist statements. I believe that what Jewett is doing is subtly but significantly different from Käsemann's "canon-within-the-canon." Instead of rejecting one New Testament writer altogether, Jewett intends to bracket some statements of a writer (Paul) which are not consistent with the writer's own main theme. Thus to be able to speak of Paul's New Testament witness at all, one must in this case employ *"Sachkritik,"* or content criticism, or be left with an unconnected collection of Pauline sentences. Needless to say, the picture would change if Jewett came to consider the Pastorals (which contain the offensive texts) as deutero-Pauline.

To approach the question from a slightly different angle, it might be said that Jewett sees the "analogy of scripture" as the "larger picture" or "general trend" of scripture. Against the general backdrop of biblical thought, one might be able to spot some minor deviant elements. To drop them in light of the larger picture would then be to preserve rather than to violate the analogy of faith. The authority of "the Bible as a whole" does not necessarily mean that every single verse is authoritative, but rather that the picture formed by biblical teaching in general is authoritative. Note the difference between this notion and that of Käsemann who doubts that there is any "general picture" at all.

APPENDIX: GETTING A NEW START

Some readers may have been taken aback at my suggestion at the end of Chapter 10, that I can deem leaving Evangelicalism a viable option. It is clear to me that there are individuals whose experience with Evangelical Christianity has been negative enough in the long run that they no longer want to identify themselves with it, even should Chapter 10's analysis make a continuing identification theoretically feasible. And then again, there will probably be readers who see the cogency of my critiques, but not of my reconstructive proposals. They may decide that a "postmodern Evangelicalism" just will not fly. They will see Evangelicalism as a sinking ship that needs to be fled. I have nothing more to say to try to stop them, so let me instead offer a few hints for a healthy and smooth exit into the outside world.

First let me warn the new ex-Evangelical about the trap of self-fulfilling prophecies. Those raised in a revivalistic setting may recall certain warnings against the evil of backsliding. "Now that you know the truth/are indwelt by the Holy Spirit, you can never enjoy a life of sin again. The Spirit will convict you of your backsliding, so you won't be able to enjoy your sin!" If the listener eventually does backslide into his old worldly ways, he probably will feel guilty, at least if he ever took his faith seriously. Whether or not the supernatural agency of the Spirit is in play, the backslider's conscience will bother him, and for easily explainable reasons. An apostate is one who no longer believes what he used to believe, but a backslider is one who acts contrary to what he *still* believes. No wonder his conscience would give him fits.

We see a similar situation with regard to the devotional practices of meditative Bible-reading and "up-to-the-minute" confession of sins, i.e., confessing your sinful thoughts to God as soon as you become aware of them. (Bill Bright, John R. Rice, John R. W. Stott, Lehman Strauss, and nearly all other fundamentalists recommend this. Peter Gillquist is one of the few who have broken with it.) The idea is that if one stops practicing these regular disciplines, he will atrophy spiritually. His unconfessed sins will distance him from God; his failure to "feed on the Word" will make him "dull to the things of God." Will they? The earnest Born Again Christian will never know, since he dares not experiment. We see here a phenomenon formally analogous to obsessive behavior, e.g., the neurotic who is always snapping his fingers to keep tigers away. If a friend points out that there are no tigers in the area anyway, the neurotic merely replies, "See how well it's working?" If however such an earnest Christian does temporarily relax his spiritual rigor, he will almost certainly feel the guilt and distance from God he was warned about. Is this due to the inherently deleterious effects of his relaxation? Maybe not; he is quite possibly the victim of a self-fulfilling prophecy. He is in the same position as the backslider. Had he been taught that a different, more casual, devotional life was permissible, he might never feel any ill effects, much less guilt, for not being so strict.

Now what does all this have to do with our ex-Evangelical friend? Presumably he no longer believes the threats and warnings of his former mentors. Could he still be prey to self-fulfilling prophecy?

Yes indeed. There is yet another version, designed especially for
him.   Back in Chapter 2, I quoted James Sire, Francis Schaeffer,
and others, to the effect that the only consistent alternative to Evangelical Christianity is nihilism, even despair.   The point of such
warnings, I suspect, is not only to back the non-believer into an
evangelistic-apologetical corner. Perhaps even more importantly, the
Evangelical   reader   is   being   warned   never to consider leaving the
camp of the faithful.   There is only darkness and despair without.
As long as the Evangelical reader is convinced of the validity of his
faith, he can breathe a sigh of relief—no existential *Angst* for him,
thank God!   But what if the day comes when the Evangelical becomes dissatisfied with his faith and its apologetical defenses?   Such
a reader may be able to identify with Sam Keen: "The issue was so
drawn for me, that the choice was between remaining Christian or
becoming honest."[1]
     Such a person, tragically, may see himself faced with the alterna-
tives of dishonest faith (worthless in anyone's reckoning) and honest despair.   Why do the alternatives seem so bleak?   Why, simply
because, even though the ex-Evangelical has rejected the Evangelical
alternative, he has not realized the need to reject the Evangelical
delineation of the alternatives!   And the latter of course is itself
part of the Evangelical alternative!   As we saw in Chapter 2, the
negation of all other views was a defense mechanism for the Evangelical worldview.   If the reader sees fit to reject that worldview, let
me remind him that he need no longer trouble himself to defend it!
In other words, he should now find himself in the position to re-
examine other viewpoints.   Their failure to conform to Evangelicalism
should, obviously, no longer count against them.   Yet this is far
from obvious to many ex-Evangelicals, who never bother taking a
second look, say, at Liberal theology.   They still take Francis Schaeffer at his word on this one point, and proceed to resign themselves
to a lifestyle of "quiet desperation."   This is not necessary.   I ad-
vise such a reader to reread Chapter 9.   There I tried to demonstrate how Liberal theology cannot be dispensed with so easily.   And
of course there are other options as well.
     Back in the Introduction, I made the observation that instead of
really leaving Evangelicalism, many de-converts actually become sort
of reverse-fundamentalists.   To call them "ex-Evangelicals" is analogous to calling someone else, e.g., a "neo-Evangelical."   All that is
different is the prefix.   They are but a different stripe of Evangelical.   The idea is that the emotional bond continues to tie them to
their faith, only in a mirror-image way.   I think I can illustrate
this with an enlightening anecdote from Richard Rubenstein.   He
recalls an ironic episode from his days in a Liberal Jewish seminary.
He sat talking with a handful of other students in the lounge when
a friend rushed in, enthusiastically brandishing his lunch. It seemed
that the seminarian was a recent convert from Orthodox to Reform
Judaism.   Exulting in his newfound freedom from Orthodox dietary
laws, he exclaimed, "Look, I'm eating a ham sandwich!"   Rubenstein
comments, "N. was, of course, unaware of the extent to which his
symbolic revolt tied him to the very religious system he wanted to
overthrow.   His need to assert his rebelliousness openly was an
acknowledgement of orthodox Judaism's continuing power over him."[2]
     Accordingly, I warn my ex-Evangelical reader that every time he

announces his repudiation of his former compatriots, each time he derides what now seem to him absurd views, every time he becomes resentful over having been "taken for a ride," he is placing himself, albeit negatively, back into his Evangelical world. Now all of this is quite understandable, even justifiable, since one must "get it out of one's system."   And, as is well known, a pendulum never stops in the middle the first time. But the ex-Evangelical should look forward to its settling down in the middle eventually.   That is, his goal is to put the whole thing behind him, not to continue to be involved with it, fighting the same old battle only on the opposite side.

James Barr has perceptively written that "just as a personal conversion is normal as an entry into fundamentalist religion, something not far short of another conversion may be needed before one can get out of it."[3] Taking Barr's hint, I want to mark out a sort of Evangelical path out of Evangelicalism for those who want to "hand back their ticket," in the phrase of Ivan Karamazov. This is going to involve the reverse application of those defense mechanisms and maneuvers discussed in Chapter 2. Now remember, I am assuming such an ex-Evangelical reader already to have discarded his old faith-stance for *cognitively appropriate* reasons. Otherwise, he would be tempted to use these defense and avoidance maneuvers as an excuse for *not* coming to an honest decision; i.e., he would be merely slipping out of his faith by a kind of unthinking osmosis. (And as you remember, this is just the kind of cop-out I criticized Evangelicals for in Chapter 2!) It would only be a more sophisticated form of backsliding.

What is really at stake in the deconversion contemplated by the ex-Evangelical is a jump from one worldview to another. Peter Berger calls such a worldview a "plausibility structure," i.e., that web of assumptions, beliefs, and values taken for granted by us and our peer-group, which provides the ground rules for our view of reality, and for our behavior in the world. The consent and affirmation of one's peer-group or community is all-important here. Psychological experiments and anthropological research have amply demonstrated that our grip on normally taken-for-granted assumptions becomes very tenuous when we find ourselves in a "cognitive minority" position.   How can you be so sure you're right if everyone around you disagrees? This is another form of the "truth by majority vote" syndrome. Obviously, such cognitive intimidation cannot answer the truth question, but if one is not careful, it often *seems* to.   We saw how Evangelicals stress the need for "fellowship" so as to keep one's convictions secure and reinforced (Stephen Board even puts it explicitly in the terms of our discussion—see his booklet *Doubt*).

If the new ex-Evangelical has made an intellectually conscientious decision against Evangelicalism, he may find it helpful to "clear his head" by at least temporarily absenting himself from the Evangelical subculture and its plausibility structure. If he doesn't, he will find himself still resident in his customary plausibility structure, but now as an alien! His new beliefs will be unwelcome, and will serve as a poor guide for conduct among Evangelicals. He will constantly be on the wrong wavelength. With all the cognitive pressure surrounding him, he may find himself almost believing absurdities like

"Evangelicalism is true, though unfortunately I no longer believe in
it"!   Besides, at this crucial stage of the game, the new ex-Evangelical needs input from the outside world.
    The ex-Evangelical is probably headed for identification with some
element of the mainstream culture or worldview.   But this cannot
come immediately.   In his first steps outside the cognitive ghetto of
his past, he will probably find very helpful a transitional peer-
group, a support-group of other ex-Evangelicals like himself.   These
people can share perspectives, work through common questions, etc.
The others can give the new ex-Evangelical the relief of realizing
"Hey, I guess I'm not crazy after all!"   Just where does one find
these other ex-Evangelicals?   If one's decision to "de-convert" has
been preceded by a period of questioning and discussion with Evangelical friends, he may have smoked out some of them already.   It
may be surprising just how many Doubting Thomases there are waiting to come out of the closet with a little provocation.   As a matter
of fact, anyone who one thinks might be interested in reading this
book would probably be a good candidate for such a support group.
Or one might try to find a local chapter of Fundamentalists Anonymous.
    Whether or not the reader can find a collection of kindred spirits,
he can take advantage of a kind of written equivalent.   There are
several fascinating books wherein a writer recounts his or others'
personal exodus from Evangelicalism, or modification of it.   Some
have not left the fold entirely.   Reading some of these books can
give an idea of options, within or without the Evangelical camp, as
well as insights as to various reasons individuals became dissatisfied
with Evangelicalism.   Here is a list:

> Skipp Porteous, *Jesus Doesn't Live Here Anymore*
> Harvey Cox, "Dialogue with Harvey Cox," *Right On*,
>   June, 1975.
> Martin Gardner, *The Flight of Peter Fromm*
> James Helfaer, *The Psychology of Religious Doubt*
> Thomas Howard, *Christ the Tiger*
> Sam Keen, *To a Dancing God*
> Shirley Nelson, *The Last Year of the War*
> C. Brandon Rimmer, *Religion in Shreds*
> Wayne Robinson, *I Once Spoke in Tongues*
> Jack Rogers, *Confessions of a Conservative Evangelical*
> Daniel Stevick, *Beyond Fundamentalism*
> Mike Yaconelli, *Tough Faith*

    If I may offer some friendly advice as to what a new ex-Evangeli-
cal might avoid, let me caution such a reader not to become an anti-
evangelist.   There is no point in carrying a vengeful chip on one's
shoulder, looking for every opportunity to challenge and refute an
Evangelical.   What a pathetic irony this would be!   Just picture the
person who has repudiated the task of trying to save people by
converting them *to* Evangelical faith, now trying to save people by
converting them *from* Evangelical faith!   A similar temptation is to
negate completely one's Evangelical past as a "life of sin," i.e., "I
once was blind, but now I see!"   Once again we would have the
mirror-image of the thing repudiated!   No, I dare say the "ex-Evangelical" wants eventually to mature past the "anti-Evangelical," to

become the "non-Evangelical." Then he will be able to appreciate the positive experiences of the past, however he may now want to explain them. He will be able to look at his former co-religionists simply as people with whom he happens to disagree, rather than as the unsaved "them," i.e., the same set of categories he used to see. As a full-fledged non-Evangelical he will not have to deny his past, nor let his past define all the issues for him.

The position of the ex-Evangelical has always reminded me of the hero of Hesse's *Siddhartha*. After a successful yet unsatisfying period of life among the Samana ascetics, Siddhartha concludes that enlightenment must lie elsewhere, back in ordinary life. Yet the distance from it all that he has gained gives him a unique perspective on common, worldly affairs. Though he no longer scorns the world, he can take it with less than full seriousness. He treats his new life in the mainstream "plausibility structure" as a kind of game to be experimented with, not a rat race in which one blindly takes one's place. I think that the ex-Evangelical starts his journey back into the mainstream on the same footing, with the same advantage. He can be purposefully selective in his embracing of the new world before him. And who can say what will come of it all? Perhaps like Siddhartha, the ex-Evangelical will find his return to the world a stage on the way to enlightenment.

FOOTNOTES

[1] Sam Keen, *To a Dancing God* (New York: Harper & Row, 1970), pp. 12-13.

[2] Richard L. Rubenstein, *My Brother Paul* (New York: Harper & Row, 1972), p. 12.

[3] James Barr, *Fundamentalism* (Philadelphia: Westminster Press, 1978), p. 38.

Printed in the United States
127777LV00001B/94/P